A Military History of Russia

Praeger Security International Advisory Board

A MILITARY HISTORY OF RUSSIA

From Ivan the Terrible to the War in Chechnya

David R. Stone

PRAEGER SECURITY INTERNATIONAL
Westport, Connecticut · London

Library of Congress Cataloging-in-Publication Data

Stone, David R., 1968–
  A military history of Russia : from Ivan the Terrible to the war in Chechnya / David R.
  Stone.
      p. cm.
  Includes bibliographical references and index.
  ISBN 0–275–98502–4 (alk. paper)
  1. Russia—History, Military. I. Title.
  DK51.S745 2006
  355.00947—dc22   2006018356

British Library Cataloguing in Publication Data is available.

Library of Congress Catalog Card Number: 2006018356
ISBN: 0–275–98502–4

First published in 2006

Praeger Security International, 88 Post Road West, Westport, CT 06881
An imprint of Greenwood Publishing Group, Inc.
www.praeger.com

Printed in the United States of America

The paper used in this book complies with the
Permanent Paper Standard issued by the National
Information Standards Organization (Z39.48–1984).

10 9 8 7 6 5 4 3 2 1

Contents

List of Maps

Acknowledgments

This book was written in 2005–2006 at the Center for the Advanced Study in the Behavioral Sciences in Stanford, California. I am deeply grateful to the Center and its staff for providing a wonderful environment in which to work. I also appreciate Kansas State University and my colleagues in the History Department for making my sabbatical year possible.

Lee Farrow, Jennifer Siegel, and David Schimmelpenninck kindly reviewed the manuscript, as did Greg Mulready and Joseph Mulready. Their helpful suggestions made this a better book.

Finally, my wife Kristin Mulready-Stone read the manuscript in its entirety and took time away from her own work to enable me to do mine. This book would simply not have been possible without her. Meredith, Julianne, and Danielle were remarkably patient with their father who spent too much time typing when he really would rather have been playing with them.

Introduction

Military history, as practiced and read, is too often cripplingly limited in its chronological and its geographic scope. The programs of professional meetings in military history, scholarly journals and popular magazines on military history, and even the offerings on the History Channel reveal a view of military history that is profoundly narrow. To oversimplify, this military history starts with the U.S. Civil War, and it stretches from the Mississippi River to central Europe. In western Europe, the picture is slightly better: it starts with the Napoleonic Wars. Both versions too often omit a great span of time and the majority of the surface of the world. I do not intend to demean the high-quality scholarship on the United States and western Europe, only to suggest that a view of military history that does not include the rest of the world, and particularly Russia, is inherently incomplete.

In this book, I intend to do several things. Two of them are basic. The first is to recount the battles, campaigns, and wars that make up an important part of Russian military history. The second is to talk about the other half of Russian military history: the complex and reciprocal relationship between the military and society in Russia. For hundreds of years, the Russian military has had an enormous impact on Russian life, and, in turn, Russian society has determined what sort of military Russia possesses. Each half by itself is incomplete.

Building on those foundations, I hope this book informs Western readers about Russia's military past. One might argue the only military history worth knowing covers western Europe and North America, but that argument is certainly misguided. The constellation of European great powers, for example, looks quite different because of Russia, which more than any other state was responsible for breaking three potential great powers: Poland, Sweden, and the Ottoman Empire. Readers may chuckle at the thought of those states as serious European powers, but that is only because Russia thoroughly demolished their territorial possessions and military potential. Even simple generalizations about twentieth-century warfare reflect misunderstandings of Russian military history: that World War I was a war of stalemate and immobility, that World War II was a "good war" with a clear line between the just and the unjust, and that the German blitzkrieg reflected German predominance in tanks and armored warfare. All those are false or incomplete, as the briefest glance at Russian military history shows. The Eastern Front in World War I was not bogged down, but offensives instead covered hundreds of miles. World War II on the Eastern Front was a contest of murderous regimes on both sides. The German Army that invaded the Soviet Union in 1941 was outnumbered at least five to one in tanks, and most of its soldiers walked across the border or rode in horse carts. The list could go on.

This book is not intended to promote triumphalism, and Russian military history is not triumphal. It includes victories and defeats, the promotion of education and human development alongside the pernicious subjugation of human lives to military ends. What I want to emphasize is the importance of Russia to a proper understanding of military history and to undermine a misconception that Russian military history is a long saga of stoic suffering, victory through snow, or passive, defensive, negative achievements. The actual story is more complex and interesting than that.

Finally, this book explores key themes: Russia's ambiguous position as a Western and a non-Western culture, Russia's struggle to overcome social, economic, and technological backwardness, the necessity and the burden of the militarization of Russian society, and, finally, the interplay between space and state capacity in Russia.

In my view, a close look at the Russian experience reveals the deep problems of simplistic notions of particular Western styles of warfare, or the inherent military superiority of the West over the non-Western world. First, Russia itself undermines the very distinction between Western and non-Western. Russian thinkers have been arguing for centuries whether Russia is or should be part of the West. Whatever the criteria for defining the West, Russia is a thoroughly ambiguous case, and that ambiguity undermines the idea that military history is best understood through a Western vs. non-Western dichotomy.

Is Russia Western? It lacks the central institutions that define the West. It has never been truly capitalist. For centuries before the communist Bolshevik Revolution of 1917, Russia's economy was based on peasant communal agriculture, with half those peasants before 1861 being serfs, permanently bound to the land. What little industry Russia had before the last half of the nineteenth century was founded, patronized, and often managed by the Russian state itself. Even when Russia began to industrialize, its political and social system was hardly capitalist. After the Bolshevik Revolution in 1917, it ceased being capitalist in any sense. Even contemporary Russia, with most of its important industries tightly bound to the state, does not look particularly capitalist.

Russia has never had a Western army of citizen-soldiers because it has not had citizens. Under the tsars, Russia's people were subjects, not citizens, devoid of rights that the tsar did not deign to grant. Free peasants could be converted into serfs at the tsar's whim. The nobility that made up the core of early-modern Russian armies called themselves slaves of the tsar, used childish nicknames to refer to themselves in their correspondence with the tsar, and did not enjoy security of property. Like their serfs, they were not free: though their living conditions were immeasurably better, Russian nobles were, until the middle of the 1700s, required to serve the state.

Russia has never enjoyed the freedom of thought and expression characteristic of the West. Under the Russian tsars, under the Soviets, and even today in the Russian Federation free speech existed to the degree that political authorities allowed it to exist. Typically, that meant no free expression at all. Particular rulers at particular times might allow particular types of expression to serve state interests, but there was never anything resembling Western notions of freedom of speech.

So Russia is certainly not Western. It has, however, regularly crushed Western powers militarily. Russia under Peter the Great ended Sweden's pretensions to Great Power status and, over a period of two centuries, was instrumental in erasing Poland, once the largest state in Europe, from the map. As is far better known, Russia broke Napoleon's power and annihilated Hitler's Third Reich. A Russian army has occupied Berlin twice and Paris once; a German army has never occupied Moscow, and a French army only as prelude to its complete destruction.

Is Russian then non-Western? Not at all. Russia converted to Christianity more than a millennium ago, and Christianity has been a central element of Russian identity ever since. Though not part of the Roman Empire, Russia received Christianity and its high culture from the Byzantine Empire, which combined the cultural traditions of Greece and Rome, and whose people called themselves and their empire Roman. The Russian word "tsar" is derived from Caesar. Russian science and culture have been at the forefront of the Western world since the 1800s. Ballet, the periodic table, the concept of conditioned reflexes, non-Euclidian geometry, and linear programming all took their modern form in Russia.

So Russia is certainly Western. It has, however, regularly been defeated by non-Western military forces. In 1240 it was conquered by Mongol hordes, beginning centuries as a Mongol vassal state. In 1904–1905 Russia was humiliated by Japan, the first defeat of a Western state by an Asian power. The Soviet Union's invasion of Afghanistan ended in ignominious withdrawal, and the present-day Russian Federation's two wars in Chechnya have brought only suffering and failure. The point of this exercise is to show that it makes little sense to study military history from a neat East-West divide. If one wishes to argue that Russia is only an exception to a clear East-West dichotomy, it is such an immense and important exception that it is unclear how much of a rule is left.

The next major theme this book explores is Russia's persistent backwardness in comparison to other European powers. This backwardness has taken many forms, whether in technology or military organization, political structures or social development. It is a recurring element in Ivan the Terrible's inability to use his light cavalry armies to take Western cities or the Soviet Union's inability to adapt its resources and tactics to fighting a guerrilla war in the mountains of Afghanistan. In general terms, Russia's shortcomings in technology and technique have been the most easily corrected. Once aware of problems, Russia's rulers have quickly and effectively acquired knowledge and resources to match Western powers. Political and social backwardness has, however, been more intractable. Authoritarian rule and a poor, illiterate population were so deeply entrenched in Russian society that correcting those problems was generally difficult or impossible. The military damage has been as serious as from outdated weaponry or organization.

This book explores militarization in Russian history. By militarization, I do not mean rule by military elites. Though states similar to Russia in their level of economic and social development have commonly had military rule, Russia has not. Though the tsars and their Soviet inheritors typically had some military experience, and military elites have played a role in power struggles, no Russian general ever put himself into power through a military coup. Instead, by militarization I have in mind the organization of society for war. From its beginnings, Russia has been a society organized for war. In the time of Ivan the Terrible, when this book opens, the Russian state was essentially a machine for organizing and supporting an army, and the Russian political class was generally identical to that army. The degree to which Russia was organized for war fluctuated over time, but war was always central to how Russian elites conceived their state and their role in it.

This militarization had terrible consequences for Russian political development and for the well-being of Russians. There was, however, little choice. East European polities that did not effectively organize for war were destroyed. Of the powers that surrounded Russia during Ivan the Terrible's reign—Sweden, the Kazan Khanate, the Crimean Tatars, the Ottoman Empire, the Habsburg (or Austrian) Empire, and Poland-Lithuania—only Sweden survived continuously as a state to the present day, with a fraction of its former extent. Kazan and the Crimea were entirely eradicated. Poland lost its existence as a state for over a century. The Ottoman and Habsburg empires disintegrated during World War I. Only Russia survives as a political unit with borders reasonably close to its greatest territorial extent. To be sure, Swedes and Austrians live lives today far better, and Poles significantly better, than Russians, but that is not the point. Governments did not make decisions based on the well-being of their subjects, but on the survival of the state, and Russia survived. Surviving with open borders, poor soil, and cold climate meant an enormous and expensive military establishment and authoritarian political culture.

Finally, this book discusses the interplay of space and state power. Russia's vast expanse has given Russian warfare a characteristic pattern. When the central state is relatively weak and unable to muster resources, projecting power at a distance inevitably means single, narrow drives, easily isolated and destroyed. In the Smolensk War, in Peter the Great's defeat on the Prut, in the Russo-Turkish War of 1877–1878, and in the Bolshevik attack on Warsaw in 1920, Russia pushed beyond its limited resources, leaving thin and fragile spearheads easily broken. When the state has, by comparison, mastered assembling men and materials, Russia's resources provide overwhelming power capable of terrible destructive force on a wide front. The 1654 Russo-Polish War, the World War I Brusilov Offensive, and World War II's Operation Bagration all display a characteristic Russian way of war: overwhelming power on a broad front.

In covering centuries of history in a short book, I have omitted a great deal. Specialists will note simplifications and generalizations on every page. Dates may seem confusing. Until 1917, Russia employed the Julian calendar, which ran several days behind the Gregorian calendar used in the West. That is why the 1917 Bolshevik seizure of power, called the October Revolution in Russia, took place in November by Western calendars. This book lists both dates: an awkward but necessary compromise. After 1917, there is no distinction. The society discussed in this book has had many names, confusing unwary readers. When I can, I try to be reasonably precise. That means using the term "Kievan Rus" for the society existing in medieval Russia, "Muscovy" for the early modern empire centered on Moscow, "Russia" or the "Russian Empire" for what Muscovy became through the reforms of Peter the Great, the "Soviet Union" or "USSR" for the new state created as a result of the 1917 Russian Revolution, and "Russia" or the "Russian Federation" for the central fragment left behind by the Soviet Union's 1991 collapse. For comprehensibility, however, I sometimes use Russia and Russian where they are not strictly correct. Cities changed names routinely. Tsaritsyn became Stalingrad and then Volgograd; St. Petersburg became Petrograd, then Leningrad, then St. Petersburg again. Place names and personal names have different spellings or entirely different names in different languages. I have generally used Russian names for places and people instead of Ukrainian, Belorussian, or Polish; I intend no offense or political judgment. I have

Westernized some well-known names for clarity: Peter the Great instead of Pyotr, Leon Trotsky instead of Lev Trotskii.

Finally, Russians do not have middle names in the Western sense. Instead, they have patronymics; the father's name is made a middle name by adding an ending: -ovich/-evich for men, -ovna/-evna for women. Thus Mikhail Sergeevich Gorbachev has the given name Mikhail, is the son of Sergei, and has the family name Gorbachev. Russian tsars were and are often referred to by name and patronymic alone.

CHAPTER 1

The Rise of Muscovy

What became the continent-spanning Russian Empire began as something very different. The first government and society for which we have any reasonable record on Russian territory is what historians have termed "Kievan Rus." Though a great deal of the history of Kievan Rus remains obscure, a careful sifting of historical chronicles and archaeological evidence gives a reasonably coherent picture. It is worth stressing, however, that almost every assertion made below is questioned by at least some scholars of early Russian history.

Kievan Rus emerged from the combination of two separate populations. The first were Slavic agriculturists, migrating east into present-day Russia and Ukraine. The Slavs spoke related languages and shared a related culture. Though their precise origin is disputed, it is reasonable to locate the Slavs' ancestors in the forests and marshes of western Ukraine, from which, around the year 600, some moved west and north, becoming the Poles, Czechs, and Slovaks; others moved south, becoming the Slovenes, Croats, Serbs, Macedonians, and Bulgarians; others, the East Slavs, moved into what are now Russia, Ukraine, and Belarus. Their migration into Russia seems reasonably peaceful; though the East Slavs lacked a written language, their knowledge of agriculture and the greater population it supported enabled them to push aside primitive Finnic and Baltic hunter-gatherers inhabiting the region. Loosely organized into tribes, the East Slavs lived in farming villages, supplementing their diet with fishing and hunting.

The second group forming Kievan Rus, much smaller in population, was Viking traders and raiders (the two occupations coexisted quite well). These Vikings used the rivers of eastern Europe to travel between their Nordic homelands and the rich cities of the Mediterranean. In particular, they traded with the Byzantine Empire, the Greek-speaking eastern half of the Roman Empire, which survived the catastrophic collapse of the western half. By traveling up the rivers flowing north to the Baltic Sea, making portages in central Russia, then traveling south downriver to the

Black Sea, these Vikings carried northern goods such as fur, wax, amber, and silver to Byzantium, returning with luxury goods and coins. They established trading posts and encampments along Russia's rivers and lakes and coexisted peacefully with their Slavic neighbors.

It is difficult to tell when the first real state, a governing authority, emerged from this Slavic-Viking society. What chronicles tell us is that at some point in the 800s the Slavic tribes of the region, tired of conflict among themselves, invited Vikings, the Rus, to rule them and bring order (Rus may be derived from a Finnic word for Viking or Swede). These Rus in turn founded a state centered on the city of Kiev: hence, Kievan Rus. These few lines in Russian historical chronicles have generated fierce controversy. An anti-Russian position, the Normanist view, concludes that political organization and civilization were brought to the Slavs only from outside, by Norsemen. A Russian nationalist position argues, by contrast, either that the Rus were also Slavs or that the story is mythical and the Slavs created a state themselves. Healthy moderation provides a clearer picture. There is no doubt that much of the Kievan elite was Viking; their names in surviving documents are Scandinavian. On the other hand, those Vikings were drops in a Slavic ocean. The modern Russian language includes almost no Scandinavian vocabulary, suggesting that there were too few Vikings to make an appreciable demographic or linguistic impact. The same sources that show us Scandinavian names also show them joined and then replaced by Slavic ones.

Almost as controversial is identifying Kievan Rus as the ancestor of present-day Russia. After all, as Ukrainian nationalist historians point out, Kiev, supposedly the capital of the first Russian state, is in Ukraine, outside of present-day Russia. Their conclusion is that Kievan Rus belongs to Ukrainian history, and the true origins of Russia lie elsewhere. While it is indeed worth remembering that Kievan Rus is not an exclusive Russian possession, it is equally true that the people of what is now Russia saw themselves as belonging to a common society and culture centered in Kiev, traced the descent of their princes to the founders of Kiev, and saw the entire region as one common Rus.

This new state, a loose and far-flung empire of Viking and Slavic traders and warriors ruling Slavic villagers, proved remarkably successful and adaptable. It brought together the Slavic tribes of the region under a single ruling elite, which used Orthodox Christianity, the faith of the Byzantine Empire, to tie together its disparate peoples. Far too large to be effectively ruled from Kiev, Kievan Rus evolved a flexible structure. The senior member of the dynasty, known as the grand prince (*velikii kniaz'*), held power in Kiev. The other members of the extended family, known simply as princes, ruled smaller and less prestigious cities while still part of a single dynasty. The title prince (*kniaz'*) belonged to male descendants of the original Viking ruling family, and each prince ruled through an armed retinue (*druzhina*). When brought together, these princes and their fighting men served as the army of Kievan Rus in clashes with nomadic tribes to the east and south. When broken up, they fought the frequent civil wars of Kievan Rus.

Civil wars, feuds inside the ruling dynasty's extended family, were a predictable outcome of the nature of succession in Kievan Rus. The ruling dynasty recognized lateral succession: that younger brothers succeeded elder brothers, rather than sons exclusively inheriting from their fathers. In theory, that meant constant rotation, as younger brothers and members of junior branches of the ruling family constantly shifted their holdings to rotate up the hierarchy of cities. In practice, this conflicted with the natural desire to establish a stable patrimony for one's sons. The characteristic political conflict of Kievan Rus pitted uncles against nephews; a son wished to inherit his father's land and title, clashing with his father's younger brothers. This produced growing political fragmentation. The economic and cultural unity of Kievan Rus was matched by political disunity, as what had been a reasonably coherent trading empire became a patchwork of feuding city-states by 1200.

The Destruction of Kievan Rus

Political disunity made it impossible for Kievan Rus to withstand an approaching disaster. As long as Kievan Rus existed, its people fought nomad raids from the southern steppes, but this did not prepare them for a much greater menace. In 1237, according to a chronicler, a horrible new threat appeared from the East. The Mongols, called Tatars in the sources, appeared at the city of Riazan and demanded tribute. When they were refused, "the foreigners besieged the town … and surrounded it with a palisade; the Prince of Riazan shut himself up in the town with his people. The Tatars took the town … and burned it all, and killed its prince Iurii, and his princess, and seized the men, women, and children, and monks, nuns, and priests; some they struck down with swords, while others they shot with arrows and flung into the flames; still others they seized and bound." Over the next few years, irresistible Mongol hordes sacked and burned scores of Russian cities, turning Russia into part of the sprawling Mongol Empire and imposing what later Russians called the "Tatar yoke." Kiev, the erstwhile center of Kievan Rus, became a ghost town.

Mongol rule produced important changes, though after the horrors of the initial onslaught, Tatar authority proved relatively mild. As long as the Mongols received tribute and deference, they left Russians alone. The Mongols did accelerate a steady population shift to the north. The flat, open southern steppe was far too exposed to attacks from the Mongols and other nomads. The northern forests, shielded from the nomads, were safer, and the center of gravity of Kievan Rus moved from the south around Kiev north toward the ancient cities of Suzdal and Vladimir and newer, smaller Moscow. The Mongols had an important impact on Russian political culture, as witnessed by Russian vocabulary. Many Russian words—money, barracks, hard labor, taxes, executioner—were borrowed from the Tatars. Russian styles of warfare, shaped by hundreds of years of fighting against nomads, were crystallized by Mongol influence. Russian city-states went to war as bow-armed light cavalry armies, like the nomads they fought and the Tatars who ruled them.

The Tatar yoke, annihilating the old Kievan system, opened up new political possibilities. The cities of the northeast, protected from nomadic attacks, now competed for dominance. Moscow, though not as old or as prestigious as some of its neighbors, benefited from remarkable leadership and became the agent of Tatar administration, collecting tribute and enforcing Tatar will. Moscow used that privileged position to expand its territory and influence. With the religious and cultural inheritance of Kievan Rus, and the hard political and military lessons of centuries of nomad warfare and steppe politics, the princes of Moscow built a territorial empire in the 1300s and 1400s. Moscow's burgeoning power enabled a gradual break from Tatar dominance, culminating in the Battle of Kulikovo Field in 1380. Prince Dmitrii Donskoi of Moscow defeated a Tatar horde, marking a fundamental change in the relationship.

The Gathering of Russian Lands

From the 1300s through the 1500s Muscovy (Moscow) was the beneficiary of a series of talented rulers. While Moscow enjoyed some geographical advantages—it was far enough north to escape the worst of the Mongol invasions, and it was on or near navigable rivers that flowed both north and south—there was nothing making it any more likely than its more prestigious neighbor Vladimir or any number of other Russian princely states to create an empire. What Moscow had, above all else, was a line of savvy, ruthless, and lucky princes who grabbed land by conquest, intrigue, marriage, or inheritance whenever opportunities presented themselves. For over 200 years, from Prince Ivan I, also known as Ivan Moneybags (*Kalita*) for amassing wealth and land, through Ivan IV, or Ivan the Terrible, the rulers of the small city-state of Muscovy pulled together a sizable empire from the fragments of Kievan Rus. Though the Kievan principle of brotherly inheritance had lapsed, Russian tradition held that all sons of a prince deserved a share in the inheritance; Moscow escaped division into nothingness by the fortunate accident that its princes had few sons, keeping the patrimony from fragmenting with each generation.

By the time Ivan IV inherited the throne at the age of three in 1533, what historians have termed "the gathering of Russian lands" was essentially complete. Muscovy exercised effective control over Russian-speaking territory, an area roughly equivalent to the present-day Russian Federation west of the Volga River. That meant that by the 1500s Russian foreign policy had fundamentally changed: Ivan's ancestors dealt largely with those like themselves: Orthodox Christian and Russian-speaking, seeing themselves as descendants of the original rulers of Kievan Rus. Though they had traded and fought with those farther west, and especially with nomads to the east and the south, the gathering of Russian lands had been a civil war among Russians, literally princely cousin against cousin.

Ivan IV's Muscovy had broader horizons, and its wars and diplomacy were conducted with those fundamentally different from the descendants of Kievan Rus: Catholic, Protestant, or Muslim, speaking Polish, German, or Tatar. His grandfather Ivan III had already recognized and signaled some of these changes. He had used the title "tsar," derived from the Roman title "Caesar," to signify that his power and prestige had reached a level above the mere princes ruling other Russian cities. Ivan III also introduced the double-headed eagle, gazing east and west, as Russia's state device—a symbol that survives today. Ivan III's claim to be tsar "of all Russia," all that had once been Kievan Rus, was not yet reality; by the time of Ivan IV, though, it was closer. Much of Kievan Rus, particularly Ukraine, still lay outside Muscovy's control. On a more practical basis, Ivan III had broadened the base of Muscovy's army and expanded its power. By recruiting more cavalrymen directly through grants of land, Ivan III created a larger army, and one more dependent on him, than in Russia previously.

To the east and south, Muscovy confronted successors of the Mongols that had once ruled Russia. When the Mongol Empire disintegrated, it split into smaller but still formidable hordes. These khanates, dominated by Muslims speaking Turkic languages, combined the horse-borne warfare of the Mongols with substantial institutions: cities and settled civilization. Muscovy bordered three important post-Mongol khanates: the Kazan khanate to the east, increasingly under Muscovite pressure and influence; distant Astrakhan to the southeast; and Crimea to the south. To the west, Muscovy had three neighbors, two strong and one weak. To the northwest, Sweden's empire included present-day Finland and dominated the Baltic. To the southwest, an enormous Polish-Lithuanian joint state stretched from the Baltic to the Black Sea and controlled much of the original Kievan Rus. In between lay Livonia (roughly present-day Estonia and Latvia), a patchwork region with a Baltic peasantry ruled over by German elites. Ivan IV's Muscovy fought all its neighbors.

Ivan the Terrible's Muscovy

When Ivan IV inherited the throne as a toddler in 1533, his ability to rule was obviously limited. When he became an adult, he had enormous power in principle, somewhat less so in reality. His better-known appellation Ivan the Terrible is, in part, a mistranslation and would be better rendered as Ivan the Dread or Ivan the Awe-Inspiring. This reflected his style of ruling and, to some degree, the power of his office. The nobility of Muscovy described themselves as "slaves of the tsar," and outside observers noted how much less power Muscovy's nobles had than proud and independent Western elites. While Muscovy's nobles were comparatively weaker, this does not mean Ivan could do as he pleased: there were practical restraints on his power, even after he reached adulthood. In particular, he had to rely on those slaves of the tsar to govern. He lacked the administrative machinery to rule without them.

The Muscovite state was a primitive institution for ruling a vast territory. Its lands formed a rough oval, stretching 500 miles east to west and 1,000 miles north to south, devoid of roads. Its administrative machinery had evolved from the princely household of a petty city-state, which Muscovy had previously been, and it still bore the marks of personal, ad hoc rule. The most important political institution, the boyar duma, was hardly an institution at all. Russian princes had always ruled in close consultation with their highest-ranking elites—nobles from rich and prestigious families called boyars. The boyars met in council with rulers to discuss important matters of state, but this council, retroactively labeled the boyar duma by historians, lacked formal rules or procedures that we can discern. It was simply a means for powerful men to discuss matters with their ruler. It also served as a reservoir of experienced and high-ranking servitors to staff Muscovy's rudimentary government. Without roads or communication, Muscovite tsars had little choice but to grant control over distant regions to powerful and politically savvy men. The boyar duma provided Muscovy with its field generals, its provincial governors, its ambassadors, and the other key positions of the state.

This boyar elite was terribly status conscious. Many of its members, those bearing the title of prince, were descended from the Viking rulers of Kievan Rus, just as Ivan the Terrible, and were proud of their ancestry and honor. Elite families long in Moscow jockeyed for position with new recruits to the tsar's service. To regulate this competition, the princes of Moscow established a system of organized and regulated precedence: *mestnichestvo*. This involved careful calculations of familial prestige and honor and dictated placement and rank in court ceremonials and government service. Appointments by seniority rather than ability were clearly inconsistent with military efficiency, so Ivan regularly decreed that *mestnichestvo* did not apply to military campaigns, and his successors typically followed the same expedient. While this boosted military effectiveness, it did nothing to eliminate cutthroat competition among elite families.

While the tsar and the boyar duma set policy, it was implemented and run through a series of offices (*prikazy*), which took clear form during Ivan's reign. Each *prikaz* had a particular function, whether combating bands of robbers or running the postal service. The ambassadorial office (*posol'skii prikaz*) controlled foreign policy. For military policy, two were most important. The *razriadnyi prikaz* kept service records of the gentry cavalry and called them for service when required in addition to handling logistics and rudimentary military intelligence on Muscovy's potential foes. The *pomestnyi prikaz* managed the land grants (*pomestie*) provided to those noble cavalry for their material support. The Muscovite bureaucracy expanded greatly under Ivan, as the territorial extent of the state, the increasing burden of war, and the growing complexity of the Muscovite army required expansion in the bureaucracy and its administrative expertise to deal with those challenges.

Muscovy did not have a standing army. Instead, its military forces were built around gentry cavalrymen who did part-time service for life, mustering for service when called to campaigns or to defend the realm. The term gentry, not a precise description, is intended to signify several things. The servitors who formed Muscovy's cavalry were men of status in society. They ranked above the hired mercenaries, generally foreign, who served as infantry, artillerymen, and engineers, and far above the townspeople and peasants who made up the bulk of the population. Their rank brought control over land, but not necessarily ownership of land. Some of Muscovy's gentry enjoyed something close to land ownership in their *votchina*: land held by right, and passed by father to son. In expansion from a small city-state to a major territorial empire, however, Muscovy's ruling grand princes had converted the land they conquered from *votchina* into something more amenable to their interests: *pomestie*. *Pomestie* land was held on condition of service, and made its possessors far less secure. The Muscovite princes granted particular lands to servitors in exchange for allegiance and military service. Should that service end, that particular serviceman had no continued right to that land. While the ruling prince might deign to pass a particular *pomestie* holding from a dead father to a living son, in principle failure to serve caused the land to be forfeited. Naturally, this land tenure, giving land, status, and livelihood in exchange for obedience and service, gave the princes of Moscow great power over their nobility. Typically, Moscow's conquest of another Russian city-state meant the transfer of that city's boyars and gentry warriors into Moscow's service, with their old *votchina* land confiscated and replaced by *pomestie* land far away. The confiscated *votchina* land was in turn granted as *pomestie* land to newly planted gentry. By Ivan the Terrible's time, this process was largely complete. While old boyar families might have extensive *votchina* land, the overwhelming majority of Muscovy's gentry, and therefore of Muscovy's army, were holders of small grants of land conditioned on their continuing loyal service as warriors of the tsar whenever called.

Under Ivan the Terrible, holding *pomestie* or *votchina* land made little difference to the concrete experience of military service. If one held land, whether conditional on service (*pomestie*) or inherited (*votchina*), one served as a cavalryman for the tsar. Whether one's holdings were large or small, the obligation still applied. Those enjoying larger tracts held a further obligation to provide additional mounted warriors, often armed slaves, depending on the extent of their land. Despite being referred to as nobility or gentry, most of the gentry cavalry lived hardly better than the peasants who sustained them. Though the boyars were tremendously wealthy, the average *pomeshchik* (holder of *pomestie* land) possessed a mere half-dozen peasant households and a small cash salary to support him and his family and pay for his weapons and horse. Some *pomeshchiki*, in fact, were so poor that they found themselves forced to sell themselves into slavery, as highly skilled military contractors for wealthier nobles obliged to bring additional warriors on campaign.

These gentry warriors, shaped by Russia's centuries of steppe warfare, fought as lightly armored cavalry. Their chief weapon was the bow, supplemented by saber and spear, and their chief tactic was raining hails of arrows on a foe. Their equipment, their small horses, and their rudimentary organization made them incapable of the shock charge with couched lances typical of European heavy cavalry. Though different from a Western European model, this force was perfectly suited for warfare against steppe nomads. Likewise, its organization for campaign and battle was rudimentary, but appropriate for the wars that Russian cities fought. The cavalry armies were generally split into five units: advance guard, main body, left wing, right wing, and rear guard. Strategy and tactics were not sophisticated. Most battles, as far as the limited sources allow us to determine, involved fluid, hit-and-run clashes of light cavalry decided by exchange of arrows, not hand-to-hand combat. Muscovy's most striking tactical innovation was the use of the *guliai-gorod,* or rolling fortress. Constructed from wooden screens on wheels, these moving defensive emplacements, somewhat akin to the wagon fortresses used by Hussite rebel forces in Bohemia in the early 1400s, provided protection and rallying points in fighting on the steppe.

Muscovy's most pressing danger was raids from the southern steppe, carried out by the Crimean Tatars for plunder and slaves. Much of the gentry cavalry did its yearly service in patrols along the southern border. As it grew, the Muscovite state established extensive defensive lines for protection, stretching hundreds of miles along Muscovy's border with the open steppe. Created from felled trees, wooden palisades, and earthen walls with ditches, these defensive lines were studded with observation posts and fortresses to repulse smaller raids and warn of larger ones. Despite occasional disasters, Muscovy's push south using its fortified lines opened up huge territories to renewed settlement. This shifted Muscovy's population back south from the forests of northern and central Russia to the increasingly secure steppes, partly undoing the results of the original Mongol attack.

Russian cities were walled for protection, with wooden and earthen outer walls shielding a core fortress or kremlin (*kreml'*) of stone or brick housing the city's ruler and government. Moscow's Kremlin, therefore, is the best-known example of something typical of Russian cities. This meant that warfare between cities required bringing down walls, and Muscovy used and built artillery from the 1400s. The growing presence of artillery meant that urban fortifications improved over the 1400s and 1500s, with earth and stone replacing wood. City fortifications grew more sophisticated with time; a particularly impressive complex at Smolensk was built at the end of the 1500s. Russian fortifications never reached the geometrical sophistication of western European equivalents, but were effective nonetheless.

Though the heart of the Muscovite army was the part-time gentry cavalry, Ivan the Terrible began incorporating regular infantry with gunpowder weapons. Firearms were not new to Muscovy; Moscow's princes had assembled such units and hired mercenaries before, but on a temporary basis. Ivan's innovation was to make these infantry (the *strel'tsy*) a permanent part of Muscovy's military. In 1550, Ivan created six companies of *strel'tsy*, each of 500 men, as standing, peacetime units, drawn from outside the noble gentry. In some ways they were professional and regular: armed uniformly with arquebus (primitive musket), long ax, and sword, dressed in long coats with units distinguished by color, and organized into a hierarchy of subunits. They were paid in part from the state treasury, a sign of the increasing capacity of Ivan's regime to extract cash from the population for state ends. Nonetheless, their salaries were inadequate to sustain them as full-time soldiers. They were provided plots of land, and many became urban tradesmen to support themselves. Despite their semiprofessional nature, these troops proved valuable in the eastern campaigns of Ivan's early reign, and they expanded over the 1500s. A large number were stationed as a permanent Moscow garrison.

The thin sources on Muscovite battles do not give much sense of how the *strel'tsy* were employed tactically. It seems they were stationed in the center of Muscovite lines to provide stationary massed fire, not to maneuver on the field of battle. That still leaves questions unanswered. In western and central European armies, firearm troops needed the protection of pikemen against cavalry charges; the slow and inaccurate fire of sixteenth-century weapons meant that cavalry attacks could not be repulsed with gunpowder alone, but only with the assistance of disciplined spearmen. The *strel'tsy* carried axes, not pikes, more for supporting their heavy arquebuses when firing than for combat. They may have relied on close support of Muscovite cavalry for protection, or *guliai-gorod* mobile fortifications.

The combination of these factors—a light cavalry army, walled cities, and primitive infantry—helps to explain critical features of Muscovite warfare: the lack of decisive battles, the accompanying importance of sieges, and, as a consequence, Muscovy's backwardness when warring against better-developed European states.

First, there is the lack of decisive battles. Contrary to the view that Western warfare has been characterized by decisive infantry clashes since the ancient Greeks, battles gave way in Europe to sieges and raiding for more than a millennium: from the fall of the Roman Empire until the seventeenth century. In early modern Europe, wise commanders avoided battles: they were dangerous, bloody, and unpredictable, as damaging to the victor as the vanquished. An army of superior strength was foolish to subject its superiority to the risk of battle: far better a predictable siege. Muscovite warfare exacerbated this tendency. Muscovy's light cavalry, admirably adapted to parrying nomad raids, was ill-suited to decisive battle. It fought by hit-and-run, launching flights of arrows and fleeing. While equipped with spears and sabers, Muscovites avoided shock action—the powerful cavalry charge—that might impose a clear and devastating defeat. Their horses were light and tough for long rides across the steppe but not for carrying the armor required for shock charges. On the other side, in the event of defeat, Muscovy's noble cavalry was capable of riding to safety, leaving any infantry behind. As a result, Muscovite military history is oddly devoid of decisive battles. Wars were not settled by victories in battle, but by sieges and exhaustion. The first decisive battle, in the sense that the course of the war and Russian history itself might have been different had the battle gone the other way, was Poltava in 1709 (discussed in Chapter 3).

Nomads from the steppe raided to steal goods and people; they did not need to be decisively defeated, only stopped and turned back. In wars against other powers, however, the things that were valuable were towns and cities, and those were fortified. Taking territory, either for one's own benefit or as a bargaining chip in negotiations, meant a siege. Muscovy's wars revolved around the sieges of key cities and fortresses, and the success or failure of those sieges determined success or failure in war, until the time of Poltava and the Northern War at the beginning of the 1700s.

So, when Muscovy fought more-developed Western powers under Ivan the Terrible, its technological and social backwardness, and resultant military backwardness, meant it had little success. Muscovy did have artillery and hired siege engineers, but those were functions of money and industrial development, where Muscovy was outpaced by its neighbors. Sieges required artillery, infantry, engineers, money, and time, and the Muscovite military machine was based on part-time gentry cavalry. There was a fundamental disconnect between Ivan the Terrible's army and the goals he wished to achieve with it.

Ivan's Early Reign

Born in 1530, Ivan was the product of an aged father's second marriage. Inheriting the throne at the age of three, Ivan played no initial role in actual governance. Instead, he became a pawn in political maneuverings among boyar clans, a situation far worse after the death of his mother in 1538. The danger and insecurity of Ivan's childhood had a pernicious influence on his personality, particularly evident later in life. In 1547, at age 16, Ivan took full power, had himself crowned tsar, and married. In his youth, Ivan was ambitious and able. Surrounding himself with capable and intelligent advisors, he began institutional, legal, and military reforms that made Muscovy capable of striking efforts at expansion. Ivan overcame the political turmoil of his childhood, married happily, established himself on the throne, and was now prepared to fulfill the promise of his title—tsar of all Russia.

Ivan's grandfather Ivan III had played kingmaker in Kazan, establishing Muscovite influence over the khanate's tangled politics, but that control slipped under Ivan's father, Vasilii III. The precise motivations that led Ivan the Terrible to make Kazan his first target of expansion are complex, including revenge for centuries of Tatar rule, a sense of Muscovy's destiny as leader of Orthodox Christianity in a crusade against Islam, and simple territorial gain. After the overthrow of a Muscovite-backed khan, Ivan personally led a Kazan campaign in late 1547. An early thaw of the Volga River, however, prevented Ivan from massing the artillery he needed to take Kazan. His troops besieged the city and ravaged the surrounding territory, but eventually had to withdraw. In 1549, the khan of Kazan died, leaving his throne to a two-year-old son. Ivan, feeling no sympathy, moved against the city in 1550, again unsuccessfully. To prepare for future campaigns, Ivan built an advance base at Sviiazhsk, on the Volga above Kazan. Crippled by internal conflict and the prospect of imminent Muscovite assault, Kazan accepted a Russian puppet as khan and freed tens of thousands of captured Russian slaves. This arrangement, however, rapidly collapsed. Wearied by the turbulence of Kazan politics and the unreliability of Muscovite agents, Ivan decided on outright conquest.

In the summer of 1552, Ivan personally joined the final campaign. Taking advantage of the distraction provided by Muscovy's push east, the Crimean Tatars launched a major raid, but were defeated by Muscovite forces outside the city of Tula. Ivan's campaign continued uninterrupted. By August, Ivan had reached Sviiazhsk and crossed to the Kazan side of the Volga. On 23 August 1552, the siege began. Outside Kazan's earth-filled wooden walls, studded by over a dozen stone towers, the Muscovites set up earthworks and fortifications of their own while maintaining a steady bombardment. Ivan's forces contained regular sorties by the Kazan garrison and destroyed Tatar forces raiding the Muscovite siege works from forests outside the city. Foreign engineers in Ivan's service tunneled under and destroyed the city's water supply, then prepared a mine with a massive explosive charge under the city walls. On Sunday, 2 October 1552, the Muscovites detonated the mine, blowing a hole in the city wall, and began a general storm. Ivan prayed for victory while his troops forced their way into Kazan in vicious hand-to-hand fighting. Though many Russians stopped fighting to loot, Tatar resistance eventually collapsed. The khan was handed over to the Russians by his own soldiers, many of whom broke and fled for their lives through the encircling siege works. In the city itself, a general massacre of resisters began, sparing women and children as prizes. On returning to Moscow, Ivan built Russia's best-known architectural landmark, St. Basil's Cathedral on Red Square, to celebrate his achievement.

Two things are striking about Ivan's success from a military point of view. First, Muscovy launched and sustained two initial campaigns, albeit unsuccessful ones, 500 miles from Moscow in the dead of Russian winter. Second, the final conquest of Kazan was an impressive feat of engineering: building siege works, erecting siege towers, filling moats, and tunneling mines. The ultimate assault required hard fighting through the streets of a major city. Both tasks were unsuited to Muscovy's noble cavalry—indeed, during the storm Ivan had ordered his personal regiment to dismount and join the street fighting. Clearly, Muscovy's armed forces had progressed rapidly in capability and sophistication under Ivan's rule.

The conquest of Kazan had a number of important consequences. It opened the door to Siberia and its staggering natural wealth. From Ivan's time on, Russian soldiers and traders pushed relentlessly toward the Pacific. Second, Muscovite troops had for the first time conquered a Mongol successor state. Mongol hordes had been defeated before, but not conquered. Third, the conquest of Kazan made Russia a multinational state. The Muscovy that Ivan had inherited had been populated almost entirely by Russian-speaking Orthodox Christians. After Kazan, he had a large population of Muslim Turks and Finnic pagans, to say nothing of Siberian tribes soon under Moscow's rule. To Muscovy's credit, its elite was remarkably open to ethnic outsiders, provided they accepted Christianity. Tatar nobles who converted to Orthodoxy were treated as equals by their Russian counterparts and often enjoyed lengthy and prestigious careers in Russian state service. The Tatars also provided a valuable supplement to Ivan's military power. Nearly a quarter of some armies in the subsequent Livonian War were Tatars. Conquering Kazan required years of pacification to bring the region's tribes and unreconciled Tatars under control. Muscovite punitive expeditions took captives, burned villages, and slaughtered resisters in large numbers.

Kazan put the upper Volga in Moscow's hands. The logical next step was to extend Ivan's power to the mouth of the river on the Caspian Sea at Astrakhan, the site of another Mongol successor khanate. In this, Ivan had the cooperation of a faction of Nogai nomads, who controlled territory between Kazan and Astrakhan east of the Volga. In spring 1554, a Russian army traveled down the Volga to Astrakhan, seizing it in July against token resistance. Ivan installed a Russian client as the new khan, and his allies won control of the Nogai horde. Astrakhan proved no more stable as a Russian satellite than Kazan had been. A second expedition to Astrakhan in 1556 imposed Moscow's direct rule permanently.

The Livonian War

Just as Ivan's twin successes meant he could be confident that his eastern border was under control, he faced twin problems to the south and west. To the south, perennial Crimean Tatar raids on southern Russia carried away captives to Mediterranean slave markets. Muscovy carried out a series of punitive expeditions, testing a concerted effort to conquer the Crimea as Kazan and Astrakhan had been taken. This was no simple task: reaching the Crimea involved a long march through inhospitable terrain. The Crimea itself was a natural fortress thanks to the Perekop, the narrow isthmus connecting it to the mainland. An attack on the Crimea was an enormous risk when a seemingly easier target was close at hand.

Despite arguments by several advisors that the Crimea was a better choice, Ivan was convinced that Livonia was an ideal opportunity for conquest. Muscovy was increasingly drawn into western and central Europe's trade networks. Grain and forest products went west; manufactured goods, particularly military technology, went east. An English vessel traveled around Scandinavia to northern Muscovy in 1553, whetting Ivan's appetite for Western ties. Muscovy's inadequate outlets to the West meant that its trade enriched Livonian ports—Reval (now Tallinn), Parnau (now Pärnu), and Riga. Though prosperous, Livonia was politically and militarily weak. It was a mosaic of towns, bishoprics, and territories loosely controlled by the Livonian Order, a crusading society of knights that had pushed Latin Christianity into pagan regions around the southern shores of the Baltic. The knights had long since lost their crusading zeal, and Livonian society was itself riven by the Protestant Reformation. Ivan saw an opportunity for easy gain in Livonia. The danger he overlooked was that Livonia had more than one rapacious neighbor. Sweden, Denmark, and Poland-Lithuania—all formidable opponents—were just as eager to seize Livonia's lucrative ports and would not let Moscow have them without a fight.

Muscovy manufactured a crisis in 1554 over the issues of tribute from the bishopric of Dorpat (now Tartu), long in arrears, and free transit for Russian merchants and goods. When the promised tribute was not forthcoming, even after a grace period of three years, Ivan invaded. When Muscovite troops crossed into Livonia in January 1558, this set in motion events producing 150 years of warfare among the powers ringing the Baltic. By the end, Denmark and Sweden were destroyed as great powers, and Poland was wiped from the map of Europe altogether, while Russia was a major force in European politics. There was nothing inevitable about that outcome, and there was no guarantee that Muscovy would become the dominant power in eastern Europe, instead of Sweden or Poland. Indeed, at several points in that long struggle, Muscovy seemed close to annihilation.

The initial January 1558 incursion was reconnaissance, not a serious attempt at conquest; it ravaged the Livonian countryside and Muscovite forces returned loaded down with plunder. In May, as ambassadors from the Livonian Order arrived in Moscow to negotiate terms, Ivan's troops seized Narva, just across the border from the Muscovite town of Ivangorod, and Ivan told the Livonian ambassadors that only complete acceptance of Muscovite hegemony was acceptable. By the end of summer 1558, Muscovite forces had captured 20 Livonian towns, leaving garrisons behind and returning to Muscovy. This ill-timed withdrawal gave the Livonian Order an opportunity to counterattack, retaking some lost towns, though not Narva and Dorpat, the real prizes. Some Livonian forces even raided into Muscovy itself, provoking Muscovite retaliation. In January 1559 a punitive expedition, not equipped for seizing cities, burned and ravaged its way through the Livonian countryside. A pattern had thus developed within a year of the war's outbreak: Muscovite forces could range across Livonia at will, devastating the countryside and taking small towns and cities, but they could not seize what was most important to Ivan: the large ports. The lesson was not one that Ivan or his immediate successors learned and applied: Muscovy's gentry cavalry was increasingly obsolete in a era dominated by sophisticated fortifications and infantry wielding gunpowder weapons. Ivan's cavalry and primitive infantry could terrorize peasants, but major ports, protected by substantial fortifications and resupplied by sea, were beyond his grasp.

As the war grew more savage, Livonia appealed to its more powerful neighbors for protection. Sweden offered nothing; Denmark purchased parts of Livonia for rule by the Danish king's brother. Poland was most willing to help, offering Livonia protection in return for territorial concessions. Poland's warning to Ivan to steer clear of Livonia went nowhere, however, laying the groundwork for general war in the Baltic. In late 1559, Muscovite incursions began again, and in 1560 Muscovy finally destroyed the remaining military power of the Livonian Order. Increasingly desperate to end Muscovite depredations, the cities and towns of Livonia sought any deal under any conditions. Reval put itself entirely under Sweden's authority in June 1561. The bulk of Livonia, by contrast, gave itself over to Poland in November 1561.

By this point, at the end of 1561, all Livonia's neighbors had seized parts of the whole. This raised the possibility of a simple partition in which Muscovy, Sweden, Denmark, and Poland would all share Livonia and end the war. A similar settlement, in fact, destroyed Poland 200 years later. For Ivan, though, ending the war along the front lines of 1561 did not give him enough to justify peace without some further attempt to gain a better outcome. The major ports of Livonia and their lucrative tolls were still out of his grasp. Ivan may, in addition, have been affected by the paranoia and irrationality soon to explode in an orgy of violence.

After years of clashes between Muscovite and Polish-Lithuanian forces in Livonia, in 1563 Ivan escalated the conflict to full-scale war by expanding the fighting out of Livonia into Poland-Lithuania proper. A Muscovite army crossed the border to attack the important city of Polotsk. While taking Polotsk would shield Ivan's supply lines to Livonia, the attack also allowed Ivan to portray himself as a crusader against heretic Catholics, Protestants, and Jews. A two-week siege destroyed the city walls and forced its surrender. Polotsk's Jews were massacred, and wagonloads of plunder went to Moscow. Poland proposed peace, but Ivan was still not willing to settle without further gains. In an attempt to cement his domestic support, in 1566 Ivan summoned a *zemskii sobor,* an assembly of the land, to consult with representatives of the Muscovite population on whether to make peace or continue war. The boyars, lower nobility, and the church hierarchy all pledged themselves to Ivan's policy: war until victory. Ivan had the political backing he desired, but never gained the outcome he sought. The war dragged on without any significant Muscovite gains, only a continuing drain of men and money.

As the Livonian War's frustrations mounted, Ivan's paranoia and frustration exploded into horrific violence against his own people. This *oprichnina,* a period of political chaos and mass terror, still provokes intense debate: was Ivan insane, or was he reacting against real dangers to his authority? If the dangers were real, were Ivan's actions a rational response or a paranoid overreaction? There is still no consensus. What is clear is that Ivan believed that his failures in the Livonian War were due to traitors among his own servitors. There was indeed opposition to the seemingly intractable war. After all, many within Muscovy had wanted a war against the Crimean Tatars instead. Some boyars broke with Ivan openly and defected abroad, fearing for their safety if they stayed. Increasingly isolated by the death of his beloved first wife and his break from his key advisor Aleskei Adashev, Ivan's suspicion grew unchecked. In a bizarre episode in 1565, Ivan announced his abdication, provoking his anxious boyars to beg him to return. Ivan allowed himself to be persuaded to take the throne again on the condition of his own absolute power. Immediately afterwards, he announced the division of Muscovy into two separate jurisdictions: the *oprichnina* under his direct rule and the *zemshchina* under the boyar duma. This meant two armies, two administrations, and enormous chaos. Ivan used his new powers over the *oprichnina* to redistribute land and create a private army of enforcers and executioners. These *oprichniki* rode Muscovy in black robes on black horses, carrying dogs' heads and brooms as symbols of their intent to sniff out and sweep away disloyalty and treason. Ivan began wholesale executions of real and suspected enemies.

While the nature and course of the *oprichnina* remain mysterious (Ivan deliberately destroyed most records), its impact on Russia's military history is clear. With Ivan at war with his own society, Muscovy's ability to carry on the Livonian campaign and protect itself from outside attack disappeared in a storm of political bloodshed. The Crimean khan invaded Muscovy in spring 1571, and despite Ivan's attempts to organize a defense, reached Moscow and burned it, killing so many, the chronicles tell us, that corpses dammed the Moscow River. The shock of this disaster sobered Ivan. He abolished the *oprichnina* in 1571 and banned any future mention of it. Muscovy was able to repel a second Crimean invasion in 1572.

The damage the *oprichnina* inflicted, however, could not be easily repaired, particularly since Ivan's diplomatic environment had taken a turn for the worse. In 1569, Poland and Lithuania, jointly ruled by the Polish king, united themselves into a single state in the face of the growing Muscovite threat. In 1570 Sweden ended its own war with Denmark, freeing itself to concentrate fully on Muscovite territory on the Baltic. Finally, after the death of Polish King Sigismund Augustus II in 1572, lengthy political maneuvers ended in the election of the talented and energetic Stefan Batory as Polish king in 1576. Ivan nevertheless continued his seemingly unending efforts to conquer Livonia. He established Magnus, renegade brother of the king of Sweden, as a puppet king of Livonia in 1570 and personally led an army into northern Livonia against Swedish-controlled territory in late 1572. Intermittent successes, including the capture of Pernau in 1575, and the conquest by 1577 of most of Livonia, kept Ivan's hopes of ultimate victory alive as the human and financial costs of war mounted.

In 1578, however, Batory turned the war decisively against Ivan. Swedish and Polish armies took Livonian towns one after another and raided deep into Muscovy. In August 1579, Batory led a Polish army to retake Polotsk, lost to Ivan 15 years earlier. The next year he captured the Russian town of Velikii Luki, threatening Ivan's communications. In 1581, Batory presented Ivan with his greatest danger by besieging Pskov. Losing Pskov would sever the connection between Muscovy and Livonia, leaving Ivan utterly defeated. At the same time, Sweden took advantage of Ivan's desperate condition to liquidate Ivan's conquests in northern Livonia, grabbing Narva and Ivangorod. On the verge of complete disaster, Ivan accepted negotiations with Batory. Over the winter of 1581–1582, Muscovite diplomats agreed to cede Livonia to Poland and accept a ten-year truce. Ivan's surrender was intended to enable him to fight the Swedes, to regain in northern Livonia what he had given up to the Poles in southern Livonia. With depleted troops and little stomach for a continued fight, however, Ivan gave up this dream and agreed to a three-year truce with the Swedes in 1583, closing the quarter-century Livonian War.

Ivan did not live to see that truce expire. Tormented by pain, disease, and guilt, he died in 1584. Despite the accomplishments of his early regime, including establishing Russia's first regular infantry and opening Russian expansion into Siberia through his conquests of Kazan and Astrakhan, his Livonian War proved disastrous. To sustain war with Western powers, financially and militarily, Muscovy needed substantial reform. In return for the costs of the war, the horrific devastation inflicted on Livonia, and the tens of thousands of Russian lives lost, Ivan had nothing. His hope had been Muscovite trade with the West through Livonia's seaports. Instead, Ivangorod, Muscovy's mediocre foothold on the Baltic, was now Swedish. The disaster did not end there. The damage Ivan had done to Muscovy's political and social system had pernicious consequences long after his death, bringing Muscovy to the brink of utter destruction.

CHAPTER 2

The Time of Troubles

Like a time bomb, the damage Ivan the Terrible did to Muscovy exploded with terrible force 15 years after his death and nearly destroyed everything the Grand Princes of Muscovy had painstakingly built for 200 years. This period of staggering upheaval, stretching from Ivan's death in 1584 through the establishment of a new dynasty in 1613, is called the Time of Troubles. The Muscovite state almost ceased to exist from rebellion, civil war, foreign war, and the famine and disease that accompany them. In a way, the Troubles showed the contradiction at the heart of the Muscovite social contract. The state was organized to support a noble cavalry class through serfdom and ruthless centralization; that serfdom and centralization bred deep social tensions that exploded into horrible violence.

From the point of view of military history, the sieges and battles of the Time of Troubles seem to blend together in a confusing morass: is there any pattern to be discerned? The length and interminable nature of the Time of Troubles give some clues as to what it signifies. The lack of decisive battles mentioned in the last chapter gives way in the Time of Troubles to the general indecisiveness of all warfare. Both Sweden and Poland invaded Muscovy during the Time of Troubles, but were unable to sustain major campaigns deep inside Muscovy. Rebel armies appeared again and again, but could not take and hold power beyond their heartland on the Muscovite southern frontier. The government in Muscovy might defeat a rebel army or take a rebel stronghold, but rebel movements shook off those defeats and raged unabated. What all these have in common is a lack of state capacity. Both established governments and rebel movements found it very difficult to muster the financial and human resources necessary to take territories and hold them intact. The chaos of the Time of Troubles fed on itself. Authorities lacked the legitimacy to expect their followers' loyalty. At the same time, political upheaval made it impossible to find the tax revenues necessary to *buy* loyalty.

What finally brought the Time of Troubles to an end is what its greatest historian, S. F. Platonov, called its national phase. A lack of state capacity brought only continuing and unresolved warfare, but a movement organized from below on a *national* basis, i.e., on a shared ethnic and religious identity in opposition to foreign and alien elements, restored order to Muscovy and ended the Troubles. By tapping into deep xenophobia as a unifying force, what the Muscovite state proved unable to do, the people of Muscovy did for themselves.

Boris Godunov

After Ivan the Terrible's death in 1584, Muscovy faced twin crises: dynastic and sociopolitical. The dynastic crisis involved Ivan's heir. Ivan killed his eldest son and heir Ivan Ivanovich in a rage in 1581, and his pregnant daughter-in-law died of shock immediately afterward. That left Ivan with only two sons as possible heirs, neither ideal. The older son, Fyodor, was mentally handicapped, and all observers agreed he was incapable of ruling alone. Ivan had another son, Dmitrii, born to his seventh wife in 1582. Though Dmitrii seemed mentally sound, Ivan's numerous marriages made Dmitrii's legitimacy doubtful in the eyes of the church, and in any event Dmitrii was not the eldest son. At Ivan's death, the throne went to Fyodor, despite his obvious shortcomings. If Dmitrii had reached adulthood, he might have threatened his weak half-brother, but that problem was solved when Dmitrii died in 1591 of a knife in the throat, ostensibly self-inflicted during an epileptic fit.

Despite Fyodor's handicap, before Ivan's death he married Irina Godunova, sister of Boris Godunov, a highly intelligent rising star in Ivan's court. When Fyodor inherited the throne, Godunov used his position as the tsar's brother-in-law to maneuver with remarkable rapidity and skill into position as the power behind the throne, ousting all competitors with ease. When Fyodor died childless in 1598, Godunov moved immediately to have himself crowned tsar, taking in name the authority he had in fact wielded for over a decade. The dynasty that had ruled Muscovy for centuries thus came to an end with Godunov, widely perceived as an interloper, as tsar. A group of powerful boyars, ambitious for status and possessing long memories, rankled under the authority of their lower-born tsar.

The sociopolitical crisis, compounding the dynastic crisis, grew out of the nature of Muscovy's gentry cavalry army. Its warriors depended on grants of land to support them and their families while also paying for their arms, armor, and horses. Two long-term trends made this untenable. First, natural population growth of the gentry meant a steadily increasing number of nobles who needed land, but the territorial expansion to provide that land was difficult to achieve. Second, noble land required peasant labor to work it. Heavy taxation, harsh landlords, and the political turmoil of Ivan's reign brought the depopulation of central Muscovy as peasants fled to newly opened territories on Muscovy's periphery, away from landlords and tax collectors. Muscovy's success in pushing defensive lines south into the steppe paradoxically created safe havens on the southern frontier for runaway peasants. In order to keep peasants in place to support its military class, the rulers of Muscovy over the 1500s had imposed increasing limitations on peasant movement while still allowing it in principle.

Godunov's remarkable political skill did much to postpone disaster. He embarked on massive public works projects. One was expanding the southern defensive lines against the Tatars; another was the fortification of Muscovy's cities, including a mammoth fortress at Smolensk, commanding the key route toward Moscow from the west. During Fyodor's lifetime, Godunov granted tax relief to the hard-pressed gentry and imposed temporary bans on all peasant movement. These temporary bans became permanent in the 1590s, creating the institution of serfdom—an unfree peasantry bound to the land—that characterized Russian history for the next 250 years. Godunov's reign therefore culminated a lengthy process of enserfment of the Russian peasantry to prop up the gentry who made up the Muscovite army. Tying peasants permanently to the land, however, only slowed the crisis. In Russia's vast spaces, with labor short everywhere, escaped peasants were difficult to track down. With the average *pomeshchik* possessing only a half-dozen peasant households, the flight of even one was an economic catastrophe.

Many fleeing peasants, along with escaped slaves and poor nobles who could not meet their service obligations, went south to enroll as soldiers along the frontier defenses. Others joined cossack bands. The cossacks, a term derived from the Turkish word for "wanderer" or "freebooter," were a heterogeneous community along Muscovy's southern borders, living in democratic and communal settlements in the no-man's-land of the empty steppe, what Russians called the "wild field" between settled Muscovite territory and areas under the control of the Crimean Tatars. In addition to an important community of cossacks along the Dnepr River in what is now Ukraine, other groups of cossacks formed farther east, particularly along the Don River. The cossacks lived peacefully through fishing and hunting and violently as mercenaries and raiders. Generally Orthodox, they more often than not sided with Muscovy against its Muslim Tatar enemies to the south and Catholic Polish-Lithuanian enemies to the west, but cared above all for their own liberties. For both Muscovy and Poland, each of which had substantial cossack communities on their southern frontiers, the undisciplined cossacks presented dangers and opportunities: the danger of a refuge for fleeing peasants and of unpredictable and combative bands that might turn against settled authority. On the other hand, the cossacks provided auxiliary troops in time of war and a valuable buffer against Tatar raids. Muscovy and Poland thus followed similar strategies to domesticate the cossacks, registering them where possible as regular servitors of the state, particularly by enrolling them as garrison troops along the frontiers. The growing numbers of cossacks, and their resistance to outside control, meant that the proportion under reliable authority was always small. The cossacks were jealous of their freedom, with an ethos of equality and liberty that coexisted poorly with any attempt at centralized control by Poland or Muscovy.

Godunov needed land to reward the *pomeshchiki* who made up his army and peasants to work that land. As a result, he steadily pushed Russian control south into the steppe, trying to recover escaped peasants and control cossacks, a process dreaded by those on the other end. Seething resentment over the relentless march south of Muscovite authority threatened to explode into open rebellion.

In terms of foreign policy, Godunov worked assiduously to maintain truces with Poland and Sweden, at least until Muscovy had recovered from the damage that Ivan had inflicted. Permanent peace was unlikely, given that Sweden held Ivangorod, a town that had been indisputably Russian for many years. Muscovy broke the truce with Sweden at the beginning of 1590. In a campaign joined personally by both Tsar Fyodor and Godunov, Muscovite troops won a quick victory outside Narva, and the Swedes agreed to return Ivangorod. Fear of Polish intervention kept Godunov from continuing the war in hopes of seizing Narva as well, and tortuous negotiations produced a permanent peace in 1595. Godunov also capably managed the Tatar threat. A Crimean invasion in 1591 reached the southern outskirts of Moscow, but a pitched battle in which the Muscovites employed *guliai-gorod* fortifications in conjunction with field artillery and *strel'tsy* infantry to resist Tatar attacks led the Crimeans to flee south, abandoning their plunder and allowing their rear guard to be annihilated. This produced a peace settlement with the Tatars, removing some of the pressure from Muscovy's southern borders.

The Pretenders

Godunov's carefully constructed regime and its 15-year run of success began to collapse in 1601. Poor weather produced crop failures and devastating famine lasting through 1603. Godunov's efforts at relief for the poor proved inadequate to deal with the disaster, and his legitimacy came into question. As the famine eased, bizarre news in 1604 made Godunov's hold even more tenuous. A man appeared in Poland claiming to be Dmitrii, son of Ivan the Terrible and Muscovy's rightful tsar, presumed dead in 1591 but miraculously saved and ready to reclaim his rightful place. Historians ever since have argued over the identity of this First False Dmitrii, though they have generally accepted that he was not in fact Ivan's son. The First False Dmitrii was a convincing impostor, carrying himself as a well-bred Russian boyar and evidently believing he was the man he claimed to be. The most recent research suggests this Dmitrii had been carefully cultivated from childhood as a weapon against Godunov. Those responsible may have been a conspiracy of boyar families, probably led by the Romanov clan, the family of Ivan the Terrible's first wife. Though the idea of a child raised in secret for years to believe himself a tsar seems far-fetched, the reality of the First False Dmitrii is far-fetched to begin with. Whoever he was in reality, the First False Dmitrii found boyars, cossacks, and discontented peasants ready to accept him, or at least pretend to in order to depose Godunov. Muscovite political culture made it difficult to conceive of any justification for rebelling against a tsar put in place by God; having a rightful tsar, wrongfully denied the throne, made that task much simpler.

Dmitrii, with the assistance of Polish nobles and secret allies in Muscovy itself, built an army and crossed from Poland to Muscovy in October 1604. Bringing only a relatively small force, Dmitrii did not head directly for Moscow, which would have required dealing with the major fortress at Smolensk. He instead swung south to the restive frontier where he readily found recruits. Gentry cavalrymen and cossacks swarmed to his banner, resentful toward Godunov and ready to back change. Towns and garrisons hundreds of miles in advance of Dmitrii's troops declared their allegiance. Dmitrii faced a temporary setback when his troops became bogged down in the siege of the fortress town of Novgorod-Severskii. Godunov dispatched an army to break the siege and bring Dmitrii's small but burgeoning army to battle. Despite a major advantage in numbers, Godunov's commander was far too timid. In the December 1604 battle, Polish cavalry attacks on the Muscovite right wing forced Godunov's entire army to retreat in disarray, producing even more defection. Still unable to capture Novgorod-Severskii, Dmitrii abandoned it and pushed farther into the heart of Muscovy.

Over the winter of 1604–1605, many of Dmitrii's Polish allies deserted him to return home, but the continuing flow of new Muscovite recruits meant that his armies grew stronger by the day. Dmitrii pressed his advantage and attacked Godunov's army at the village of Dobrynichi in late January 1605. Just as in the first battle, Dmitrii's cavalry attacked and routed the Muscovite right wing, whereupon the rest of his forces attacked the center of the Muscovite line. This time, however, Dmitrii crashed directly into a mass of *strel'tsy* and other infantry, protected by a *guliai-gorod*. Dmitrii's cavalry charged into a withering blast of fire and fled in chaos, pursued by the remaining Muscovite cavalry. Godunov's forces captured Dmitrii's artillery and thousands of prisoners; all Muscovite subjects found in Dmitrii's service were executed. Punitive operations against rebellious regions followed. Dmitrii himself barely escaped capture, his army in ruins.

Despite this defeat, Dmitrii was not finished. He rebuilt his forces from southern Muscovy, drawing cossacks and others from regions where Godunov had recently imposed centralized control. Godunov's commanders were passive, doubting their own soldiers' loyalty. They spent months besieging the small but strategically seated rebel fortress of Kromy, on the road to Moscow from the south, rather than pursuing Dmitrii's main army.

At this moment, with spreading rebellion along Muscovy's southern frontier and his army bogged down at Kromy, Boris Godunov died suddenly on 13/23 April 1605. Godunov's 16-year-old son Fyodor inherited the throne, but boyars who had been unable to match the father's political skill had no qualms about abandoning the son. The army besieging rebel forces at Kromy broke with Fyodor Godunov and declared its allegiance to Dmitrii. With the connivance of sympathetic boyars, Dmitrii sent agents to Moscow. In June 1605, they instigated a popular riot against Fyodor Godunov, who was murdered along with his mother. The First False Dmitrii entered Moscow in triumph as the tsar of Muscovy and got the real Dmitrii's mother, Ivan the Terrible's seventh wife, to proclaim him genuine.

The new tsar Dmitrii was by all accounts active, cosmopolitan, liberal, and merciful, traits that led directly to his downfall. His Polish customs, open tolerance of Catholics, Protestants, and Jews, and May 1606 marriage to a Polish Catholic all turned Muscovite opinion against him. The boyars who aided Dmitrii's path to get rid of Godunov no longer needed him and plotted his downfall. Prince Vasilii Ivanovich Shuiskii, a boyar of impeccable family credentials and despicable morals, had nearly been executed for disloyalty to Tsar Dmitrii before being spared on the chopping block. Shuiskii repaid Dmitrii's mercy by recruiting factions of the army, church, and boyars to a conspiracy, using Dmitrii's Polish connections to stir up resentment. In May 1606, Shuiskii's conspirators assembled a mob on Red Square, seized the gates to the Kremlin, then stormed inside. Attempting to flee, Dmitrii fell from a high window, and the boyars shot and hacked him to death. Over a thousand Poles were massacred, along with hundreds of Russians from Dmitrii's fallen regime. Shuiskii, leader of the conspiracy, had himself proclaimed tsar, and systematically discredited his predecessor. The pretender's body was burned, and his ashes were blown from a cannon back toward the Polish border.

Tsar Shuiskii's new regime was fragile from its beginning. The social and dynastic crises that had plagued Godunov's reign were worsened by the First False Dmitrii's invasion and tawdry murder. The discontented cossacks and gentry who flocked to Dmitrii showed no loyalty to his murderer. Southern Muscovy, which had defied Moscow's authority under Godunov, did the same under Shuiskii, a regicide, a usurper of a usurper, and a well-documented liar.

This rebellion became even more dangerous. Ivan Bolotnikov, a wandering soldier, took it over, using his natural talent as a leader. Believing himself an agent of Tsar Dmitrii, Bolotnikov organized the seething cossacks of southern Muscovy into a revolutionary army. Despite the antielitist ethos of his cossack followers, large numbers of dissatisfied gentry, disgusted with Shuiskii, joined Bolotnikov as well. His armies were a blend of gentry and cossacks, i.e., those who had some status in Muscovy and had something to lose. A struggle between Shuiskii and the rebels to control the towns south of Muscovy raged over the summer of 1606 until Shuiskii's weary and dispirited armies began to collapse and withdraw north. More and more gentry abandoned their nominal obedience to Shuiskii. By October 1606, Bolotnikov had ringed Moscow to the west and south, with his main forces encamped just south of the city at Kolomenskoe.

At this point, the rebellion's heterogeneous makeup began to work against it, as gentry rebels grew increasingly uncomfortable with cossack radicalism. A rebel in the name of Tsar Dmitrii, Bolotnikov could as yet produce no Dmitrii to back his case. As Bolotnikov urged social revolution against the privileged, many of his gentry allies deserted him and returned to Shuiskii, or simply went home. Shuiskii improved his chances further by appointing his young, talented nephew Mikhail Vasil'evich Skopin-Shuiskii to command his troops. Bolotnikov's failure to completely encircle Moscow allowed Shuiskii to move supplies and reinforcements into the city through a northeastern corridor. Sensing Bolotnikov's weakening grip, Shuiskii's army moved south from Moscow to attack him at Kolomenskoe. Under Skopin-Shuiskii, the tsar's forces met Bolotnikov's in a decisive clash in December 1606. In the midst of the battle, as part of a prearranged scheme, Bolotnikov's second-in-command defected along with his men. The rebel forces broke and ran, with Skopin-Shuiskii pursuing them closely, capturing and slaughtering rebels by the thousands. Bolotnikov withdrew south to Kaluga to regroup and was trapped there by Muscovite troops.

The reservoir of discontent along Muscovy's southern border meant that Bolotnikov's campaign was not over. Though Bolotnikov himself was trapped in Kaluga, his movement drew continued support. Another pretender appeared in the south, this one claiming to be the entirely fictitious Peter, nonexistent son of Tsar Fyodor. This False Peter gathered an army at Tula, 100 miles south of Moscow and only 60 miles east of besieged Kaluga. A push by the False Peter's troops met Shuiskii's besiegers on the Pchelnia River 25 miles from Kaluga in May 1607. Much like Bolotnikov's defeat at Kolomenskoe, the clash was settled by a betrayal. This time, however, a number of Shuiskii's cossacks switched their allegiance to the False Peter, leading to the almost complete annihilation of Shuiskii's army. Kaluga's encircling forces lost heart with news of the defeat, allowing Bolotnikov to lead a decisive sortie that sent Shuiskii's soldiers fleeing in terror. Bolotnikov, now free, withdrew to Tula alongside the False Peter.

The civil war seemed no closer to resolution. Shuiskii remained ensconced in Moscow; Bolotnikov's rebels controlled southern Muscovy from his new headquarters at Tula. Recognizing his desperate situation, Shuiskii spared no effort to pull every last man from the areas of Muscovy still under his control, including drafting peasant conscripts (*datochnye liudi*) devoid of military experience to fill his armies. False Peter and Bolotnikov made Shuiskii's task easier by an ill-advised offensive against Moscow. Shuiskii's army caught this expedition in June at the Vosma River. Once again, treachery decided the battle; several thousand rebels defected, leading to the destruction of the rebel army. This permitted Skopin-Shuiskii to trap Bolotnikov, the False Peter, and the rest of the rebels inside Tula. After attempts to storm the city failed, Shuiskii's army deliberately dammed the Upa River, flooding the city. After a four-month siege, the Tula rebels surrendered on 10 October 1607. After Bolotnikov and the False Peter were paraded through Moscow, the False Peter was tortured and publicly hanged; Bolotnikov, now a folk hero, was kept under arrest in reasonably good conditions until February 1608 when he was blinded and drowned on Shuiskii's orders.

Even as Bolotnikov's cossack rebellion was brought under control, a *second* False Dmitrii appeared in Poland. Other pretenders had sprung up across Muscovy, but this one enjoyed significant Polish backing. Unlike the First False Dmitrii, the second knew he was an impostor and was a puppet of his important supporters. His masquerade was a cynical ploy for support, which he indeed received: from Polish adventurers eager to regain what they had lost with the First False Dmitrii's murder, and from cossacks continuing their opposition to Moscow. The Second False Dmitrii invaded Muscovy in September 1607. Shuiskii's focus on taking Tula and capturing Bolotnikov allowed this new Dmitrii to win quick successes, gathering recruits steadily. With Shuiskii's resources and will dwindling, the Second False Dmitrii easily reached Moscow. Unable to breach the city's formidable fortifications, he settled his army in June 1608 at Tushino, just north of the city. The war had shifted from cossack uprising to Polish intervention, but was no closer to resolution.

The Second False Dmitrii's siege of Moscow brought another stalemate. He was unable to capture Moscow and eliminate Shuiskii; Shuiskii could not defeat the pretender. This created two separate governments. The south was entirely out of control after years of rebellion; the pretender seized the still relatively prosperous north to strip it of resources; Shuiskii controlled Moscow and some territory in eastern Muscovy but little else. Muscovy's elites, deprived of any sense of principle by years of political turmoil, shifted their allegiance back and forth in keeping with their immediate calculations of self-interest.

Shuiskii was desperate for assistance, and Charles IX, king of Sweden, was eager to prevent any expansion of Polish influence. Skopin-Shuiskii negotiated a deal in 1609 for Swedish intervention. Sweden provided 5,000 mercenaries and another 10,000 the next year in return for a permanent alliance against Poland and Muscovy's surrender of all claims to Livonia. In addition, the Second False Dmitrii's extortionary tactics in northern Muscovy, particularly his use of Polish troops, turned the population against him and in favor of Shuiskii. A resistance movement centered on the town of Vologda spread across northern Muscovy.

Using Swedish troops and native Muscovites, Skopin-Shuiskii methodically pushed south from Novgorod in 1609 to relieve Moscow, heading for the False Dmitrii's base at Tushino. The second False Dmitrii was in a poor position to halt Shuiskii's onslaught, since his own movement was disintegrating. His Polish sponsors, disgruntled Russian gentry, and cossack rebels had little in common, and feuded with each other as much as with Shuiskii. By the end of 1609, undermined by faction and dissension, the second False Dmitrii fled south for safe haven in Kaluga. Skopin-Shuiskii entered Moscow in triumph in March 1610, having saved his uncle's regime.

Shuiskii's respite was illusory. Swedish intervention had driven Sigismund III, king of Poland, to abandon all pretense and invade Muscovy himself, besieging the border fortress of Smolensk, recently expanded by Boris Godunov. Those Muscovite nobles who had burned their bridges with Shuiskii and found themselves abandoned by the second False Dmitrii now gave their allegiance to Sigismund, agreeing to grant the office of tsar to Sigismund's son Wladyslaw, providing he converted to Orthodox Christianity. This was hypothetical as long as Shuiskii still reigned as tsar in Moscow—but not for long.

Skopin-Shuiskii, whose military and diplomatic skills kept Shuiskii on the throne, collapsed in April 1610 and died soon after. Convinced Shuiskii had murdered a potential rival, the tsar's remaining supporters abandoned him. Shuiskii's troops were soundly defeated by an invading Polish army at Klushino when foreign mercenaries deserted the Muscovites and went over to the Poles. Seeing little point in staying, Shuiskii's Swedish allies abandoned him as well. The Second False Dmitrii, sensing Shuiskii's weakness, rebuilt his own army south of Moscow. Finally, a Moscow mob incited by anti-Shuiskii boyars seized Shuiskii in July 1610, and forcibly made him a monk (in Muscovite culture, an irreversible step, one removing him from politics forever). Shuiskii had used up the last of his political lives. Given his history of deceit, double-dealing, and murder,

Shuiskii was fortunate to escape so lightly. As bad as things had been for Muscovy, they had just gotten worse; no one stepped forward to take up the office of tsar. With Shuiskii's putative Swedish allies now seizing Russian territory, the Second False Dmitrii just outside Moscow, and a Polish army marching toward the city, a group of boyars in the capital repeated the previous offer of the throne to Wladyslaw, son of the king of Poland. Polish troops entered the city in September 1610 to prepare for Wladyslaw's takeover, and Moscow's boyars swore allegiance to him. Polish forces began fighting the Second False Dmitrii's resurgent army for the right to take control of the empty shell of Muscovy.

Neither Wladyslaw nor the Second False Dmitrii became tsar. The pretender was murdered by his own bodyguards in December 1610, and Wladyslaw's father Sigismund made it clear he wanted the throne of Muscovy for himself and for Catholicism. Fear of a Catholic tsar stirred a national movement united around Orthodoxy and rejection of foreign rule. The cossacks who had eagerly fought against Godunov and Shuiskii were discomfited by the specter of Polish domination. Provincial gentry and cossacks built an army to expel the Poles holding Moscow and recreate Muscovy. In March 1611, Moscow was consumed by fighting between Polish occupiers and the resentful population. Muscovite forces were unable to dislodge the Poles from their stronghold in the center of Moscow, and just as the Second False Dmitrii's army had been torn apart by its tensions between privileged gentry and radical cossacks, the anti-Polish movement was riven as well by clashing interests and ambitions. Disasters over the summer of 1611 made it appear all hope was lost. The long-besieged fortress of Smolensk had its walls breached and was finally taken by storm by the Poles in June. In July, Swedish forces, whose alliance had been with the now-deposed Shuiskii, captured Novgorod by stealth, allowed through a gate by a treacherous resident. The gentry and cossacks of the nascent anti-Polish movement tore themselves apart with feuds and assassinations.

Even after all these disasters, the national movement was not finished. Allegiance to Orthodoxy and resentment of foreigners were still strong, strong enough to serve as the bedrock of a resurgent Russia. A new national movement arose in Nizhnii Novgorod in late 1611, organized by Kuzma Minin, a trader, and Prince Dmitrii Pozharskii, a noble servitor and veteran of the anti-Polish movement. It attracted support over the course of 1612 up and down the Volga River. Minin's financial acumen and Pozharskii's military skill combined to create a movement with more staying power than previous efforts. Their goal was the reestablishment of old Muscovy, and they welcomed support from all sides, including rebellious cossacks. After a slow and deliberate advance on Moscow, Pozharskii's national force arrived in August 1612, joining the cossacks keeping the Polish garrison trapped in the city. Pozharskii's motley army met a

Polish relief force southwest of Moscow. Three days of fighting finally forced the Polish column to return home. Bereft of hope, the Polish garrison and their Russian allies finally capitulated in October. Though Muscovy was devastated, with its key border cities of Novgorod and Smolensk in foreign hands, and much of cossack territory to the south still out of control, the worst of the crisis was over.

CHAPTER 3

The Early Romanovs

The end of the Time of Troubles left unfinished business. In particular, vital cities were in foreign hands: Novgorod to the northwest in Swedish; Smolensk to the west in Polish. The Crimean Tatar threat to the south was as dangerous as ever. To make matters worse, the military means to deal with those threats were lacking. The experience of the Livonian War and the Time of Troubles made it clear that a light cavalry army along traditional Muscovite lines was inadequate for defending Muscovy against its Western neighbors. What military historians have termed the "military revolution" was transforming warfare. European states were refining the tactics and technology of gunpowder weaponry while building ever larger and more sophisticated armies and fortifications. At the same time, "absolutist" European states were consolidating and centralizing their governments to extract tax revenues and conscripts more efficiently. This absolutism did not mean absolute control, for poor communications and rudimentary bureaucracies made such power impossible to achieve. Instead, absolutist rulers sought to eliminate or disarm all domestic rivals for power, whether powerful regional elites or obstructionist representative institutions, in order to increase their capacity to wield power.

The Muscovite state had to change and adapt to survive. The 1600s in politics were a period of consolidation at home and abroad. Abroad, the tsars of Muscovy worked to regain the territories they had lost during the Time of Troubles and gain ascendancy over their Polish, Swedish, and Tatar neighbors. Domestically, they reestablished their own power and strengthened the structures of serfdom that maintained the gentry cavalry. And, finally and ironically, while they propped up the gentry, they reformed the Muscovite army along European lines, making that gentry cavalry increasingly obsolete. Muscovy compensated for its military weakness by adapting Western technology and tactics, but resisted Western innovations in society and culture.

Founding of the Romanov Dynasty

In 1613, a hastily called *zemskii sobor,* assembling representatives of all Muscovy, elected as the new tsar Mikhail Romanov. He was the son of Filaret Romanov, a boyar who had assembled a record of treason and double-dealing remarkable even by the lax moral standards of the Time of Troubles. Filaret had been closely associated with the various pretenders to the Russian throne, and he may even have groomed the First False Dmitrii for his grab at power. In 1613 Filaret was a Polish prisoner, paying for a failed flirtation with the Poles during the Troubles. His son Mikhail's youth and weakness recommended him for the office of tsar, making it unlikely he could dominate the boyars. Mikhail made up for the Romanov clan's history of dabbling with pretenders and foreigners by his kinship to Ivan the Terrible's first wife, giving him a personal link to the last time there had been no doubt who rightfully held the throne. Though Mikhail was too young to make policy (and not especially bright), his government moved to clean up the messes left by the Troubles, though the devastation presented serious obstacles. Large sections of Muscovy were not under Moscow's control, and some cossacks still owed allegiance to whatever pretender they could find. The last remnant of those pretender movements, the toddler son of the Second False Dmitrii, was finally captured along with his cossack sponsors and hanged from the Kremlin wall.

Though the cossacks had been largely controlled, the tsar and his government were more comfortable with them constructively occupied in fighting abroad, ideally against Poland. Much remained unsettled: Mikhail's father Filaret languished in Polish captivity, Smolensk was in Polish hands, and Poland still claimed the Muscovite throne. During 1613, Muscovy recaptured some lost territory in the west and even besieged Smolensk. Boris Godunov's fortifications proved too skillfully constructed, however. Poland invaded again, and Wladyslaw, still dreaming of the Muscovite throne, joined Polish forces personally. Muscovy's feeble new regime barely scraped together the soldiers to defend Moscow, aided by Wladyslaw's problems paying his mercenaries. Wladyslaw managed to reach Moscow in September 1618. Though he failed to take it, his army remained intact in the heart of Muscovy. With both sides near exhaustion, Poland and Muscovy reached agreement at Deulino in December 1618 to end hostilities. Not a perpetual peace but a 14-1/2-year truce, their accord ceded large sections of western Muscovy, including Smolensk, to Poland. It provided for the return of Muscovite prisoners in Polish hands, including Filaret Romanov. Filaret returned after nearly a decade in Polish captivity to take over government on behalf of his son the tsar.

Sweden still controlled much of northwestern Russia, including the economically significant Baltic Sea coast and the trading center of

Novgorod. Inconclusive fighting from 1613 to 1616 changed little; the Muscovites were unable to win back Novgorod, let alone the Baltic coast. Swedish troops besieged Pskov from the summer of 1615, but that city's heroic resistance kept it out of Swedish hands. The two sides were forced into a peace of exhaustion, the Treaty of Stolbovo, in 1617. Muscovy regained Novgorod at the bargaining table, but was still barred from the Baltic shore, and had to surrender any remaining claims on Livonia.

The Smolensk War

The devastating Thirty Years' War in Germany (1618–1648) produced a series of military innovations no state could ignore. While intervening in Germany, Gustavus Adolphus, king of Sweden, put together a number of improvements to make Sweden a dominant power. By regularizing and standardizing tactical units, making his field artillery lighter and more maneuverable, adopting the musket with its longer range and greater penetrating power, and employing his cavalry for shock, using the saber rather than pistol shot, he revolutionized warfare. Perhaps most important was his grasp of linear tactics in gunpowder warfare. Before gunpowder, when what mattered was the mass, impetus, and cohesion of an infantry unit, depth meant power. Infantry formed in columns or squares had great advantages in their assault's shock—its physical impact—but only a small proportion of their numbers could actually employ their weapons; most were buried deep in the formation, providing pressure and weight but little else. The increasing use of firearms, though, promoted linear tactics—wide and shallow formations, providing substantially increased firepower. Those thin, fragile lines, as opposed to deep squares or columns, required protection from cavalry attacks, discipline to follow orders when not surrounded by hordes of fellow soldiers, and direction to fire when and where appropriate. That implied professional soldiers, thoroughly trained and competently commanded. Part-time *strel'tsy*, and levies of gentry cavalry slowly gathered from their estates, were simply not professional enough to use new tactics, as the Muscovites came to realize. If Muscovy were to compete with Poland or Sweden, it needed regular infantry and regular cavalry, equipped and trained along European lines.

The Deulino truce was certain to result in renewed warfare when it expired. Smolensk was too grievous a loss for Muscovy to accept, and Poland's King Sigismund and his son Wladyslaw had never renounced their claims to the Muscovite throne. Filaret Romanov returned from Polish captivity with a deep hatred for Poland and a burning desire to regain Smolensk. In preparation for Deulino's expiration, Muscovy imported enormous quantities of weaponry, along with the iron and lead needed to prepare the weapons and ammunition needed for the war to come. At the same time, Muscovy began systematically developing its domestic production of metals and weapons, a process that continued through the rest of the century and beyond.

In addition, Mikhail's government upgraded Moscow's army through the creation of "new-style" regiments along European lines, beginning the long process of adopting Western norms of organization and equipment to bring Russia's military to Western standards. In 1630 and 1631, Filaret hired thousands of foreign mercenaries, recruiting officers throughout western and central Europe. They organized and trained new-style regiments as an alternative to the noble levies and *strel'tsy*. Many Muscovites were unhappy with these developments. In addition to a deep-seated mistrust of foreigners and foreign ways in Muscovite culture, the increasing importance of infantry threatened the distinctive position of noble cavalry. Given gentry reluctance to serve in new-style infantry units, they were recruited instead from other free people (that is, not serfs): volunteers first, then conscripts. Ranging in size from 1,600 to 2,000 men, the new-style infantry and cavalry regiments were intended to have training and discipline lacking in the irregular noble cavalry. From 1630 to 1634, 17,000 soldiers, making up ten regiments, were recruited to the new units. They were trained in new linear tactics, particularly along Dutch lines. The infantry regiments initially included pikemen for protection from cavalry, compensating for the slow rate of fire of their muskets, given the lack of bayonets.

In April 1632, King Sigismund of Poland died just before the Deulino truce expired. Filaret took advantage of the chaos surrounding the election of a new Polish king by launching his war to regain Smolensk before preparations were complete. Contrary to expectations, Sigismund's son Wladyslaw was quickly elected Poland's new king without undue complications, depriving Muscovy of the domestic turmoil it needed.

Muscovy's invasion force of 30,000 soldiers, 9,000 from new-style regiments, was too small for the war Filaret envisaged. Muscovy was still weak from the Troubles and could not assemble the manpower needed for a successful campaign against Poland. Instead, the Muscovite plan was limited to a single narrow grab at Smolensk. Mikhail Borisovich Shein, commander of the Muscovite army, captured a number of small border towns and reached Smolensk at the end of October 1632 to begin its systematic bombardment and reduction. Shein had been appointed due to his experience as commander of the Smolensk garrison during the Polish siege 20 years before. Shein was thus old, probably too old for effective command. To make matters worse, the premature attack meant Shein lacked heavy artillery, making the capture of one of the largest fort complexes in Europe a difficult task. Shein's men built batteries ringing Smolensk, which sat on the southern bank of the Dnepr River. Shein established his own main camp east of Smolensk, on the south bank of the river. With the arrival of siege guns, Shein's forces smashed large sections of Smolensk's walls to rubble.

Though the siege progressed well, Wladyslaw's rapid election meant Polish response was swift. Polish raids on Muscovite lines and infiltration of troops and supplies into Smolensk began in spring 1633. Wladyslaw himself reached the city with around 20,000 men in August 1633. Faced with this new challenge, Shein halted the siege and consolidated his forces at his main camp east of Smolensk. His passivity doomed the army. A Polish raid destroyed Shein's key supply dump at Dorogobuzh, farther east. Wladyslaw then seized the high ground adjoining Shein's camp and used his cavalry to keep the Muscovites pinned against the Dnepr. Running short of food and ammunition, under constant bombardment, and pressured by his foreign mercenaries to capitulate, Shein surrendered. He and his men marched out of camp on 19 February/1 March 1634, free to return home but forced to abandon their weapons and supplies. Shein's foreign mercenaries had to swear not to fight against Poland; many went directly into Polish service. Upon Shein's return to Moscow, bringing only a quarter of the troops he had taken to Smolensk, he was tried and executed, not only for incompetence but for the trumped-up charge of being a Polish agent.

There was little point to continuing after the defeat at Smolensk. Filaret had been desperate to win the city, but died in October 1633. The Poles might have driven a hard bargain, but their retaliatory push toward Moscow bogged down, and they feared an attack by the Crimean Tatars while they were embroiled in Muscovy. The Peace of Polianovka, ending the war in June 1634, generally confirmed the prewar status quo, though Muscovy paid a large indemnity to Poland in return for Wladyslaw's surrendering all claims to the Muscovite throne.

The Thirteen Years' War

For Muscovy's gentry, accustomed to traditional warfare and traditional hierarchies, the new-style regiments were an affront to their honor and place in society. Despite the new units' respectable performance, they were dissolved after the war, and foreign mercenaries were sent home. The shortsightedness of this policy became clear in 1637 when new-style regiments were recreated, only to be disbanded again shortly thereafter. The units were permanently established only in the 1640s, as the end of the Thirty Years' War created a glut of underemployed mercenaries capable of training Muscovites in new tactics. Under the next tsar Aleksei Mikhailovich, the new-style regiments grew steadily, reaching nearly 100,000 soldiers by the reign of Aleksei's son Fyodor. Despite the influx of foreign officers and instructors to train and command these units, and the steady import of European technology and techniques, Muscovy's army remained distinct in one key respect from other European armies: it was almost entirely a national army, with the rank and file all Russian, despite its international officer corps. Other European armies, by contrast, were largely made up of mercenaries with no connection of birth, faith, or ethnicity with the country they served.

Tsar Mikhail died in 1645 and was succeeded by his son Aleksei Mikhailovich. Pious and dutiful, Aleksei continued the patient work of rebuilding Muscovite finances and military power. Both Mikhail and Aleksei maintained Godunov's precedent of defending the status of the gentry against economic pressure. Mikhail allowed the wives and children of gentry cavalrymen killed or imprisoned to keep their estates. Aleksei in turn codified and systematized Muscovite law, making Godunov's improvised serfdom into a permanent legal principle of Muscovite society and, by implication, guaranteeing a livelihood to his nobility.

Aleksei Mikhailovich's opportunity to win back Smolensk and to seize Kiev, reclaiming the full heritage of Kievan Rus, came through an explosive cossack uprising. The cossacks that had proven so dangerous to Muscovy during the Time of Troubles now threatened Poland. The empty lands south of Poland and Muscovy had been steadily colonized over the late 1500s and early 1600s; the land along the Dnepr River, under Polish rule, was deeply riven between wealthy Catholic, Polish magnates and poorer but more numerous Orthodox, Ukrainian cossacks. In 1648, Bogdan Khmelnitskii led a revolt against Polish rule, setting off a massive uprising throughout Polish Ukraine. Khmelnitskii had been a cossack in Polish service, provoked to revolt by a feud with a Polish landowner. Khmelnitskii united cossacks, peasants, and townspeople in a war against Polish domination, a war that slaughtered many of Ukraine's Jews, despised as agents of Polish authority. Poland's registered cossacks, those officially enrolled in Polish service, defected to Khmelnitskii. This left Poland with almost no forces to bring Ukraine back under control, especially after Khmelnitskii destroyed a Polish army in September 1648.

Though Poland's prospects of forcing Khmelnitskii to submit looked bleak, full independence for Ukraine was not an option. Poland's decentralized political system, with a weak king and powerful nobles, now showed signs of serious strain. Poland's structure had worked effectively through the 1500s and the first half of the 1600s. Now, the relative weakness of the Polish monarchy and the lack of a standing army made it hard to bring Ukraine back. On the other hand, Khmelnitskii's Ukraine was riven by internal fissures and lacked the resources to exist as an independent power. His cossacks had little in common with townspeople and peasants besides opposition to Polish Catholic cultural influences. As a result, his aim was not an independent state, but the defense of cossack rights and autonomy against Polish infringement. He settled with Poland in August 1649. Though Khmelnitskii won substantial concessions for the cossacks, underlying tensions were not resolved. Cossacks still resented their nominal Polish overlords, while deeply split themselves between the wealthy cossack elite and the poorer rank and file.

Fighting flared again in 1651, and temporary cossack successes did not alter the clear verdict that lasting victory against the Poles required outside aid. Khmelnitskii's delicate position as a middleman between the Polish state and Ukraine was simply not sustainable. The only real alternative to Polish rule was the Muscovite tsar. A shared Orthodox faith and Muscovy's antipathy toward Poland led Khmelnitskii to turn to Aleksei Mikhailovich for aid. Though Aleksei had been cautious in response to Khmelnitskii's appeals in 1648 and 1649, taking several years to prepare the country for war, he finally decided there was no better chance to win back what had been lost to Poland during the Time of Troubles. Muscovy declared war on Poland in autumn 1653. In January 1654 at Pereiaslavl Khmelnitskii signed an agreement with Aleksei's representatives providing for cooperation against Poland. The precise nature of this agreement—what the cossacks gave up and what Muscovy promised in return—has been a matter of dispute for 350 years. From Aleksei's point of view, and that of subsequent Russian nationalist historians, Khmelnitskii gave himself and his cossacks over to the tsar as loyal subjects. Khmelnitskii, by contrast, clearly believed that he retained traditional cossack autonomy. The Crimean Tatars, apprehensive about Muscovy's growing power, joined Poland against the cossacks.

The initial campaigns of the Thirteen Years' War proved that Muscovy's military capability had advanced far beyond that of the Time of Troubles or the Smolensk War. In keeping with the substantial growth in army size characteristic of the military revolution, 100,000 Muscovite soldiers, well equipped with firearms and artillery, carried out a multipronged invasion of Poland-Lithuania. Yet this Muscovite army was still a mixture of old and new. Aleksei Mikhailovich's reign saw the steady growth of new-style regiments, but those served alongside increasingly obsolete gentry cavalry and strel'tsy. By contrast with 1632, when Shein commanded a single narrow thrust at Smolensk, Muscovy now launched a campaign of breathtaking scope. Since Aleksei Mikhailovich's aim was not aiding the cossacks but winning territory, his main forces headed for Smolensk. To the north, 15,000 soldiers moved on Polotsk and Vitebsk, covering the right flank of the main attack; the main force of 40,000 attacked Smolensk; to the south 15,000 protected the left flank of the main attack and moved toward Roslavl and a link with the Ukrainian cossacks. All three armies were intended to support the war's main goal: to cut off and seize Smolensk. For Khmelnitskii, by contrast, there was only a limited

Muscovite force to assist him, far less than what Aleksei threw against Smolensk.

Stretched to its limits by Khmelnitskii's uprising and unable to match Muscovy's manpower mobilization, Poland assembled only token forces to defend Smolensk. The Muscovites reached Smolensk in June 1654, with Aleksei personally participating in the siege. Though an initial attempt to storm the fortress failed, steady bombardment left the weakened garrison with little hope. After the defeat of a Polish relief column, the city surrendered that fall, leaving Aleksei Mikhailovich in firm possession of Smolensk and its surroundings as campaigning ceased for the winter.

The next spring Aleksei prepared for an ambitious campaign beyond Smolensk into the Lithuanian half of the Polish state. The Muscovite main army pushed west toward Minsk before swinging north to Vilnius, seizing it in summer 1655. For Poland, the war had turned from defeat into disaster. Already weakened by the bloody cossack revolt and full-scale war against the ever-growing power of Muscovy, Poland faced annihilation as Sweden invaded in summer 1655, taking advantage of Polish weakness to occupy Warsaw by September. Aleksei's calculations changed as Poland disintegrated. A weakened Poland shorn of Smolensk and Ukraine was one thing; a Poland entirely conquered by Sweden was quite another. In late 1655 Aleksei eased his pressure on Poland in hopes of winning election to the Polish throne. In May 1656 he declared war on Sweden and invaded Swedish Livonia as Ivan the Terrible had done nearly a century earlier. As in that earlier campaign, Muscovite troops were unable to capture a major port. In a demonstration of how far Muscovite military modernization still had to go, Aleksei's troops besieged Riga but failed to conquer it either by bombardment or by storm. Aleksei returned home in autumn 1656 without Riga, but with significant other gains. Poland had managed to recover during its brief respite from Muscovite pressure. Mindful of the growing expense of war, Aleksei abandoned his campaign against Livonia, signed a truce with Sweden in 1658, and reopened his war with Poland.

As the war dragged on, Aleksei's relationship with his cossack allies worsened. For the cossacks, the war meant devastation. The right (west) bank of the Dnepr, main theater of fighting in the south, was essentially depopulated by the war. Poles and Jews fled northwest to Poland proper for safety, while cossacks and peasants crossed the Dnepr to relative security on the left (east) bank under Muscovy's protection. Khmelnitskii and his cossacks became increasingly disillusioned with the tsar, who fought the war for conquests in Belorussia and Lithuania, not cossack autonomy in Ukraine. Khmelnitskii died in 1657, disgusted with Muscovy and the tsar. His death produced a civil war between the cossack elite, favoring renewed Polish ties, and the rank and file, sympathetic to Muscovy. After the victory of the pro-Polish faction, Aleksei shifted his forces south from the Belorussian-Lithuanian campaigns to bring the cossacks back under control in Ukraine.

By 1659 and 1660, the war that had begun promisingly for Aleksei turned sour. The economic and social burdens of warfare on a scale undreamt of earlier in Muscovite history took their toll. Aleksei had expanded the network of *prikazy* to handle his new army, but the system's ad hoc nature showed signs of strain. To build and maintain his armies, Aleksei introduced regular conscription, mass levies from Muscovy's peasant population. In the winter of 1658–1659, for example, Aleksei ordered every 100 households to produce six conscripts for the army. This principle of requiring peasants to select a quota of unfortunate draftees from among their number would persist for 200 years. The initial levy produced 18,000 men for Aleksei's new-style regiments, but those regiments required competent officers to lead them, either from Russia's gentry or foreign recruits. Continuing losses to combat, disease, and desertion meant that Aleksei repeated his unpopular levies. Heavy casualties meant that the new-style regiments were increasingly manned by newly conscripted and poorly trained peasants. The expense of war also forced Aleksei to debase his currency by the extensive minting of copper coins. The resulting inflation and counterfeiting provoked riots in summer 1662 that threatened Aleksei's personal safety, and which he crushed with brutal force.

The easy successes of the first years of the war were not repeated. At Konotop at the end of June 1659, a Muscovite army was nearly annihilated by cossacks. Poland, recovering rapidly from Swedish conquest, went on the offensive to win back some of the eastern territories it had lost, inflicting a major defeat on the Muscovites at Polonka in June 1660. Later that year, yet another Muscovite army was caught by cossacks and Tatars in open country west of Kiev. Using a rolling fortress of linked wagons, the army tried to make its way east to the relative safety of the Dnepr River and the Muscovite garrison at Kiev, but was caught and forced to surrender; 10,000–20,000 soldiers went into Tatar captivity.

Muscovy and Poland were both reaching exhaustion, though the war would linger on for years before the final truce in 1667. As discussed in previous chapters, state capacity, though greater than in previous generations, was still too limited to enable states to inflict clear and unequivocal defeat. The war reached a stalemate, with Poland and Muscovy each controlling their bank of the Dnepr River. Each could attack across the river, but not sustain campaigns to seize and hold ground. This provided the basis for a settlement. By early 1667, Polish and Muscovite negotiators at Andrusovo, near Smolensk, had reached a 13-1/2-year truce, preserving Moscow's gains of Smolensk and large sections of Belorussia, and dividing Ukraine along the Dnepr River, with Muscovy controlling the left bank and Poland the right. The city of Kiev, though on the right bank, was awarded to Muscovy for a two-year term (upon the expiration of that term, Muscovy refused to surrender the city). Though Muscovy's victory was limited, it was nevertheless substantial. It had pushed its frontiers west, regained the key border city of Smolensk, and established its dominance over left-bank Ukraine.

Razin's Uprising

The temporary respite from war afforded by the Andrusovo truce did not last. Cossack uprisings in eastern Ukraine became almost routine, but the most serious disturbance came from a different cossack community farther east, in the valleys of the Don and Volga rivers. Discontent was rife by the close of war. Just as in Ivan the Terrible's time, war, conscription, and taxation forced thousands of peasants in central Muscovy to flee south and east to escape their government and landlords. Aleksei's continuous efforts to improve his frontier defenses made this only easier by making the southern steppe safer. Anxious to maintain his tax base and keep his nobles' estates stocked with labor, Aleksei engineered brutal campaigns to track down runaway serfs. Aleksei had also backed religious reforms, altering certain details of church ritual, which many Russians rejected as the work of the Antichrist. As Muscovite authority steadily pushed south, poor cossacks and peasants dreaded the future.

Stenka Razin, a Don cossack turned pirate, transformed this widespread discontent into open rebellion, much as Bolotnikov had done during the Troubles. Razin spent years on the lower Volga and the Caspian Sea as a bandit. In 1670, he began open rebellion against tsarist authority, while careful to limit his abuse to the tsar's evil advisors, not to the tsar himself. His appeals to destroy landlord oppression and restore cossack freedom had enormous resonance with Russia's long-suffering poor. His cossack army captured the Volga town of Tsaritsyn (later Stalingrad) and then ambushed and wiped out a *strel'tsy* regiment sent down the Volga against him. The garrison at Astrakhan, at the mouth of the Volga, sent *strel'tsy* north against Razin, but those mutinied, joining Razin instead. Razin then moved down the Volga to take Astrakhan itself. Though Astrakhan was a substantial fortress with a sizable garrison, Razin's charisma dissuaded most of the town's troops from fighting him, and supporters opened the gates to his rebel army. Razin's cossacks gleefully slaughtered government officials and nobles.

Razin returned up the Volga to prepare for the inevitable showdown with tsarist forces. As he moved north, towns fell without a fight, and peasants took Razin's approach as a signal to murder landlords and join him, enlarging his army but hurting its quality. In keeping with Muscovite rebel tradition, he produced a pretender to legitimize his movement:

Aleksei Mikhailovich's recently dead son Aleksei. Detachments of cossacks ranged in all directions to slaughter nobles and proclaim rebellion. Razin's advance stalled at the Volga town of Simbirsk, well fortified and ably defended. Arriving in September 1670, Razin was met outside the walls by a government cavalry detachment, which after a day-long battle retreated north to Kazan to summon reinforcements. The garrison withdrew to Simbirsk's inner kremlin, leaving the outer city open for Razin. Razin first tried to burn out the defenders. Two further attempts to storm Simbirsk under cover of darkness failed in vicious hand-to-hand fighting.

By October, reinforcements finally arrived from Kazan. Razin met them outside Simbirsk, leaving part of his forces pressing the siege. Razin's ill-disciplined cossacks and peasants, adept at slaughtering noble families or pillaging small towns, were no match for regular troops trained to European standards and honed by 13 years of warfare against Poland and Sweden. Muscovite artillery blew gaping holes in rebel formations, panicking Razin's peasants into headlong flight. Razin's cossacks left behind were overwhelmed by disciplined infantry. Two further pitched battles demonstrated the utter inability of Razin's rebel mob to fight a real army. Merciless reprisals followed.

After Razin's defeat, punitive expeditions ran down and wiped out scattered rebel bands with extraordinary brutality. Razin himself fled to his home on the Don River. Cossack elites, troubled by the disorder Razin brought and the specter of massive Muscovite intervention, arrested Razin and turned him over to Aleksei. After torture, Razin was executed in Red Square. He had the misfortune of rebelling against Moscow's power in the immediate aftermath of war with Poland, meaning that Muscovy had large numbers of veteran soldiers at its disposal. Later cossack rebellions when Russia was actively involved in foreign wars were much more dangerous.

Dynastic Crisis

Aleksei Mikhailovich died in 1676. The tsar who had done so much to build Muscovite military power left behind a family dilemma, similar to that after Ivan the Terrible's death, which threatened to destroy everything he had created. From his first marriage, Aleksei had a weak and sickly eldest son Fyodor, a physically and mentally handicapped younger son, Ivan, a remarkably intelligent and astute daughter, Sophia, and a number of other daughters who played no political role. From his second marriage, he had a healthy and vigorous son Peter, only three years old at the time of Aleksei's death, and two additional daughters. Sophia and Peter, those best suited to rule Muscovy, were disqualified from the throne, in Sophia's case by her sex, in Peter's by his age and place in the line of succession. Despite Fyodor's chronic illness, his status as the presumptive heir ensured he took the throne without incident in 1676. Though he married twice, Fyodor fathered no surviving children and died in 1682.

In military terms, Fyodor's reign saw the first major, direct confrontation between Muscovy and the Ottoman Turks. As Muscovy's power grew and Poland's waned, Moscow's horizons expanded. Poland was so weak it was no longer an opponent to be fought against; rather, it was a satellite to be propped up as a buffer against more dangerous neighbors. This new alignment became clear in 1672 when an Ottoman army, assisted by contingents from the Crimean Tatars, invaded Poland. Poland's inability to resist spurred Muscovite fears for the safety of the newly acquired Ukrainian territories, and to a lesser degree for the integrity of Poland. Muscovy now saw the Ottoman Turks and their Crimean vassals as the main foreign threat. Ukraine stopped being an arena for conflict with Poland and instead became a battleground for warfare between Muscovy and the Muslim states to its south. Muscovy had fought against the Crimean Tatars for centuries, but Moscow's hegemony over Ukraine heightened Ottoman fears of a new potential rival. The indecisive Russo-Turkish War from 1676 to 1681 centered on control of the fortress of Chigirin, just west of the Dnepr River. Possession of the town seesawed back and forth in a war that was the opening skirmish in a centuries-long struggle for control of the shores of the Black Sea.

Fyodor's 1682 childless death brought the dynastic crisis that had only been delayed in 1676. Since Sophia could not inherit, that left the manifestly incapable Ivan and the bright and vigorous ten-year-old Peter. The Muscovite crowd (supported by most of the court elite) shouted for young Peter to take the throne. Peter became tsar with the government in the hands of his mother, Natalya, Aleksei's second wife. This left one key faction unhappy: the Miloslavskii clan, the family of Aleksei's first wife, and particularly Peter's older half-sister Sophia. Resentful at the elevation of her half-brother and stepmother, Sophia and her Miloslavskii kin turned to the *strel'tsy* for aid. The *strel'tsy* were routinely discontented. Their military role was displaced by new-style regiments, and their inadequate pay was routinely in arrears. Carefully cultivating *strel'tsy* resentments, Sophia and the Miloslavskiis unleashed an uprising on the pretext of halting a plot to assassinate Ivan and Peter. The *strel'tsy* stormed into the Kremlin in May 1682 and butchered the key figures of Natalya's regime, sparing her and Peter. The conspirators engineered a new proclamation of dual tsars, Ivan as senior and Peter as junior, and installed their sister Sophia as regent.

Sophia was no figurehead. From 1682 through 1689, she was the central political figure in Muscovy. Though there was no precedent for a woman tsar, she cultivated the idea that her sex need not bar her from the position for which she was manifestly qualified. Where being a woman prevented her from exercising the duties of a tsar in diplomacy or warfare, she relied on her lover and political partner Prince Vasilii Vasil'evich Golitsyn.

Sophia continued the evolution of Muscovite foreign policy from anti-Polish to anti-Turk. The Ottoman sultan unsuccessfully besieged Vienna, capital of the Austrian (Habsburg) Empire, in 1683. In the wake of Turkish defeat, Austria, Poland, and Venice formed a Holy League against their common enemy: the Ottoman Turks. Moscow joined the League on condition of Poland making the temporary truce of Andrusovo permanent, and acknowledging Muscovite possession of Kiev and the left bank of the Dnepr. Poland accepted in 1686. Sophia committed Muscovy to attack the Crimean Tatars, key Ottoman allies, as its service to the League.

Golitsyn, Sophia's lover, commanded the 1687 expedition against the Crimea. Sophia's government assembled an army of 100,000 soldiers. Recruiting went slowly, as it took months to call the gentry cavalry from their estates. Part of the purpose of the gentry cavalry was fighting wars on the open steppe; they now proved ineffective even at this. Golitsyn's force set out in May, inching south at four miles a day, and by June reached the steppe only to find the Tatars had set it afire, destroying the grass Muscovite horses depended on. Short of water and fodder, the army turned back to Moscow 100 miles short of the Crimean isthmus, achieving nothing.

In fall 1688 Golitsyn prepared a second campaign, intended to begin in early spring and avoid the dry summer steppes that had beaten the first campaign. This second army of over 100,000 men moved south in early 1689 with snow still on the ground. In mid-May, Golitsyn fought initial skirmishes against Tatar cavalry well north of the Perekop, the isthmus connecting the Crimea to the mainland. The artillery Golitsyn's army hauled south effectively kept Tatar cavalry well away from the main force. These indecisive clashes allowed Golitsyn's army to crawl south with Tatar cavalry ringing the horizon. By the time Golitsyn reached the Tatar fortifications at the Perekop, his army had no water and no prospect of attaining more. Golitsyn bluffed, opening negotiations with the Tatars to win by diplomacy what his weakening troops could not win by force. When the Tatars proved unyielding, Golitsyn had no choice but to turn back for a long, dry march north through the steppe. With only a few dozen men killed in battle, Golitsyn's army lost tens of thousands to disease and thirst on the march home.

These twin Crimean defeats contributed to Sophia's growing crisis. Muscovy might acquiesce in her rule so long as her brothers were incapable. Ivan could never rule, but by 1689 Peter was an adult, married with a pregnant bride, and obviously capable of serving as tsar. In August 1689, fearing an attempt on his life by the *strel'tsy,* Peter fled Moscow to the nearby Trinity Monastery. In the resulting showdown with Sophia,

Moscow's elite decided *en masse* to align themselves with Peter, and her support melted away. She was hustled off to a convent for the rest of her life, and Golitsyn was exiled to the far north. Peter bore no grudge against his half-witted half-brother Ivan, allowing him to hold the title of joint tsar until Ivan's death in 1696. After Sophia's defeat, the 17-year-old Peter was now tsar in fact as well as in title and was ready to change Muscovy, change it so dramatically that we can now call it by its present name: Russia.

CHAPTER 4

Peter the Great

Untangling the military history of Peter the Great's reign is quite complex. In contrast to previous eras of Russian history, our sources are rich; the problem lies elsewhere. Peter's reign was consumed by war, his government preoccupied with the men, money, and materiel necessary to fight, and his reforms shaped by military priorities. There is little in Peter's eventful reign that can be meaningfully separated from war and the military. Though Peter is best known as a reformer, many signature reforms came late in his reign, after his greatest war was over. To give some sense of Peter's parallel military campaigns and domestic reforms, and the enormous energy and activity they required, this chapter interweaves the stories as much as possible.

Despite Peter's well-deserved reputation as a reformer, his military reforms were clearly more the continuation and evolution of previous efforts than his cultural reforms, which were by comparison far more radical. For example, Ivan IV created regular infantry, conducted sophisticated siege warfare with the assistance of numerous foreign specialists, and contended on equal terms with Western powers in Livonia. Peter's father, Aleksei Mikhailovich, converted Muscovy's armies to predominantly new-style regiments along European lines and even constructed Russia's first Western-style warships (on a limited scale). Peter consolidated the military reforms of his predecessors rather than breaking with the old order completely. In political terms, Peter continued the development of the particular Russian brand of absolutism originated by his father, improving the efficiency and extractive capacity of the Russian state in order to boost its power.

By contrast, his cultural and social initiatives were startlingly original. As Lindsey Hughes has pointed out, in the century before Peter, the number of secular books printed in Russia could be counted on the fingers of two hands. Not only did Peter single-handedly create a secular culture in Russia, he abolished the office of Patriarch, head of the Russian Orthodox church, and replaced it with a government department. He changed

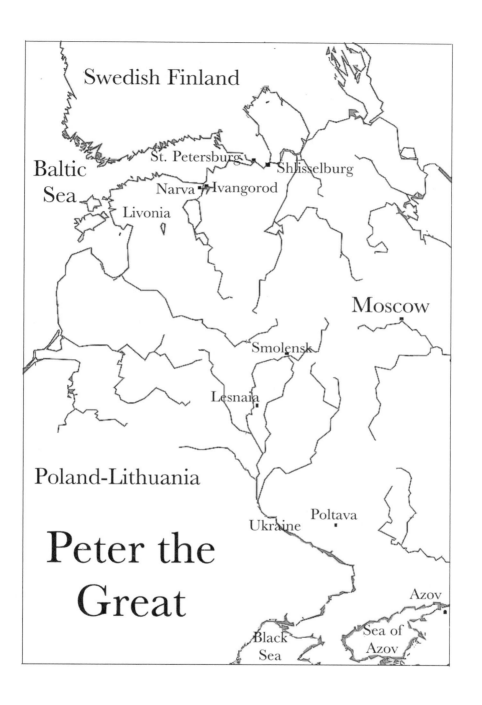

Swedish Finland

Baltic
Sea

St. Petersburg
Shlisselburg

Narva Ivangorod

Livonia

Moscow

Smolensk

Lesnaia

Poland-Lithuania

Ukraine   Poltava

Peter the
Great

Azov

Black
Sea

Sea of
Azov

the clothing, grooming, and daily life of the Russian elite beyond recognition. His military reforms were nowhere near so original, but far more devastating in their impact on the Russian population through conscription and taxation. In terms of Russia's perennial lag behind Western powers, by the end of Peter's reign Russia's military technology and organization, as well as its elite culture, was thoroughly European. Its social and economic arrangements, still centered around serf agriculture, remained far behind those of western Europe.

During Peter's childhood, it was in the best interests of Sophia, Prince Vasilii Vasil'evich Golitsyn, and the Miloslavskii clan to keep him out of political life. His presence would only remind Russians there was a male heir available. This isolation, and Peter's manic levels of energy, let him cultivate his own interests. Though highly intelligent, Peter was neither intellectual nor refined, and his hobbies ran to practical arts: working with his hands, and particularly boating and military matters. Peter's fascination with boats and sailing is legendary, and it drove his promotion of a Russian navy. His interest in military matters had a direct impact on the politics of his regime. Peter and his playmates, the sons of noblemen and servitors, formed "mock troops" (*poteshnye voiska*) to play war. As they grew, the games became increasingly elaborate, including organized units, fortifications, and live ammunition. As adults, the men of the mock troops became Peter's officers and administrators. In particular, Aleksandr Danilovich Menshikov, a former stableboy, became Peter's closest associate through his affiliation with the mock troops. In the late 1680s and early 1690s, the mock troops evolved into Russia's first two elite guard units, the Preobrazhenskii and Semenovskii guards, regiments with a large contingent of Russia's highest nobility among their officers and men. The core of Russia's army during Peter's lifetime, they played a central role in politics after his death. They became, in effect, a school for officers as well. Young nobles serving as rank-and-file soldiers learned the military life in these regiments before becoming officers elsewhere.

Peter's youthful isolation freed him to indulge his fascination with foreigners and foreign ways. Though Muscovy had liberalized under Aleksei Mikhailovich, it was still an insular and xenophobic place, with foreign officers and technical experts segregated in a Moscow suburb. Peter had a number of close contacts among the foreign specialists. Between the play regiments and his foreign friends, Peter's entourage was almost exclusively military.

Peter's Army

The military machine Peter inherited had progressed a great deal toward Western models, and Peter continued the organization of new-style regiments. In Muscovy, the gentry had been the core of the army, but Peter made the nobility an officer class, leading units of European-style infantry and cavalry recruited from among non-nobles. Peter's vision for noble service was somewhat egalitarian: in 1712, for example, he stipulated the nobility should serve as rank-and-file soldiers before becoming officers. Peter still saw the nobility as the natural leaders of his new Russian army, though worthy commoners might serve that role as well. Not all nobles became officers; illiterate nobles, unqualified for officer rank, served as common soldiers. Peter did not intend for educated nobles to remain in the ranks, only to have practical experience before rising to command. For Peter's nobility, permanent escape from service came only with death; old age and disability transferred nobles from active military service to garrison duty or civil administration. Peter governed by the principle that all served, including Peter himself, whether by growing crops, fighting in the army, or administering the state. There was no right to leisure.

Despite Peter's principle of universal, lifelong service for Russian nobles, he still relied on foreign expertise. The Russian nobility simply lacked a sufficient number of men with the education and sophistication to handle modern warfare. The same shortage of educated men hampered Peter's efforts to build a well-run state. Peter established a network of schools to train his new elite, while dispatching large numbers abroad for education. This dearth of qualified Russians meant that while nominal command over a campaign was often held by the old boyar elite, command of regiments and other subunits went to either foreign recruits or newly trained Russian officers.

For common soldiers, Peter recruited volunteers with substantial pay and the possibility of freedom for serfs (though with lifelong service in the army). Given the near certainty of death from disease or wounds in a military career, this was inadequate to produce the number of soldiers his wars demanded. Peter turned to conscription, just as his father had, beginning in December 1699 with the call-up of one soldier from every 50 peasant households. This first levy was repeated again and again, as his government grew adept at ferreting out previously untapped manpower, including freed slaves, priests' sons, and enemy deserters. Over his reign, Peter imposed 53 separate levies, bringing 300,000 soldiers into service from a population of only 15–16 million. Because of this reliance on conscription, Peter's army remained more a national force than its European counterparts, which recruited heavily from Europe's mercenary market.

Peter continued the evolution away from *strel'tsy* and gentry cavalry without discarding them entirely. Nonetheless, his clear priority was building more and better green-coated new-style regiments, making his army more European with every year. Peter provided common,

European-style uniforms with knee breeches, tricornered hats, and long coats. Peter's forces were not particularly specialized. His cavalry were dragoons, cavalry trained to move on horseback but fight as infantry on foot, and not otherwise differentiated by function. For light cavalry missions—skirmishing, raiding, and scouting—Peter relied on irregular formations of cossacks and of nomads from the north Caucasus and central Asia. Rather than serve alongside commoners, many nobles maintained their distinctiveness by serving in exclusively noble cavalry units.

Peter eliminated much of the Muscovite governmental system. The boyar rank, central to Muscovite politics, fell into obsolescence as Peter ceased appointing new ones. His father Aleksei had begun an absolutist evolution away from the boyar duma and its potential check on the tsar's power, relying instead on smaller groups of key advisors. Peter continued this. The boyar duma ceased to meet, and Peter substituted instead a privy chancellery: key advisors and the heads of *prikazy*. The elites who had been boyars under previous tsars remained as vital to Peter as they had been before, but the boyar rank and the boyar duma were now obsolete. Peter supplemented Muscovy's old elites with outsiders. Foreign officers, always trusted technicians, now joined the tsar's inner circle. A number of lowborn Russians moved into the elite, most notoriously Menshikov. On the other hand, Boris Petrovich Sheremetev, a boyar of old family, generally served as Peter's top field commander.

The Azov Campaigns

Peter's first years as tsar were spent drinking and carousing. Only in the mid-1690s did he take his duties seriously, and that meant foreign war and territorial expansion. Peter had inherited the Holy League's war against the Ottomans, a war that had been quiet during his early reign. Since Golitsyn's failed campaigns had demonstrated the difficulty of a direct attack on the Crimea, Peter instead focused on Azov, a Turkish fortress at the mouth of the Don River. Peter's plan, developed over the winter of 1694–1695, envisaged a two-pronged attack. As a diversion, a large cavalry force moved against Turkish fortresses on the lower Dnepr River. A smaller, infantry-heavy force, accompanied by Peter himself as an artilleryman, moved down the Don, arriving at Azov in early summer 1695.

The siege of Azov went poorly. The Russians first had to capture two Turkish watchtowers guarding heavy chains stretching across the Don and preventing Russian movement by water. During that process, the Turks launched a successful sortie capturing several Russian siege guns. Steady Russian bombardment and two attempts to storm Azov were unsuccessful, and there seemed little chance of starving the Turks into submission. Regular deliveries of supplies by water kept the fortress functioning longer than Peter could sustain an army outside its walls. By late September, three months after the siege began, Peter decided to withdraw.

Peter then displayed one of the central marks of his character: unflagging pursuit of a goal once set. Since resupply by sea had sustained Azov, Peter built a fleet to isolate it. Peter assembled a galley fleet at Voronezh on the upper Don, then launched it in April 1696 for a second attempt at Azov. The galleys accompanied a ground force of 70,000 troops, double the previous year's army. The second siege went better, cutting off sea access as Peter planned. After a month of bombardment, 2,000 cossacks rushed the walls. Failing to penetrate Azov's inner defenses, they nevertheless captured sections of the outer works. Realizing the futility of further resistance, the Turkish garrison surrendered honorably in July 1696. Peter had won his first triumph.

Inspired by his hastily built fleet and his lifelong affection for boats and seafaring, Peter built a navy far more impressive than his father's. Peter's father, Aleksei, had begun a navy, but with laughably poor results. Stenka Razin had burned the one true ship Aleksei had built (as opposed to a galley or small boat), the three-masted *Eagle*. Azov gave Peter the opportunity to contest Ottoman control of the small Sea of Azov and, beyond it, perhaps even the Black Sea. Peter also had designs on the Baltic. For both goals, he needed a seagoing fleet. In 1700, Peter founded an Admiralty *prikaz* to manage shipbuilding and naval artillery. Authority over the navy went to Fyodor Matveevich Apraksin, an aristocrat and competent and judicious figure. More than anyone else, he built Peter's fleet. Peter required the church and the nobility to build him ships, but shipbuilding and seamanship required far more foreign expertise than the army did. Peter himself had studied both extensively, and he required the same of many Russians sent abroad or trained by foreigners at home. Since western Europe possessed the knowledge Peter needed, he organized a Great Embassy in 1697 to recruit shipbuilders and navigators while taking Russians abroad to learn Western trades.

The Great Embassy also had foreign policy implications. The Holy League's alliance against the Turks was in ruins, as Austria pursued a peace settlement and left the Russians without allies. Peter was also recruiting partners for a war against Sweden, reopening the Russian quest for ports on the Baltic. Peter accompanied the Great Embassy abroad in spring 1697 under the polite fiction that he was the humble Peter Mikhailov, a ruse that fooled no one but spared Peter formal court ceremonial. While en route he intervened in the election of a Polish king on behalf of the successful candidate Augustus II, elector of Saxony, who soon proved an ally of dubious worth. He traveled through Germany to the Netherlands, where he occupied himself with carpentry, shipbuilding, sailing, and the dissection of corpses. Hearing of the high art of shipbuilding in England, he crossed the Channel for a three-month stay in London. His return journey passed through the Austrian Empire, where he heard news from home requiring his immediate return.

In the summer of 1698, Peter received word from Moscow of a *strel'tsy* uprising—the same *strel'tsy* who put his sister Sophia into power in 1682. He hurried home, arriving in August to find the revolt already squashed. He brought with him Western ways, greeting his boyars informally and shaving their beards. He dealt with the rebellious *strel'tsy* personally, participating in their interrogations and uncovering some connection with Sophia. Hundreds of *strel'tsy* were executed, a number of Moscow regiments disbanded, and Sophia's status was changed from residing in a convent to actually becoming a nun. The bodies of executed *strel'tsy* were hanged outside her window to remind her of the consequences of disloyalty.

The Great Northern War

Peter was ready for expansion in Europe, and Sweden seemed a propitious target. Charles XI, king of Sweden, had died in 1697, leaving the throne to his teenaged son, Charles XII. Charles's youth and inexperience, together with Sweden's hold on Baltic ports, made the Swedish Empire ripe for partition by its neighbors Denmark, Poland, and Russia. Encouraged by discontented Livonian nobles, Peter conferred with newly elected King Augustus II of Poland on his return from the Great Embassy, then discussed an alliance with the Danes. He began conscription to fill out the ranks of his army at the end of 1699. The newly formed coalition planned on attacking Sweden in early 1700, though Peter had to wait until he reached a settlement with the Ottomans. Peter's negotiators preserved his conquest of Azov in a summer 1700 agreement with the Turks, finally freeing Peter for his war with the Swedes.

By the time Peter joined the war, his alliance was already collapsing. The Great Northern War had begun in early 1700 with Danish attacks on Swedish allies in Schleswig-Holstein and Polish attacks on southern Livonia. Charles XII proved to be a gifted commander and a far more formidable opponent than his neighbors had expected. In July 1700, Charles moved a Swedish force of 15,000 across the sound to Danish territory, driving Denmark out of the war in a month. Ignorant of this, Peter declared war in August 1700, leading an army of 35,000 against Narva, on the west bank of the Narova River just south of the Gulf of Finland. In September Peter built fortifications around Narva to keep the city under siege and prepare for Charles's efforts to relieve it. Charles had decided to deal with Peter and Russia next, saving Augustus and Poland for last. As Charles's small army approached Narva, Peter left the scene to organize reinforcements, taking himself out of harm's way.

Arriving on 18/29 November 1700, Charles was outnumbered three to one. The Russians did not anticipate an attack, expecting Charles to wait on reinforcements to even the odds. Instead, Charles attacked the Russian siege works under cover of a snowstorm early the next morning. His assault caught the Russians thinly stretched around Narva to the west, vulnerable to breakthroughs by disciplined and experienced Swedish columns. The Swedes easily penetrated the Russian perimeter in several places, breaking the Russian line into indefensible pieces and panicking Peter's officers and men. Many fled to the Narova River to drown in the freezing water, while the Swedes rolled up the remainder of the Russian line with ease. Only Peter's precious guards regiments, the Preobrazhenskii and Semenovskii, managed to make a stand in good order with the aid of fortifications improvised from supply wagons.

The Battle of Narva was an utter humiliation for Russia and for Peter personally, but Charles spared Peter further defeat. Having removed the immediate threat to Narva, Charles chose *not* to follow with a final push to knock Russia out of the war. After capturing a large share of Peter's artillery and senior officers, Charles assumed Peter was no longer a threat and instead turned south. He first wrecked a Polish invasion of Livonia, then continued into Poland itself to finish off Augustus, the final member of the anti-Swedish coalition.

Peter responded to Narva with a three-part policy. First and most importantly, he raced to repair and rebuild the Russian army, which had so convincingly demonstrated its incapacity to stand up to a European power. Second, as Charles moved south into Poland after Augustus, Peter snatched up Swedish possessions around the Gulf of Finland. Finally, he dispatched expeditionary forces to Poland to bolster resistance to Charles.

Rebuilding meant replacing the officers and men lost at Narva. Officers could be hired abroad or trained from the Russian nobility; replacing common soldiers meant repeated levies of peasants from the civilian population, allowing Peter to build an army of 200,000 within a few short years. Given the far-flung theaters of war, Peter's army was much heavier on cavalry than the European norm. Peter melted church bells for artillery pieces. To pay for the army, Peter scrounged sources of revenue wherever possible, raising existing taxes, adding new ones, monopolizing the salt trade, debasing the currency—whatever might bring in cash. In 1705, most notoriously, he taxed beards. Peter's military required weapons, and he actively promoted Russian industry, producing a qualitative leap in the size and sophistication of Russia's metal production and metalworking factories.

The second part of Peter's plan was taking advantage of Charles's Polish detour to seize Swedish possessions on the Baltic shore. In Livonia and Ingria, he had a welcome opportunity to temper his army fighting small Swedish detachments with Charles far away. Once it was clear

Charles had turned south, Peter's field general Sheremetev unleashed his cossacks and nomad cavalry to devastate Swedish Livonia. At the end of 1701, Sheremetev inflicted a painful defeat on the Swedes at Erestfer, west of Pskov, boosting Russian confidence. Driven by Peter to inflict the most possible damage on Livonia, Sheremetev repeated his feat, nearly annihilating an outnumbered Swedish force at Hummelshof in July 1702. Relying heavily on Sheremetev's skill and experience, Peter transferred him from Livonia east to Ingria, where Sheremetev mopped up Swedish outposts in the narrow isthmus between the Gulf of Finland and Lake Ladoga. In October 1702, Sheremetev took the Swedish fortress Nöteborg, where the Neva River flows west out of Lake Ladoga. Peter rechristened it Shlisselburg.

At the beginning of May 1703, Sheremetev took another Swedish fortress downriver where the Neva flows into the Gulf of Finland. Peter chose this spot, surrounded by marshes, to build a fortress of his own and a new city, St. Petersburg, as his window on the West. Sheremetev continued his run of successes in 1704, taking the inland town of Dorpat in July 1704 by breaching the walls with artillery. Narva was next. Supplemented by the artillery that had been pounding Dorpat, Peter's forces forced a breach in the city walls. The Swedish commander refused terms, in violation of the protocols of early modern warfare that encouraged honorable surrender once further resistance was pointless. The resulting Russian storm on 9/20 August 1704, therefore, became a massacre. The victories at Dorpat and Narva combined with economic damage to Livonia and the resulting loss of port revenues put increasing financial pressure on Sweden while Charles was embroiled deep in Poland.

Charles wasted valuable time dealing with Poland. To keep Charles there, Peter sent fast-moving Russian detachments to prop up Augustus. Charles had held his own election for king of Poland in February 1704, putting Stanislaw Leszczynski on the throne as his puppet and remaining to keep him there and prevent Augustus from returning to power. His Polish detour began drawing to a close in early 1706. Charles confronted Peter's army, dug in around the Polish city of Grodno. Having fought no major battles against Charles on Polish territory, Peter was still unwilling to risk a decisive clash and ordered his main forces to return home. Charles gave Peter still further time to prepare by moving back west into Germany in pursuit of the unfortunate Augustus, who had fled to his homeland of Saxony. Charles caught him in autumn 1706, forced him to renounce the Polish throne, and extracted funds to support the Swedish army on its chase back east after Peter. Unfortunately for Charles, Menshikov and a Russian corps caught part of the Swedish army without Charles at the Polish town of Kalisz in October 1706 and inflicted a substantial defeat, further demonstrating Russian troops' steady improvement.

By 1707, Charles had cleared Russians out of Poland, deposed King Augustus, and established his own candidate on the Polish throne, leaving him finally ready to settle accounts with Peter. Deciding against retaking the Baltic territories Peter had seized, Charles planned an invasion of Russia itself. With only 40,000–50,000 troops, Charles did not dream of conquering all of Russia. Instead, he counted on discontent within Russia to produce his victory. Charles was confident boyar opposition to Peter would depose him in favor of his son Aleksei.

Charles had good reason to believe this. Peter's radical cultural changes, including shaving beards and imposing Western dress, combined with the burdens of conscription and taxation to produce widespread discontent. A *strel'tsy* uprising in distant Astrakhan in 1705 slaughtered the local commander and hundreds of nobles, forcing Sheremetev to travel south to quell it. Peter's prestige was further damaged by Sheremetev's string of victories, while Peter instead presided over the humiliating withdrawal from Poland. The growth in power and wealth of Peter's lowborn and notoriously corrupt favorite Menshikov irritated the boyar elite, who saw in Peter's son Aleksei Petrovich a more congenial tsar, one less likely to trample elite interests in pursuit of grandiose goals. Peter conscripted peasants by the tens of thousands for forced labor projects, including constructing St. Petersburg, building his new navy, and fortifying Azov.

Finally, in October 1707, a cossack uprising broke out under the leadership of Kondratii Bulavin, reprising Bolotnikov's and Razin's earlier rebellions. Bulavin tapped resentment of Peter's efforts to recover runaway peasants and maximize tax revenues and conscripts. As regular government troops pulled from the defense against Charles XII closed in on Bulavin in May 1708, he captured the cossack stronghold of Cherkassk on the Don just above the Sea of Azov and then moved down the river in a failed attack on Azov itself. As Bulavin's movement faltered, meeting defeats where it tried to expand, dissension grew among Bulavin's supporters. Some conspirators attempted to seize him for relay to the tsar, but Bulavin shot himself in early July 1708. The remnants of his rebellion were mopped up over the next several months.

Despite this domestic turmoil, Peter was unwilling to surrender his foothold on the Baltic, while Charles would not make peace on any terms less than full restoration of the Swedish Empire. A military showdown was inevitable. Peter, well aware of Charles's invasion plans, was not ready to risk his army in battle with Sweden's veteran soldiers on foreign territory. He withdrew deeper into Russia, leaving only cavalry and light troops to lay waste to the territory in Charles's path and harass his pursuit wherever possible. In August 1707 Charles began his slow march across Poland.

By summer 1708 Charles was in Lithuania, ready to cross into Russia. On the direct road to Moscow, though, he faced the major fortress of Smolensk and countryside deliberately laid waste and devoid of food and forage. Harassed by Russian raids and still awaiting supplies and reinforcements, Charles decided in September against a direct drive east to Moscow. He instead moved southeast into Russian-controlled Ukraine, preferring to winter at Russian expense in the fertile territory of Ukraine while reserving a move against Moscow for the next year. In addition, Charles anticipated that the cossack *hetman* Ivan Mazeppa would rebel against Peter and provide him with welcome troops and provisions.

Instead, Charles's invasion of Ukraine was a disaster. The supply train Charles needed slowly trailed him south from Riga along with 12,000 reinforcements. Peter's wide-ranging cavalry caught it in fall 1708. After several days' chase, Peter's forces ran down the supply column on 28 September/9 October 1708 at Lesnaia in Poland. After a day-long running battle, the Swedish commander burned his wagons, buried his cannon, and fled to catch up with Charles. Only half the soldiers made it through to the main Swedish army, giving Charles additional mouths to feed but no supplies to feed them. Charles spent the winter of 1708–1709 encamped east of Kiev as his soldiers died from cold and disease. The cossack assistance Charles had counted on proved illusory. The cossacks had indeed suffered terribly in Peter's service, waging war far from home and finding themselves incapable of standing up to European regular armies. When Peter failed to protect Ukraine from Charles's invasion, Mazeppa defected to Charles with 3,000 followers in October 1708. The betrayal might have been more damaging without Menshikov's ruthless and timely intervention. As retribution, and a lesson in the consequences of disobedience, Menshikov seized Baturin, Mazeppa's capital, and slaughtered 6,000 men, women, and children. Peter replaced Mazeppa with a new *hetman* and used loyal Russian troops to ensure that Ukraine remained firmly under control.

Poltava

Running out of time and options, Charles became bogged down in the siege of the fortress town of Poltava in eastern Ukraine in spring 1709. Peter was still wary of meeting Charles in open battle. He slowly closed in, moving from fortified camp to fortified camp to confront the Swedes. Charles, supremely confident in his outnumbered troops' superiority to the Russians, and marooned 1,000 miles from Stockholm, willingly accepted the burden of attack in hopes of defeating Peter and ending the war. With his 25,000 troops, Charles believed his skill and veteran soldiers could overcome exhaustion, lack of supplies, and Peter's 40,000 soldiers.

Peter prepared the battlefield carefully. He could afford to be patient, for Charles's army dwindled each day. The forested and swampy ground directly between Poltava and the Russian camp to the north meant that a Swedish attack would require sweeping in a giant arc west from Poltava, north across clear ground, then back to the east to attack the Russian camp from the west. To slow the Swedish assault, Peter built field fortifications: six earthen redoubts stretching east to west across the open ground the Swedes had to cross to reach their staging area in front of the Russian encampment. On the eve of battle, Peter continued this construction, building an additional line of four redoubts running south from the first line, like the stem of a T, to further disrupt the Swedish approach.

When the battle opened on the morning of 27 June/8 July 1709, the Swedish army followed precisely the script Peter laid out, partly because Charles was not exercising his usual powers of command. He had been shot in the foot 11 days before the battle and was carried on a litter during the engagement. In preparing a plan for an attack on the Russian camp, Charles was well aware of the threat posed by the line of Russian redoubts. He decided to speed through them, not pausing for a fight. Charles left almost all his field artillery behind to achieve maximum speed. Surprised by the additional, newly built redoubts, though, Charles wasted valuable time in the morning redeploying his troops from unwieldy lines, superb for fire but slow to move, into columns, swifter across open ground. The arrangement cost Charles any conceivable advantage of surprise.

Having prepared his troops in columns, Charles moved them north at dawn toward the base of the Russian T. The plan quickly went awry. The Swedes took casualties from Russian fire as they swept past the redoubts, and a number of battalions became so entangled in desperate struggles to capture them that they never rejoined the main battle. Acrid gunpowder smoke and the dust thrown up by clashes between Russian and Swedish cavalry ahead of the Swedish main force made it difficult for Charles to coordinate his army. After Charles's columns had moved north along the stem of the T and crossed through the bar, they swung west, away from the Russians, to regroup in a low, wooded area. There Charles put them into broad lines for the final rush east across an open plain to the main Russian encampment.

As Charles regrouped, Peter prepared. Russian cavalry shifted north, preparing to attack the Swedish left flank as it pushed toward the Russian camp. Russian infantrymen left their camp to draw up in line to meet the Swedish charge. Nearly 20,000 Russian soldiers stretched across the center under Sheremetev's command, and Menshikov commanded the remaining cavalry on the Russian left. Hoping to regain the initiative, Charles decided to attack, counting on his own troops' steadiness and Russian fragility. Charles's right wing led the attack, driving back the

Russians opposite them and seizing a number of guns. The weight of Russian firepower against the undermanned Swedes and the more rapid advance of the Swedish right wing, however, opened a fateful gap in the advancing Swedish line. Russian troops, now fully capable of exploiting such an opportunity, wedged themselves into that gap, breaking the Swedish army in two. Charles's men broke and ran. Of Charles's 25,000 soldiers, 10,000 were killed or captured.

The remnants of the Swedish army scattered. Exhausted by the battle, the Russians were in no condition to pursue immediately. Most of the Swedish survivors retreated south to the banks of the Dnepr, where they were caught a few days later by a cavalry detachment under Menshikov. Charles and a few hundred others escaped into Turkish exile.

Poltava was perhaps the first decisive battle in Russian history, in the sense that the entire course of the Northern War and Russian history itself might have changed had the battle gone the other way. Widespread opposition to Peter's radical reforms could easily have become active support for Peter's son Aleksei and a reversal of Peter's innovations had Peter lost the Battle of Poltava, more so if he had been killed or captured. Instead, Peter's triumph gave him the political capital to face down domestic opposition. The Battle of Poltava was not decisive, however, in the sense that it did not end the Northern War, which was not even half over.

Peter hastily exploited his victory and destroyed Charles's empire. He sent troops to Poland to restore Augustus and garrison the country. Swedish possessions around the Baltic fell like dominoes. In June 1710 Peter captured Vyborg, just north of St. Petersburg. In July Sheremetev captured Riga, in September, Reval, quickly followed by all of Livonia. Not only did this mark concrete gains for Peter, but the financial damage to Sweden from lost taxes and tolls made it almost impossible to rebuild its shattered army. This also demonstrates the progress of Russian military capacity. Artillery and siege engineering had advanced sufficiently to allow the rapid reduction and conquest of cities that Russian armies had been trying to take since Ivan the Terrible.

The Turkish Detour

Peter's victory almost led to disaster at the hands of the Ottoman Turks. Overconfident in his talents and the abilities of his army, he pushed the Russian military far beyond its limits. The Ottomans, apprehensive over Peter's growing power, declared war on Russia in late 1710. Peter himself was enthusiastic and shifted troops across the length of Russia from north to south, pulling his old reliable Sheremetev away from Riga to run the campaign. This war, however, repeated the failures of Peter's grandfather's 1632 Smolensk War. The size of the theater and distance to Turkish territory were not commensurate with the forces Peter could employ. The single army that Peter led on a single, narrow penetration far into Ottoman territory was terribly vulnerable to being isolated and cut off. Only later tsars, commanding greater resources and not distracted by other wars, would be able to bring Russian power to bear against the Turks effectively.

Russia had fought the Turks before and would again over the next two centuries, but a new element marked this war. Peter actively played the Balkan Christian card against the Turks. The peasant population of the Balkans was mostly Orthodox. Aligning himself with Ottoman possessions Moldavia and Wallachia, Peter employed that religious bond against the Turks both to justify the war in Russia and recruit Balkan Christians, something Russia did consistently in future Turkish wars.

By spring 1711, the Russian plan was set. An expedition, accompanied by Peter and his fiancée Catherine, a Livonian innkeeper's daughter, knifed southwest from Kiev through Poland, skirting well to the west of the Black Sea coast, and crossing the Dnestr into Moldavia to detach it from Turkish rule. Stymied by the enormous distances involved, Peter's force of 40,000 was instead trapped on the River Prut by 130,000 Turks. The campaign's single major battle on 9/20 July 1711 inflicted horrific losses on the attacking Turkish troops, unaccustomed to the firepower of Peter's new-style regiments and field artillery. Nonetheless, Peter was still trapped far from home and had no choice but to come to terms with the remarkably lenient Ottomans. The treaty required Peter to surrender Azov, the first prize of his reign, as well as other Russian fortifications on the Don and the Dnepr. Peter had to promise noninterference in Polish affairs—an utterly meaningless guarantee.

End of the Northern War

After the humiliation of his Ottoman War, Peter was happy to return to the Northern War and the steady dismantling of the Swedish Empire. In 1713, Menshikov was given a delicate diplomatic and military mission: to roll up Swedish possessions on the northern German coast and pressure the Swedes to end the war, while at the same time ensuring the other powers of Europe were not so alarmed by Russia's burgeoning power that they intervened on Sweden's behalf. The same year, Peter's soldiers and his galley fleet skillfully executed a lightning amphibious campaign to clear Finland within six months. Peter accumulated prizes and territory, but the expense of war and the danger of too much success prompting foreign intervention made Peter want an end to the war.

Peter's navy had been relatively ineffective while the outcome of the Northern War was still in doubt, but was much more important in the consolidation of Russian gains after Poltava. Though predominantly a galley fleet, not a sailing ship navy, this was an advantage in amphibious warfare in and around the islands dotting the Finnish and Swedish coasts. After expelling the Swedes from Finland, in July 1714 Peter's navy defeated the Swedish fleet off Hangö in a major action.

Peter's reforms continued during the methodical dismantling of the Swedish Empire. In 1711, Peter established the Senate to serve as the center of Russian government, particularly during his absences on campaign. He continued rationalizing Russia's local government. This had already begun in the 1680s, as a succession of Russian tsars ordered and systematized the administration of Russia's southern frontier and its military garrisons. Peter continued this by shaking up local administration throughout Russia, dividing the country into eight huge provinces (*guberniia*) and passing many government functions to them. The old Muscovite *prikazy*, with their haphazard division of labor and antiquated methods, bothered Peter's sense of order and industriousness. Beginning in 1715, he explored replacing the *prikazy* with colleges, based on a Swedish model. The colleges he established from 1718 to 1720, using Swedish prisoners of war to staff them, were the equivalent of government departments or ministries in Western systems. The term "college" had no educational meaning, but came instead from the principle of collegiality. The colleges' decisions were made collectively by the leading personnel, the collegium. Peter wished to inculcate reasoned decision making and collective responsibility while reducing corruption. In an effort to balance loyalty and technical competence, his colleges divided authority, often having a native Russian as president, a foreign servitor as vice-president. Peter maintained political balance by predominantly appointing newly elevated, lowborn favorites to the new colleges, while granting provincial governorships to old boyar families. War and the army fell under the Military College [*voennaia kollegiia*], with Menshikov as president. A separate Admiralty College, under Apraksin, handled the navy.

The Northern War did not end with Peter's liquidation of the Swedish Empire in Livonia. Part of the problem was Charles XII himself. Languishing in exile in Turkey, he burned to return to Sweden and resume his war. He left Ottoman custody in autumn 1714, traveling incognito to join Swedish forces on the southern coast of the Baltic, where he fought to preserve his empire. Charles's stubbornness was not the only explanation for continued war: Sweden had lost so much, including its most important revenue sources, that there was little point in making peace. The war was such a disaster that there was nothing left to lose. Charles did begin negotiations with Russia in late spring 1718, but the lack of Swedish concessions suggested to the Russians that Charles was not taking them seriously. Many in Sweden, exhausted by war, came to the same conclusion. In late 1718, Charles was neatly shot through the head, perhaps by one of his own soldiers, while overseeing the siege of Frederiksten on the Swedish-Norwegian border.

Even this did not end the war, as the Swedish government sought allies to regain what Sweden had lost. This search proved hopeless, and Russian forces began regularly crossing the Baltic to raid Sweden itself. With cossacks ravaging the suburbs of Stockholm, the Swedish government accepted the Peace of Nystad in June 1721. Peter was more generous than he might have been; while he kept Swedish Livonia, along with St. Petersburg, Vyborg, and the surrounding territory, he returned most of Finland. He could afford magnanimity. Sweden's power was broken, and it would never return to the ranks of the European great powers. Peter, by contrast, had forced Russia into the first rank of European states, alarming many western Europeans with Russia's staggering potential power.

The end of the Northern War did not halt Peter's efforts at foreign expansion or domestic reform. His reign had one last quick war against the crumbling Persian Empire for trade routes and territorial gain along the eastern shores of the Caspian. Accompanying a fleet down the Volga in spring 1722, Peter led a joint land-sea campaign that seized the port city of Derbent before supply shortages forced his troops to return to Astrakhan that fall. Though Peter did not rejoin the effort himself, Russian forces additionally captured Resht in late 1722 and Baku the next summer before establishing a final peace with the Persian shah.

At home, Peter established a system for regulating advancement through Russian state service. In the past, Muscovite elites had moved constantly and seamlessly from military commands to diplomatic assignments to provincial governorships with little functional specialization. The *prikazy* had technical specialists, but that was separate from the upper reaches of Muscovy's nobility. By Peter's time, old ranks were disappearing. Peter appointed no new boyars, and the last would die in 1750. In addition, Peter's brother Fyodor had during his brief reign abolished *mestnichestvo,* the Muscovite system of honor and precedence. This created a new problem of how to mark and record advancement in rank through service, not birth. Peter's ad hoc approach to appointments and ranks had by the end of the Northern War clearly become unsustainable.

Peter's answer was a Table of Ranks, established in 1722 from Danish, Prussian, and Swedish models. Complex in presentation and execution, it established three branches of state service: civil, court, and military, with the military split into four subbranches: infantry, guards, artillery, and navy. Each branch was divided into a maximum of 14 ranks, 1 the highest, 14 the lowest, providing a system for determining relative rank and authority across different branches of service. Not all ranks were filled for all branches of service. For infantry and cavalry, for example, a field marshal was rank 1, down to lieutenant (*poruchik*) at rank 12, sublieutenant (*podporuchik*) at rank 13, and ensign (*praporshchik*) at rank 14. Rank-

and-file soldiers and sailors were outside of the Table of Ranks altogether. Though the ranks would be adjusted over the centuries, Peter's Table persisted as the framework of rank and status in Russia until the 1917 revolution. The Table also established that service brought with it nobility. Any military officer rank, even the lowest, qualified the holder for noble status, something not achieved in civilian ranks until rank 8.

Peter's reforms gave structure to the lives of the Russian nobility. They were required to educate their sons, serve the state, and advance through the Table of Ranks. While the Table of Ranks required competence and training commensurate with each rank, it was not a pure meritocracy and in no way undermined their dominant position in society. What it forced them to do, however, was to learn, dress, think, and act as western Europeans. Peter's educational institutions and the strictures of service allowed nothing less. The decades after Peter's death consolidated and solidified this transformation, which created a noble culture sharply divided from the lives of most Russians. The common identity that Peter imposed on his nobility began the creation of a self-conscious noble class that would flower and become increasingly important to Russian political developments over the remainder of the eighteenth century.

CHAPTER 5

After Peter

Peter's death in 1725 left no son to take the throne. His son Aleksei Petrovich by his first wife was nothing at all like what Peter wanted in a son, i.e., nothing at all like Peter himself. Aleksei was passive, bookish, and uninterested in state affairs: in Peter's view not tsar material. In 1716 Aleksei offered to give up all right to the throne. Peter, furious, summoned Aleksei to a personal confrontation, whereupon Aleksei fled to Austria. Brought back to Russia by Peter's agents, Aleksei was arrested, charged with conspiracy, tortured, and died under questioning in 1718, leaving behind a small son, Peter Alekseevich. With his second wife, Catherine, Peter fathered a number of sons, none of whom survived to adulthood. After the death of Aleksei Petrovich, Peter made incomplete preparations for the succession. In 1722 he declared it was the choice of the tsar, not a matter of genealogy, but did not name an heir. In 1724, he proclaimed his second wife, Catherine, Empress of Russia. While this strengthened Catherine's claim to power, Peter never specifically named her as heir. Peter's rejection of his son Aleksei as lacking manly virtues meant, ironically, that Russia was ruled by women and children for all but six months of the next 81 years.

When Peter died, Catherine easily took the throne. She enjoyed the support and affection of the politically vital guards regiments, which she had accompanied on a number of campaigns with Peter. Peter's associate Menshikov backed her as well. As Tsar Catherine I, she had no interest in ruling, and Menshikov took over government as head of the Supreme Privy Council, a small group of Peter's inner circle. Catherine and Menshikov cultivated the guards regiments while cutting taxes and army expenditures to reduce the unsustainable burden Peter's military machine had placed on Russia.

Catherine outlived Peter by only two years, and her death in 1727 raised the issue of succession once again. Peter and Catherine had two surviving daughters, but Menshikov engineered the succession of Aleksei's son Peter, grandson of Peter the Great, as Tsar Peter II. Menshikov overreached by engaging Peter to his own daughter, bringing Peter into his household, and one by one eliminating his rivals on the Supreme Privy Council. Menshikov's bald grasp for power and astounding corruption alienated a growing proportion of the high nobility, who managed to turn Peter II against Menshikov. He was exiled to Siberia and died in 1729. Peter II did not live much longer, dying of smallpox in 1730. Neither Catherine I nor Peter II had much impact on Russian military history. Their chief contribution was a negative one: reducing Peter the Great's military burden by discharging large numbers of officers and soldiers and allowing the navy to lapse into disrepair. Russia's expansionist wars of the 1730s ended the army's decay, but the navy continued its decline for most of the eighteenth century.

After the death of Peter II, no obvious candidates for tsar remained. The Supreme Privy Council's choice was Anna Ivanovna, widow of the Duke of Courland and daughter of Peter the Great's handicapped brother, Ivan V. Her chief attraction was her political weakness as a woman and widow, and the Council made its offer conditional. To receive the crown, Anna agreed to cede to the Supreme Privy Council the right to make war and peace, promulgate new taxes, create new generals, and control the guards regiments. The conditions, had she abided by them, would have gutted the autocratic power of the Russian tsar and created an oligarchy under the Supreme Privy Council.

The prospect of domination by the oligarchs of the Council was terrifying to the rest of the Russian nobility, and they communicated to Anna their opposition to the conditions. As niece to Peter the Great, she enjoyed a natural following among the guards regiments, which she carefully groomed upon her return to Moscow in February 1730. With her political support in place, she publicly tore up the conditions the Privy Council had imposed, dissolved the Council, and proclaimed full restoration of her autocratic powers. Though the guards regiments played a key role in her triumph, she nonetheless balanced their power by creating a third guards regiment, the Izmailovskii Guards.

Despite this tour de force, Anna's widowhood and her time outside of Russia in Courland forced her to rely heavily on the Baltic German elites who had served her there. Her largely German government was dominated by her favorite, the deeply unpopular Ernst Bühren. Foreign policy was the purview of another German: Heinrich Ostermann, a Westphalian who had already been a high-ranking diplomat under Peter the Great. As with Ostermann, Anna inherited from Peter the Great her chief administrator in the Russian army: Burchardt Christoph Münnich.

Münnich had long experience in European armies, fighting in the War of the Spanish Succession before Russian service as an engineer for Peter the Great. He appealed to Anna because of his German background and his relative independence from the powerful noble families that had attempted to limit her power. Tireless, efficient, and power hungry, Münnich used Anna's backing to protect himself from the hostility he generated. Beginning from the post of Master of Ordnance, Münnich first used Anna's backing to become in 1730 head of a Military Commission to investigate and reform the army, then in 1732 President of the War College.

Münnich had an ambitious agenda. One element was cutting expenditure, difficult in the face of wars in Poland and Turkey. He did eliminate superfluous personnel and improve financial management, while continuing his predecessors' policy of allowing the navy to rot at anchor. Despite popular perceptions of a pro-German government, Münnich promoted native Russian nobility, establishing a Cadet Corps in 1731 for officer training of noble youth, effectively removing Peter the Great's requirement for nobles to serve in the ranks first. He equalized the pay of Russian and foreign officers, eliminating the premium foreigners had enjoyed. Münnich also set a 25-year limit on noble service; while still a draconian demand, this improved on the theoretically limitless service Peter the Great had required. While he did introduce some cosmetic elements of drill and uniform along German or specifically Prussian lines, those were outweighed by the substantive improvements he made in the living conditions of Russian officers and soldiers alike.

Münnich also altered Russian infantry and cavalry to make them more flexible and effective. He increased the number of artillery pieces in infantry regiments and broke up separate units of grenadiers to distribute these grenade throwers among the troops. He expanded the types of cavalry in the Russian army to enable a wider variety of functional roles. Before Münnich, all Russian cavalry had essentially been dragoons, intended to move on horseback but fight on foot: Russian doctrine forbade dragoons to fire their weapons while mounted. In addition, Russia had plentiful light cavalry for raiding, scouting, and pursuit. Cossacks filled these roles, but the light cavalry also included several regiments of hussars, manned by Hungarians, Serbians, or other foreigners. This left a gap—Russia lacked heavy cavalry capable of a decisive shock attack. For this purpose, Münnich formed an elite guards cavalry regiment to match the three guards infantry regiments, and several regiments of cuirassiers, heavily armed and armored cavalry, named for the heavy breastplate or cuirass that they wore, and requiring larger and stronger horses than had been typical for Russia.

The War of the Polish Succession

The first test of the post-Petrine Russian army, not an especially difficult one, came in Poland. King Augustus II, Peter's ally in the Northern War, died in February 1733, requiring a new election. Augustus's son (also named Augustus) inherited the family's Saxon possessions in Germany smoothly. The Polish election, however, in early fall 1733 handed the crown to the French-backed candidate Stanislaw Leszczynski, Charles XII's puppet king in Poland during the Northern War. Russia and the Austrian Empire agreed that a pro-French Polish king was absolutely unacceptable and settled on the younger Augustus as the best practical alternative. Russia and Austria intervened to depose Leszczynski and give the younger Augustus his father's throne.

The physical distance between France and its ally meant the War of the Polish Succession was an anticlimax. Anna's government massed troops on the Polish border under General Peter Lacy, an Irish exile long in Russian service, and invaded even before Stanislaw's actual election. Lacy carefully managed a second election that named the younger Augustus king of Poland. Leszczynski fled to temporary refuge in Danzig (now Gdansk). Lacy besieged him there in early 1734, then handed the siege to Münnich. France could do little to support its distant client besides desultory attacks on Austrian territory in western Europe. It sent a fleet to the Baltic that landed tiny ground forces, only 2,000 men, on the Polish coast. After Polish and French efforts to break the siege of Danzig failed, Leszczynski fled to a final refuge in France. Poland was confirmed as a Russian-dominated buffer state where Russian troops intervened at will. France and Austria continued to fight in Germany and Italy, and a small Russian force under Lacy went west to support Austria but saw no action. From Russia's point of view, the war ended entirely satisfactorily.

The Russo-Turkish War, 1735–1739

Almost immediately after the fighting ended in Poland, Russia launched another war as part of expansion aimed at the Ottoman Empire and its vassals the Crimean Tatars. Provoked by continuing Crimean raids, and encouraged by Ottoman entanglement in a war with Persia, Russia declared war on the Ottomans in 1735. Münnich devised ambitious plans for cumulative campaigns to win Constantinople, the Ottoman capital, for Russia. He was confident that the superior discipline and firepower of well-drilled Russian troops could master anything the Ottomans might throw in their way. He was not wrong, but premature. In this and future Russo-Turkish wars, Russian control advanced inexorably counterclockwise around the Black Sea's western shores.

After a failed Russian raid on the Crimea in 1735, the war's first major campaigns came in 1736. Münnich faced a number of strategic obstacles. First, Russia's objectives were distant both from Russia and each other. The road to the heart of Ottoman power lay around the western edge of the Black Sea. The Turkish fortress of Azov, controlling the mouth of the

Don River, lay to the east. The Crimean Tatars between them, though relatively less powerful than in previous centuries, dominated the north shore of the Black Sea. Efforts against any one target lay open to attack from another to cut lengthy supply lines back north. This forced the Russians to haul masses of supplies with them south across the steppe. Furthermore, Russian troops faced formidable natural and artificial obstacles. The Crimea's geographic defenses had stymied Russian armies before. The Ottoman Turks were shielded by major rivers flowing into the Black Sea from the north and the west, each in turn garrisoned by imposing Turkish fortresses.

Münnich's plan for 1736 thus delayed a move against Constantinople until he dealt with Azov and the Crimea. The main Russian forces under Münnich himself moved down the Dnepr to the Isthmus of Perekop guarding the Crimea. His troops stormed the Tatar fortifications with ease in May 1736 and moved into the Crimea. Once there, however, Münnich was unable to bring the Tatars to battle, as most fled into the Crimean mountains. Münnich laid waste to the countryside, but lost large numbers of men to thirst and disease. He withdrew that autumn. Lacy's subsidiary attack on Azov went much better. After a brief siege, Azov's powder magazine exploded and the fortress surrendered in June. Encouraged and alarmed by Russian successes, the Austrian Empire joined the war against Turkey to share and limit Russian gains in the Balkans.

With Azov captured, the Russian war effort shifted west for the 1737 campaign. Lacy's troops infiltrated the Crimea *not* through the Perekop, but instead via the narrow sandbars and spits just east of the peninsula. Breaking into eastern Crimea in May 1737, Lacy's 40,000 troops shattered a Tatar horde and carried out the usual ravaging of the countryside, but just as in the previous year, sickness and thirst forced them to withdraw. While Lacy was in the Crimea, Münnich marched southwest from the Dnepr River across the steppe to the Bug River. With 80,000 men, he crossed the Bug well upstream, then moved down its right bank to Ochakov, a major Turkish fortress. A hasty bombardment and improvised assault in July brought another fortunate powder magazine explosion, allowing the Russians to take the fortress quickly. Shortages of supplies and fodder, as well as the plague endemic to the region, forced Münnich to leave a garrison at Ochakov and withdraw back northeast.

In 1738, Russia accomplished very little. Lacy mounted the third Russian invasion of the Crimea in as many years, but without any more lasting results. Münnich skirted far west of the Black Sea with 100,000 soldiers, crossing the Bug easily and reaching the next river barrier, the Dnestr, that summer. Once again, plague and short supplies, as well as Turkish screening forces, forced him to withdraw.

For the 1739 campaign, Münnich moved his main forces even farther west, cutting through Polish territory to cross the upper reaches of the Bug, the Dnestr, then the Prut. Moving so far inland and so deep into Ottoman territory, like Peter the Great in 1711, Münnich left himself vulnerable to being cut off by the Turks and the fast-moving cavalry of their Crimean Tatar allies. Exactly that happened in August 1739. Believing Russian discipline and firepower could extract him from this trap, Münnich launched a skillful attack on the main Turkish fortified encampment at Stavuchany on 17/28 August 1737. After a diversionary blow on the Turkish right wing, Münnich carefully massed his troops for a decisive attack on the Turkish left. He utterly smashed the Turks, capturing the encampment with its supplies and artillery, then seized the fortress of Khotin on the upper Dnestr without a struggle.

At the peak of Münnich's success, a separate Austrian peace with the Turks cost Russia its only ally. Unsure of the potential for further gains, Russia agreed to terms. Despite its string of battlefield victories, the Russian army had suffered enormously from disease. The cost of the war in lives and money meant that Russia did not gain much from the peace settlement, winning some empty steppe north of the Black Sea and regaining Peter the Great's old prize Azov. Even that was not especially valuable: the condition was that Azov had to remain unfortified.

Despite its inconclusive result, the war signaled a number of developments that would persist through the ensuing decades. First, Turkish forces were incapable of standing up to much smaller numbers of Russian troops. Though Münnich's strategic goals had been too ambitious, he was absolutely correct that Russian firepower and discipline would overmatch the slowly modernizing Turks. Second, terrible losses to disease and insoluble logistics problems gave Russian campaigns a particular pattern: battles won and fortresses captured did not produce sustained gains, for the Russian army was still incapable of seizing distant territory and staying. In the approaching Seven Years' War, Russian battlefield accomplishments were rendered meaningless by the need to retreat, refit, resupply, and replace casualties.

Empress Elizabeth

Anna had been widowed almost as soon as she married, and so she had no children, a matter that grew more pressing as she aged. She chose as heir her newborn grandnephew Ivan, the son of Anna Leopoldovna, her older sister Catherine's daughter. As Anna lay dying in 1740, she appointed her unpopular favorite Ernst Bühren as regent for the new infant tsar Ivan VI. Bühren's magnanimous gestures got him nowhere with the many enemies he had made the previous decade, and he was arrested and exiled to Siberia after Anna's death. The regency passed to Ivan's mother Anna Leopoldovna for only a year, after which a coup led by Peter's daughter Elizabeth Petrovna, backed by the guards regiments, seized the throne. Ivan, only a toddler, was arrested and imprisoned along with his family.

The legacy of her illustrious father gave Elizabeth the support she needed to take the throne, but she was very unlike Peter the Great. Elizabeth's interests were clothes, dancing, and men, and she happily surrendered government to others, particularly her vice-chancellor Aleksei Petrovich Bestuzhev-Riumin, an unpleasant and neurotic character but an able administrator. Elizabeth's reign transferred power away from the Baltic Germans who had dominated under Anna Ivanovna to native Russians, and her government deliberately portrayed itself as a return to Russian roots. Ostermann and Münnich were both arrested, tried for treason, and sentenced to death, sentences commuted to Siberian exile on the chopping block. Antiforeign feeling, particularly anti-German feeling, ran high.

Elizabeth inherited a war with Sweden when she took the throne. Anti-Russian factions inside Sweden, supported by France, had declared war on Russia in summer 1741 to take advantage of Russia's political turmoil, but with a thin justification of defending Elizabeth's right to the throne.

This created the palpable absurdity of a war waged on behalf of the person now ruling the country being attacked. Sweden was entirely unprepared for war, with only tiny forces in Finland to withstand the inevitable Russian counterattack. Peter Lacy led a lighting raid into Finland in early fall 1741, using troops seasoned in the arts of destruction. French attempts to mediate and prevent the further humiliation of its ally proved fruitless.

While diplomacy failed to settle the war, Russian arms were ravaging Swedish Finland. The cossacks did what they did best, ransacking and pillaging the Finnish countryside. Lacy launched a second invasion in summer 1742, masterfully coordinating a rapid march west along the Finnish coast with supply deliveries and amphibious landings by the Russian galley fleet. In August 1742, Lacy's army cut off the Swedes' retreat outside Helsingfors (now Helsinki). Caught between Lacy's army on land and the Russian fleet at sea, 17,000 Swedish troops surrendered. The Russians occupied both Helsingfors and Finland's then-capital Abo. The Swedes were so disgusted with the performance of their generals that they were executed for dereliction of duty. By late 1742, Sweden's defeat was complete; the only question was whether Sweden would be able to rescue something at the bargaining table. By spring 1743, Elizabeth was ready to end the war, fearing as usual a European coalition to defend Sweden. Russian and Swedish negotiators in Abo agreed in summer 1743 on the cession to Russia of several provinces of eastern Finland, leaving the bulk of the country in Swedish hands in a surprisingly generous treaty.

The Seven Years' War

For most of the 1740s and the early 1750s, Russia avoided the growing tensions in central Europe. One of the key developments destabilizing Europe was the rise of Prussia. Under a series of careful and talented kings, it had become a military power in fragmented Germany far out of proportion to its small size and population. Prussia's king, the confident and cultivated Frederick II, Frederick the Great, possessed both striking military talent and the extraordinary military machine his ancestors had created. Frederick was a gifted commander, and he had drilled his troops to be more flexible and maneuverable than any in Europe. Frederick's innovations included deliberate asymmetry on the field of battle—overloading one side of his line to overwhelm an enemy flank, or maneuvering his troops quickly against an enemy flank—to win a battle before his own weaknesses were exposed. This required speed and precision, and by relentless training and discipline the Prussian army was close to achieving Frederick's ideal of winning a battle without firing a shot, simply by maneuvering the enemy into a losing position.

Frederick saw in the Austrian Empire a ripe target for Prussian aggrandizement. The death in 1740 of Austrian Emperor Charles VI gave Frederick his opening. He protested the succession of Charles's daughter Maria Theresa as Austrian empress and invaded the rich province of Silesia. Frederick's cynical grab unleashed the War of the Austrian Succession, as France and Bavaria joined Frederick's efforts to benefit from Austrian weakness. Britain intervened on Austria's side to prevent French aggrandizement. The war finally ended in 1748, with Prussia's hold on Silesia still firm. Russia had sent troops to Austria at the end of the war, but they arrived after peace negotiations were already under way. Their presence nevertheless signaled a more active role for Russia in European politics.

The Russian army continued to grow in power and expertise under Elizabeth. With Münnich's dismissal, Elizabeth's military was run by Peter Ivanovich Shuvalov, one of a trio of brothers who played key roles in Elizabeth's regime and in her personal life. Elizabeth and Shuvalov eliminated German cosmetic innovations introduced during Anna's reign, but as war approached in the 1750s, Shuvalov sought to re-Prussianize the Russian military by imitating Frederick the Great's intricate and complex use of maneuver. Shuvalov attempted to improve the doctrine and training of Russian troops, still run by outdated field manuals, but had much greater success with cavalry than with infantry, where he was too enamored of complex and artificial maneuvers. He lacked the skilled officers and the well-drilled troops to make them possible. To cope with the new demands of the European battlefield, Shuvalov converted some dragoons into heavier cuirassiers and mounted grenadiers. Dragoons could not meet European cavalry on equal terms, while cuirassiers and grenadiers could carry out shock charges on the battlefield. Shuvalov was particularly effective in improving Russian artillery, though he tended to get carried away by dubious technical gimmicks.

Russia, though generally supportive of Austria, avoided European war through the 1740s. After the War of the Austrian Succession, though, the entire structure of European international politics changed in what historians term the "diplomatic revolution." An Anglo-Austrian partnership against France, the cornerstone of European politics for decades, evaporated as the Austrians decided to focus on their large contiguous empire in eastern Europe, not their small and vulnerable possessions in western Europe. The most pressing threat to Austria was no longer France, but the growing power of Prussia. This new Austrian view of France as a potential ally against Prussia, not a rival, left the British without their traditional continental partner to balance the military might of France. The British turned instead to Prussia. Led by Elizabeth's chancellor Bestuzhev-Riumin, the Russians were both concerned about Prussian power and eager for expansion in eastern Europe at Prussian expense.

Though Bestuzhev-Riumin had been pro-British, Britain's friendship with Prussia undermined his position and opened the door to an alliance between Russia and France. By spring 1757, a new system of alliances was firmly in place: France, Austria, and Russia against Prussia and Britain.

In 1756, what were in effect two separate wars broke out, linked together under the general name of the Seven Years' War (in American history, the French and Indian War). Britain and France went to war in a worldwide struggle for colonial domination, particularly in North America and India. In central Europe, Frederick recognized the preparations for war against him by France, Austria, and Russia and preempted their attack. In late summer 1756, Frederick occupied Saxony in central Germany, removing a threat to his capital Berlin. The next year, the war began in earnest.

With Britain lacking a significant army, and preoccupied by the global war against France, Frederick faced overwhelming odds in his struggle against Europe's three largest military powers. His situation was not, however, as hopeless as it seemed. British financial subsidies kept Frederick's army provisioned and manned. The coalition against him was far from united. For France, the war against Prussia was secondary compared to fighting Britain. Though France maintained an army in Germany as part of the coalition against Prussia, the burden of the war fell more heavily on Austria and Russia. Those two powers were also working at cross-purposes: Austria wanted to regain the lost province of Silesia, while Russia looked to expand its own domination of eastern Europe. Frederick's strategic skills made the problem worse, for he used Prussia's central position and interior lines to shift his forces from one front to another to prevent his enemies from concentrating their troops against him. This established the basic dynamics of the war. Frederick's enemies sought to gain territory at the least possible cost to themselves by putting the burden of fighting on their allies; Frederick desperately raced from front to front to survive against overwhelming odds.

Though Russia had fought Poland, Sweden, and Turkey since Peter the Great's time, the Seven Years' War marked its test against a first-class European army. The results were mixed, particularly early in the war. Tactically, Russian soldiers demonstrated great reserves of courage and endurance, standing toe-to-toe with the best soldiers in Europe in bloody exchanges of volley after volley without flinching. Their commanders did not acquit themselves so well. Overall coordination of the war, given Elizabeth's disinterest in matters of state, fell to Bestuzhev-Riumin and a Conference attached to the imperial court. Inefficient and consumed by the micromanagement of armies at the front, it fell far short of Russia's needs. Russia's army commanders also proved generally ineffective. Though they never lost a decisive battle against the Prussians, they were entirely incapable of exploiting victories to turn battlefield success into political advantage. Russia's supply services were poorly prepared for sustaining a war in central Europe. Part of the reason for the Russian inability to sustain momentum and exploit victory was the perennial need to withdraw home during the winter to keep the Russian army fed and clothed.

In 1757, the war intensified. In spring, the Austrians prepared an invasion north. Frederick, well informed of how slowly France and Russia were moving to attack him, decided on a full-scale invasion of Austrian Bohemia by over 100,000 men in four columns. Austria gave up its offensive, stringing out its forces in a thin and brittle cordon along its northern border. After Frederick's easy breakthrough, Austrian troops fled in disorder as Frederick pursued them toward Prague, already anticipating diverting his troops to deal with the French. He screened a sizable Austrian garrison in Prague while using his main forces to confront the Austrian army east of the city. In a terribly bloody and closely fought battle, Frederick smashed the Austrians, then besieged Prague. Losing an equally bloody battle at Kolin in June to an Austrian relief force, Frederick withdrew north to regroup. While Frederick's Bohemian invasion was turning sour, a French army invaded Germany from the west, beating Prussia's British and Hanoverian allies.

While the war was raging in western Germany and Bohemia, Russian troops were still on Russian territory. The main Russian army of 100,000 troops under Stepan Fyodorovich Apraksin crept toward Frederick's isolated enclave of East Prussia. Well connected politically, Apraksin was an aesthete with little practical military expertise. East Prussia was lightly garrisoned and should have been an easy prey, but Apraksin's dilatory pace almost brought disaster. The Prussians caught him by surprise at the village of Gross-Jägersdorf on 19/30 August 1757. Outnumbered two to one, the Prussians found the Russians strung out in their line of march, stretching more than two miles from northwest to southeast. The Prussians attacked from the southwest, with their cavalry striking both extremes of the Russian line and the Prussian infantry wedging itself into a wood in the center. As the Russians rushed to deploy from marching columns into battle formations, the Prussians threatened to repeat what the Swedes had done at Narva: break through a thin Russian line and then roll up and destroy the individual pieces. The situation was salvaged by Peter Aleksandrovich Rumiantsev, later to become Catherine the Great's best commander. He rallied the regiments in the center of the Russian line and sent them into the wood, clearing the Prussian infantry and ending the threat of a decisive breakthrough and defeat. The weight of Russian numbers, and particularly the firepower of Russian artillery, forced the Prussians into retreat as the Russian troops organized a coherent defense. The Prussians had lost more than they could afford from their small East Prussian forces, but Apraksin had no stomach for further fighting.

Shocked by the bloody battle, he halted the invasion and withdrew to winter quarters. He was relieved of command and put on trial before conveniently dying the next year.

Despite the Russian reverse, Frederick's situation looked desperate by autumn 1757. He faced the armies of three great powers, an empty treasury that British subsidies could not fix, and a butcher's bill that Prussia's small population could ill afford. An Austrian detachment even raided his capital Berlin, while other Austrian forces snatched up Silesian fortresses to regain the lost province. Matters quickly turned Frederick's way: a spectacular victory over French forces and their German allies at Rossbach gave Frederick some security from threats from the west. He followed that with an equally impressive though more costly victory over the Austrians at Leuthen in Silesia, convincing the British to throw their support more fully behind Prussia's war effort. The prospects for 1758 seemed much brighter for Prussia.

But early 1758 also saw a renewed Russian invasion of East Prussia, this time under Villim Villimovich Fermor, a sober and intelligent Baltic German, solicitous of his troops' welfare. Moving with speed and dispatch, Fermor's well-disciplined troops took the province without difficulty. Fermor's initiative left him, however, when it came time to push west toward Prussia proper. Unable to salvage East Prussia, Frederick temporarily turned to knocking Austria out of the war. A desperate scrounging for soldiers managed to build Frederick's armies back up to 160,000 men. In spring 1758 he invaded Austrian Moravia, but found the Austrians unwilling to meet him in the open field. Without a battle, Frederick could not use his battlefield skill to make up for his ongoing strategic nightmare. By late summer, he turned back to dealing with the Russians.

Frederick met Fermor's troops in the wooded and marshy hills outside the village of Zorndorf, just east of the Oder River. Approaching the Russian position from the north, Frederick engaged in a daring night march around the Russian right flank to attack the Russians from the rear. The Russians simply reversed in place, facing south instead of north, negating much of Frederick's advantage. They were now, however, at much greater risk from any defeat, with their backs against swamps and a small stream that would turn any retreat into disaster.

Having lost surprise, Frederick now planned an attack from the south on the Russian right flank. On 14/25 August 1758, after two hours of bombardment, his massed assault troops on the Prussian left moved north through dust and smoke into a murderous close-range exchange of volleys with the Russians. Frederick's supporting troops, intending to follow the initial attack on the Russian right, instead drifted east toward the center of the Russian line, depriving the main Prussian assault of support. This shift to the center left the Prussian left flank open, an opportunity that Russian cavalry seized, sending Frederick's entire left wing fleeing in disorder. Only a prompt counterattack by Prussian cavalry stabilized Frederick's left and staved off complete defeat. In the afternoon, Frederick's right wing moved forward in attack, but was met head-on by a Russian cavalry counterattack and went nowhere. The battle degenerated into a slugging match beyond the control of either commander. As night fell, both armies broke off contact, shocked by over 30,000 casualties from among perhaps 80,000 engaged. Neither side wished for a further fight, and the Russian army withdrew east unmolested, preceded by Fermor who had fled the battle much earlier.

Fermor's retreat allowed Frederick to return south to fight the Austrians, illustrating once again how interior lines and poor allied coordination allowed Frederick to sustain a war effort seemingly far beyond his country's capabilities. Frederick nevertheless met disaster when an Austrian attack almost overran his army encamped at Hochkirch, though he was able to retreat with his army largely intact. Still, at the end of 1758 Frederick's strategic situation was no better, the year's battles had cost him his best soldiers, and his enemies demonstrated a new ability to stand up to the best Frederick could throw at them.

By the beginning of 1759, Frederick was clear that waiting on enemy attacks would bring disaster. The Russians and Austrians were improving the coordination of their moves, and even the French pressed forward in western Germany. A methodical Austrian advance in Silesia and an equally slow Russian move west into Prussia threatened to grind Frederick between them. The Russian army was under its third commander in three years: Peter Semyonovich Saltykov. Though in his 60s, Saltykov was much more aggressive and skilled than his unfortunate predecessors. By summer 1759, Frederick had left the Russian threat to a subordinate, taking the Austrian theater for himself. This was a mistake: the Prussian army blundered into a frontal assault against Saltykov's well-prepared troops at Paltzig, just inside the Prussian border, on 12/23 July 1759. They succeeded only in smashing repeatedly into impregnable Russian positions, where Prussia's well-drilled troops were slaughtered by Russian artillery. Frederick was forced to take over the defense against the Russians personally.

After Paltzig, Saltykov's forces dug in around the village of Kunersdorf on the Oder River, where they were joined by an Austrian corps sent to cooperate against Frederick. The allied forces had over 60,000 men between them. Anticipating an attack from Frederick, they constructed an elaborate series of field fortifications on a ridge running from southwest to northeast. Commanding only 50,000 men east of the Russian position, Frederick believed he could swing around the northeast extreme of the Russian position to attack its vulnerable flank, not realizing the true extent and strength of the Russian entrenchments. After repositioning his troops, Frederick attacked on the morning of 1/12 August 1759, following lengthy artillery bombardment with an infantry assault at noon up three sides of the hill anchoring the northeastern end of the Russian line. After clearing those heights in a bloody fight, he then threw his army against the next hill in the chain, immediately to the southwest, only to find densely packed Russian and Austrian infantry facing him across the small valley separating the hills. The smoke and dust of the battle prevented any coordination of the overall attack. An assault by Prussian cavalry on the southeastern face of the Russian position was repulsed by Rumiantsev's cavalry. As the grinding attack against stubborn Russian-Austrian defenses dragged on, growing numbers of Prussians deserted to safety in the surrounding woods until Frederick's army finally melted away. Russian cavalry sweeping through the low ground southeast of the Russian line completed the rout. Frederick was convinced his reign was over and that there was no escaping his allies' combined might.

The carnage of Kunersdorf—30,000 dead and wounded—and the growing divergence of interests between Russia and Austria meant that Saltykov did not take full advantage of his victory. His army had been almost as badly battered as Frederick's. Berlin was close and undefended, but Saltykov only halfheartedly crept closer to Frederick's capital and did not attempt to destroy Frederick's shattered forces, allowing the Prussians to rebuild an army. By October, Saltykov withdrew into winter quarters in Poland, allowing Frederick still more time to rebuild. Prussian desperation spurred frantic efforts to scrape together 100,000 men. At the same time, Russia's desire to retain East Prussia after the war caused growing unease in Austria.

The Russian plan for 1760 envisaged active cooperation with the Austrians to clear Silesia entirely of Prussian troops and use of the combined weight of the two armies to crush Frederick if he attempted to stop them. Despite better strategic coordination, the campaign itself proved frustrating, as the two armies still could not force Frederick into a final confrontation. Saltykov was relieved of command and replaced by Fermor, who had not improved his nerve and initiative in his time out of power. Hoping to salvage a lost year, the Russians adopted a French proposal for a lightning raid on Frederick's capital Berlin, left undefended by Frederick's concentration of troops in Silesia. A joint Russian-Austrian force, with large quantities of cossacks and light cavalry, swept rapidly up the Oder River in September 1761, assembling outside Berlin. Seeing the impossibility of defending the city, the Prussian garrison evacuated and Russian troops occupied Berlin on 28 September/9 October 1760. Eager to score political points, the Russian troops were exemplary in their restrained treatment of the population and the mild conditions they imposed. The flying corps that had taken the city was too distant from its infantry and supplies to hold Berlin and withdrew two days later.

Though a remarkable public relations feat, the brief occupation of Berlin did nothing to conclude the war. Though Prussian reserves of manpower neared exhaustion, so did the resources of every other power. In 1761, the Russians returned to their previous strategy of a drive west to the Oder River, this time under Aleksandr Borisovich Buturlin. Unlike his predecessors, who at least fought the Prussians before losing their nerve, Buturlin made only a halfhearted push west before once more pulling his troops east for the winter. The only positive result of the year was Rumiantsev's successful sea and land siege of the fortress of Kolberg on the Baltic Sea. Rumiantsev's campaign introduced of a new type of light infantry recruited from hunters and intended for skirmishing in broken terrain: the jäger or hunting battalions (in Russian, *yegerskii*). The capture of Kolberg in December 1761 offered hope for the next year: the logistics problems that forced Russian withdrawal each winter might be solved by supplies transported to the Prussian coast by sea. Even worse for Frederick, Britain was halting the financial support that kept Prussia afloat. The year 1762 promised to be disastrous for Frederick.

Frederick was saved by a remarkable stroke of luck. Tsar Elizabeth had been ill for years. Without legitimate children of her own, she had chosen as successor her nephew, her sister's son Peter. Raised in Germany as a Lutheran, Peter was deeply unhappy about coming to Russia to learn a strange language and convert to a strange religion. His marriage to Sophia of Anhalt-Zerbst, renamed Catherine with her conversion to Orthodoxy, was a spectacular failure. An impassioned admirer of Frederick the Great, Peter was the center of opposition to Elizabeth and the Seven Years' War inside Russia. At least part of Russia's inability to crush Frederick came from the reluctance of Russian commanders to alienate the heir to the throne, their future tsar. On a more principled basis, others within the Russian elite, particularly vice-chancellor for foreign affairs Mikhail Illarionovich Vorontsov, regarded the complete destruction of Prussia as harmful to the European balance of power and Russian interests and noted the desperate state of Russian finances. When Elizabeth died on 25 December 1761/5 January 1762, Peter came to the throne as Peter III. He promptly took Russia out of the war, requested no compensation from Prussia for doing so, returned all Prussian territory, made Russia a Prussian ally, and provided Frederick with 20,000 troops. Austria saw no prospects in continuing alone and concluded a peace on the basis of the status quo at the outbreak of war, leaving Silesia in Prussian hands.

Though the Russian army fought Frederick the Great toe-to-toe, taking and inflicting enormous losses, calling up 250,000 conscripts, and losing 100,000 dead, Peter had abandoned the war at the moment of victory. Increasingly conscious of their identity and status as skilled and professional commanders, Russian officers did not forgive Peter this betrayal.

CHAPTER 6

Catherine the Great

Catherine the Great ruled Russia for the final third of the eighteenth century. She earned her sobriquet "the Great" through relentless and successful territorial aggrandizement. Her career perfectly illustrates the opportunities and costs of foreign policy in an era of amoral balance-of-power politics. Contrary to theories that suggest balance-of-power politics produce stability, the eighteenth century in fact displays a ruthless and relentless struggle for military advantage and territorial expansion, with the only alternative decline and destruction. In that arena, Catherine employed Russia's immense human resources well. Her reign demonstrated a mastery of effective and rational absolute rule. She took advantage of the increasing sophistication of Russia's administrative machinery to extract resources and turn them efficiently to achieve foreign policy ends. Her power, and Russia's power, were based on serfdom, but that was no hindrance. Before the Industrial Revolution, a servile labor force and an army drawn from unwilling and illiterate serfs was no handicap. Indeed, under Catherine Russia suffered fewer military consequences from its economic and social gap with western Europe than at any time in its history. Catherine suffered, during her lifetime and after, from lurid allegations about her notoriously immoral and disordered personal life. In fact, her personal life was quite ordered: temporary but passionate monogamous relationships with a series of court favorites. In that sense, she was as restrained as most European monarchs and more upright than many. Her personal conduct was noteworthy only because she was a woman. Had she been a man, no one would have noticed or cared. The true amorality (not immorality) of Catherine's life was her conduct of foreign policy. She played the game by the rules of her time and played it very well.

Peter III ruled Russia only six months. He fell to a coup organized by and on behalf of his wife Catherine, with whom he shared only mutual detestation. Pregnant with another man's child when Peter took the throne, Catherine knew herself to be extremely vulnerable. Peter's

German sympathies and withdrawal from the Seven Years' War were highly unpopular with segments of the Russian elite, as was his confiscation of vast land holdings from the Orthodox church. He moved Russia toward war with Denmark not in defense of Russian interests, but those of his ancestral home Holstein. Though Catherine later attempted to paint her husband as unstable, even insane, the contemporary evidence is more complex. All this was not itself enough to bring a coup. That required Catherine's active intervention in the personal and factional politics at court. Catherine relied above all on contacts and friends among the officers of the guards regiments, with whom she seized power in St. Petersburg on 28 June/8 July 1762 before Peter, outside the city, even knew what was happening. After a brief attempt to flee, Peter meekly surrendered. Catherine's coconspirators then murdered him.

Peter's brief reign produced a major change in the status of the Russian nobility, all of whom in principle were lifelong servants of the state, generally as military officers. In 1736, Tsar Anna Ivanovna had granted the right to retire after 25 years in service and had allowed noble families to keep one son home as estate manager. All tsars had in practice granted lengthy leaves to allow nobles to tend to their estates and families. Peter III went beyond that. On 18 February/1 March 1762, his emancipation of the nobility granted a host of rights that had before only been gifts of the tsar. No noble was obliged to serve, and nobles in service could generally retire whenever they wished. Peter's goals were professionalizing the officer corps and improving estate management and local government through the greater physical presence of the nobility in the countryside. His emancipation ably served those goals and lasted much longer than Peter himself. As military service still brought prestige and social advancement, large numbers of nobles continued to serve, while the Russian army supplemented them as before with foreign professionals. Peter's action was immensely popular among the nobility; the Senate voted to erect a golden statue in his honor.

Despite Catherine's systematic effort to blacken her late husband's name and character, she reversed none of his policies. She kept the lucrative church lands he confiscated, kept noble military service optional, and formally confirmed this right in her own Charter of the Nobility in 1785. Moreover, Catherine was in no hurry to bring Russia back into the Seven Years' War. The war's expense and her empty treasury led Catherine to embark on conservative consolidation. Catherine gracefully and delicately solidified her position on the throne while repairing the worst damage done by Peter's arbitrary foreign policies.

Catherine retained oversight of foreign affairs, but gave its management to Nikita Ivanovich Panin. Panin's foreign policy in the early years of Catherine's reign was a "northern system." This alliance with Prussia and Denmark was intended to counter the French-Austrian alliance in southern Europe, influence events in Poland, and prevent any attack by Sweden. Centered around a 1764 alliance with Prussia, Panin's system functioned rather well. It protected Prussia against war with Austria, while providing both countries valuable time to recover from the Seven Years' War. The system's chief weakness, aside from British hostility, was the paradoxical nature of Catherine's interests in Poland. On the one hand, as Russian tsars before her, she wanted a stable and weak Polish buffer state, a view shared by her new ally Frederick the Great. A number of Polish elites, however, recognized how vulnerable Poland's weak central government made it and jockeyed to rewrite the Polish constitution to make Poland stronger and more capable. The harder Catherine worked to prevent constitutional reform in Poland and plant a reliably pro-Russian candidate on the Polish throne—through bribery, intimidation, and military intervention—the more she generated Polish resentment and efforts to eliminate Russian influence entirely.

The Russo-Turkish War, 1768–1774

The turmoil generated by Catherine's meddling in Poland led to her first war, against the Ottoman Turks. An internal Polish dispute about the rights of Protestants and Orthodox in that predominantly Catholic country exploded into violence in volatile right-bank Ukraine. The combination of a Russian troop presence in Poland, the spillover of violence by Orthodox cossacks into Crimean and Ottoman territory, and substantial support from France led the Ottoman Turks to demand full evacuation of Russian troops from Poland in October 1768. When Russia refused, the Turks declared war.

Catherine took an active and personal interest in the war, unlike her predecessors. She made a priority of territorial expansion; though the Turks started the war, the security and economic development of southern Russia depended on finishing it on Russian terms. Catherine was central to the war's strategy and decision making, consulting regularly with key military and political advisors. Though Russia's intervention in Poland left few troops for active operations in 1768, Russia was fundamentally in good shape for war. Army strength was roughly equivalent to that available to Peter the Great at his death in 1725: 200,000 regulars, plus irregular, militia, and cossack units. Catherine expanded this by additional conscription from peasant households for lifetime service in the army. Despite Russia's immense armed forces, maintaining troops in the distant theaters of the Turkish wars required repeated and painful levies of new peasant soldiers. Long marches through the war-ravaged and desolate territories of western Ukraine and the Balkans meant that a substantial proportion of any Russian army was lost well before reaching the theater of war.

The Russian and Turkish armies were both in the midst of long and difficult reforms to bring themselves up to modern standards. As the war's campaigns demonstrated, the Russians were much further along. Enormous Turkish forces, greatly outnumbering their Russian opponents, were brittle and undisciplined, unable to sustain heavy combat. Part of this had to do with the high proportion of cavalry in Turkish armies, making flight from battle too easy while hindering positional defense. Furthermore, much of the Turkish cavalry consisted of a feudal levy, something the Russians had been gradually abandoning for over a century. The Russian officer corps had been hardened by the Seven Years' War against the best army in Europe; the Turks were no match.

In particular, Peter Rumiantsev, Catherine's most successful commander, was highly innovative and adaptable. In the wake of the Seven Years' War, the Russian army had dramatically expanded its jäger light infantry, which Rumiantsev used to counter the maneuverable Tatar cavalry. He also emphasized discipline, organization, and shock, particularly night and bayonet attacks, to take advantage of poorly managed Turkish troops. His specific tactical innovation was the use of divisional squares in both defense and attack. These hollow squares, each consisting of several regiments of infantry and studded with field artillery, were used for both defense and attack. Their all-around defense protected them from circling multitudes of Turkish and Tatar cavalry, but allowed sufficient firepower and shock for attack. The firepower lost in forming squares as opposed to lines was a price worth paying against the Turks, though it would have been suicide against a Western army. In battle, Rumiantsev's squares maintained open space between them to allow for maneuverability, while remaining close enough for mutual support. The gaps between squares were covered by cavalry or light infantry, which could if necessary take refuge inside the larger divisional squares. Given the brittle and relatively undisciplined Turkish troops, Rumiantsev disdained heavy cavalry as unwieldy, trusting instead in firepower and infantry attacks to break enemy will. Strategically, Rumiantsev avoided the crippling loss of time and resources involved in annual treks from winter quarters to the front by maintaining his forces as far forward as possible year-round.

Initial Russian operations in 1769 were extremely successful, so successful that Russian forces found themselves overextended. Over the course of 1769, a Russian army, under first Aleksandr Mikhailovich Golitsyn and then Rumiantsev, who replaced Golitsyn that autumn, swept south in a wide arc around the western edge of the Black Sea, crossing the series of rivers that ran into it: the Bug, the Dnestr, and the Prut. This left intact a series of major Turkish fortresses along the Black Sea coast: Ochakov, Akkerman, Izmail, and especially Bender on the Dnestr River.

Failing to screen or reduce those fortresses left Russian armies vulnerable to being cut off deep in Turkish territory. As a result, Catherine's government devised a new plan of campaign for 1770. The two Russian armies were to move in parallel, with Rumiantsev's First Army moving slowly south farther inland, while the Second Army (led by Nikita Panin's younger brother Peter) concentrated on clearing Turkish fortresses along the Black Sea coast.

Outnumbered by the Turks, Rumiantsev moved quickly to defeat separate Turkish contingents before they could unite into an overwhelming force. Russian aggressiveness also prevented the Turks from taking advantage of their superior manpower. Confident in the organization and discipline of his troops, Rumiantsev used rapid and night maneuvers to catch the Turks unawares. Rumiantsev's tactics during this campaign, particularly his use of squares and clever employment of flanking attacks, were inspired. Rumiantsev's 40,000 troops caught a Turkish army of 75,000 at Riabaia Mogila on 17/28 June 1770. Despite being outnumbered nearly two to one by Turkish troops in a strong position, Rumiantsev coordinated a multipronged attack. He led the bulk of Russian forces himself in a frontal assault, while a smaller detachment under Grigorii Aleksandrovich Potemkin crossed the Prut River shielding the Turkish left flank to place itself across the Turkish line of retreat. At the same time, a stronger detachment, including most of the Russian cavalry, attacked the Turkish right. Confronted by Russian firepower and attacked from three directions, the Turkish position dissolved into disordered flight. Rumiantsev maintained his aggressive tempo, moving down the Prut and catching a second Ottoman army where the Larga River flows into it. Behind the Larga 80,000 Turkish and Tatar soldiers were dug in. Using the cover of darkness, Rumiantsev crossed the Larga upstream with most of his forces to launch a surprise attack on the Turkish right flank. As the Turks shifted troops to their right, a smaller detachment Rumiantsev had left behind pushed directly across the Larga River, seizing the heart of the Turkish position. The Turkish army disintegrated in confusion. In both battles, Rumiantsev was so successful that he inflicted very few casualties on the Turkish forces. They broke and ran before Russian firepower could inflict significant damage.

While Panin's army besieged Bender, Rumiantsev met the Turkish main forces on the Kagul (Kartal) River, north of the Danube River, on 21 July/ 1 August 1770. With only 40,000 troops to the Turkish grand vizier's 150,000, Rumiantsev continued his offensive tactics, hoping to beat the Turkish main forces before the arrival of additional Tatar cavalry. Launching a frontal attack on the Turkish camp early in the morning, Rumiantsev's strengthened right wing drove back the Turkish left, but a counterattack by the Turks' fearsome janissary infantry smashed the center of the Russian line and temporarily tore a wide hole into the Russian formation. Rumiantsev himself joined the reserves hastily thrown in to plug the gap. Once the janissaries had been blasted into oblivion by Russian firepower, the rest of the Turkish army again broke and fled, leaving supplies and artillery behind them. Rumiantsev detached forces for an energetic pursuit, which caught the fleeing Turks at the Danube. Only a tiny fraction escaped to safety on the far side. From this point, the Turks were forced to remain entirely on the defensive, hoping for outside intervention to rescue them from the war they started.

The Turkish catastrophe was not finished. The Ottoman fortresses along the Black Sea fell rapidly into Russian hands after the Kagul victory: Izmail, Akkerman, and Bender. To make matters worse, Catherine's lover Grigorii Orlov hatched an ambitious plan to bring a Russian fleet into the Mediterranean to attack the Turks from the south. This meant repairing and rebuilding the Russian fleet, dilapidated from decades of neglect, but Catherine threw immense financial and diplomatic resources into the project. When the Russian fleet arrived in Turkish waters in spring 1770, it attempted unsuccessfully to stir Greece into rebellion against Turkish rule. It finally brought the Turkish Aegean fleet to battle on 24 June/5 July 1770 at the fort of Chesme off the Anatolian coast. Despite being outnumbered and outgunned, the Russians' attack threw the Turkish ships into confusion and disarray, and the Turks withdrew into Chesme harbor. A night raid into the harbor with fireboats torched the Turkish fleet, destroying it completely.

The overwhelming successes of 1770 were followed by a historic triumph in 1771. Rumiantsev's First Army consolidated its position and continued to capture Turkish fortresses, but did not push decisively south across the Danube. Instead, the Russian Second Army, now commanded by Vasilii Mikhailovich Dolgorukii, pushed into the Crimea in June 1771 against scattered resistance and conquered it, a feat that had escaped every previous Russian army. Catherine set up a puppet khan and a treaty granting the Crimea formal independence, but committing it to eternal friendship and permitting Russian garrisons. Instead of a base for raids on southern Russia, the Crimea had become a *de facto* Russian possession.

Despite Catherine's staggering run of successes, she was increasingly anxious for peace. Even victories were costly. Bubonic plague raged west of the Black Sea and even in Russia itself, where it killed hundreds of thousands. The conscription and taxes to maintain her army were increasingly unpopular. In addition, Austria and Prussia submerged their differences in common alarm over the extent of Russian victories and were eager to limit Russia's gains. The Ottomans asked for Austrian and Prussian mediation in 1770; both governments moved with alacrity to assist, but peace negotiations went nowhere. Though Catherine wanted peace, she would not settle for less than her battlefield successes had earned.

First Partition of Poland

Under the principles of eighteenth-century diplomacy, Prussia and Austria wanted compensation. A gain for any great power, in this case for Russia from Turkey, should be matched by gains for the other great powers. In this case, there was a ready store of territory available for compensation: Poland. Until the 1770s, both Russia and Prussia recognized the benefits of a weak Polish buffer state. Despite the benefits of this arrangement, some within Russia called for the outright annexation of Poland, not merely the maintenance of a puppet. In 1764, Catherine engineered the election of her former lover Stanislaw Poniatowski as the new Polish king, but he proved surprisingly committed to Polish reform. The heavy-handed tactics of Catherine's agents in Poland provoked the creation of an anti-Russian confederation in 1768 and ongoing rebellion against Russian domination. It was, in fact, the spillover from this fighting that had triggered the ongoing Russo-Turkish War.

Catherine's entanglement in Poland while fighting the draining Turkish war allowed Austria and Prussia to take advantage. Frederick the Great proposed a mutually satisfactory outcome: Prussia, Austria, and Russia would each take territory from Poland, punishing it for instability and maintaining the European balance of power. All three parties were amenable, and the Poles were forced to accept the loss of a substantial portion of their country. Russia's share, confirmed by treaty in 1772, brought in 35,000 square miles along the frontier with Lithuania and 1.3 million Orthodox Belorussians. In effect, Russian gains at Ottoman expense resulted in compensation for Austria and Prussia at Poland's expense.

While the partition was finalized, the Russo-Turkish War dragged on. Rumiantsev briefly raided south across the Danube in June 1773. The key significance of that year was the emergence of Aleksandr Vasil'evich Suvorov as an aggressive and innovative commander, who later inherited Rumiantsev's place as Russia's most talented field general. Repeating the cross-Danube raid one year later, Rumiantsev's advance guard under Suvorov stumbled into Turkish troops near Kozludzha on 9/20 June 1774. Pursuing them through dense, hilly terrain, Suvorov's forces emerged into a direct confrontation with the Turkish main force. Forming their accustomed squares, Suvorov's troops pushed forward slowly against the Turks, who broke and ran in the face of Russian firepower and Suvorov's direct assault.

Kozludzha was the final blow. The Ottomans requested a cease-fire, and the peace treaty was signed at Kuchuk Kainardzhi a month later. Frederick the Great was unimpressed with the Russian victory, dismissing it as "one-eyed men who have given blind men a thorough beating." This is mistaken on two counts. First, it ignored the scale of Russian gains. In addition to freedom of transit for Russian trade, Catherine won a portion of the northern coast of the Black Sea, leaving the Turks Moldavia, Wallachia, and Bessarabia. The Crimea received nominal independence under Russian hegemony. The Ottoman sultan was forced to protect his Orthodox Christian subjects, a clause that gave future tsars a ready issue to exploit, while the Ottomans retained protective rights over the religion of the Crimean Tatars. Catherine now controlled the Dnepr to its mouth, though the river's rapids disappointed her hopes for exports. Second, the Russian army had shown an impressive capacity to fight battles and campaigns at a great distance from its bases, while displaying tactical ingenuity and flexibility that clearly pointed toward the developments Napoleon later employed so effectively.

The Pugachev Rebellion

While Catherine finished her Turkish war, she faced the most serious cossack-peasant uprising in Russian history. Emelian Ivanovich Pugachev, renegade Don cossack and veteran of the Seven Years' War and the Russo-Turkish War, appeared in the winter of 1772–1773 among the Yaik River cossacks north of the Caspian Sea, claiming to be Peter III. Following in the tradition of earlier uprisings, Pugachev combined his claim to be Russia's legitimate tsar with an appeal to poor cossacks resentful of both their richer brethren and governmental authority. Pugachev assembled a cynical inner circle with whom he developed a political program and launched his uprising in September 1773. After seizing forts along the Yaik River, he besieged Orenburg, the regional administrative center. Since Catherine was unable to spare large numbers of troops from the Turkish war, Pugachev easily defeated the first detachments to reach him, boosting his prestige. He benefited from deep opposition to Moscow's rule among non-Russian peoples of the Urals, particularly Bashkirs. These often directed their hostility at foundries and factories, the tangible evidence of Russian presence. Factory serfs, peasants attached to an industrial enterprise instead of the land, were also eager recruits. His movement grew large enough that he established a rudimentary government and royal court with himself as Peter III.

Government forces defeated Pugachev's cossacks and their allies in two battles at Ufa and at Tatishchevo in March 1774 and lifted the siege of Orenburg. Pugachev's movement between the Volga and the Yaik collapsed. Pugachev himself remained at large, and with his remaining followers, he swept north through the factories of the Ural Mountains, sacking and burning the city of Kazan. A smaller government force reached Kazan just after Pugachev and smashed his army a second time. Pugachev escaped again and headed for his homeland among the Don cossacks.

Defeated twice, Pugachev changed tactics. He now appealed to peasants to murder their masters and end serfdom. This message, spread by Pugachev's cossack followers and peasants themselves, spread destruction down the Volga as government troops chased him south and tried to restore order. Several thousand nobles, government officials, and priests were butchered by Pugachev or rebels acting in his name. Pugachev continued down the Volga, reaching Tsaritsyn in August 1774. By this time, Pugachev's chances of success were dwindling rapidly, as the end of the Turkish war released large numbers of troops. Catherine's forces, led by Peter Panin, finally caught Pugachev just south of Tsaritsyn, defeating his peasant army for the final time. Pugachev's remarkable series of escapes continued, and he returned to the Yaik where his fellow cossacks turned him over to government authorities. In a show of mercy, Catherine commuted Pugachev's sentence of quartering alive, allowing him to be beheaded first.

The Russo-Turkish War, 1787–1792

The end of the first Turkish War marked the emergence of Grigorii Potemkin, able cavalry commander, as a central figure in Catherine's life, and through that, in the Russian army and government. Among Catherine's many lovers, none matched Potemkin's political influence, and only Potemkin was Catherine's equal in intellect and force of personality. They may have secretly married, and even after their affair cooled Potemkin remained Catherine's most important advisor until his death. Potemkin became through Catherine's favor first a vice-president of the War College and then its president from 1784. He also served as governor-general of Catherine's newly acquired Ukrainian territories.

Though charismatic and intelligent, Potemkin had little patience for discipline or orderly procedures. His experience under Rumiantsev fighting the Turks made him a committed advocate of speed and initiative, not careful staff work. Catherine's military administration suffered as a result, particularly the development of a general staff. As a favorite of Catherine's, he in turn promoted favoritism within the War College. At the same time, he showed genuine concern for his troops and their needs. He simplified the uniforms of the Russian infantry, keeping the traditional Russian green but removing the decorative flourishes that hindered speedy action. He deemphasized heavy cavalry as inappropriate for Russia's military tasks and controlled and disciplined the useful but rambunctious cossacks of the frontier.

Catherine's territorial expansion continued over the next decade, though she avoided entanglement in the wars of western and central Europe. Turbulent Crimean politics led Catherine to intervene in 1776 to restore Russian domination. Russia was nearly pulled into the Anglo-French conflict surrounding the American war for independence, and in 1780 Catherine engineered the League of Armed Neutrality with Denmark and Sweden to protect neutral shipping from British interference. Catherine also dreamt vaguely of Russian satellite states in Greece and the Black Sea Straits, naming her grandson Constantine in a nod to his future throne in Constantinople. Pursuing that goal required better relations with Austria in the Balkans, and Catherine established an alliance with Austria in 1781. It also necessitated naval power in the Black Sea, and Catherine accordingly expanded and modernized the Russian flotilla in the Sea of Azov, and at the newly established city of Kherson at the mouth of the Dnepr. Under the able leadership of Fyodor Fyodorovich Ushakov, this became the Black Sea Fleet. Faced with a joint Austrian and Russian threat, the Ottoman Turks unhappily accepted Catherine's 1783 full annexation of the Crimea. In the same year, she established a protectorate over the kingdom of Georgia. Russia built a military highway through the Caucasus Mountains to link Georgia with Russian territory and stationed troops in its capital Tbilisi. Russia's rapid development of its newly acquired Ukrainian territory, its Crimean annexation, its infractions of Ottoman honor, and Catherine's triumphant tour of her conquered southern territories finally led the Turks to declare war in August 1787.

The second Russo-Turkish War of Catherine's reign opened poorly. Catherine was unable to take the war to Turkish territory, fearing an amphibious invasion of the Crimea. Suvorov, hero of the first Turkish war, ably defended the seaside fortress of Kinburn, on the Dnepr estuary, against two Turkish amphibious assaults in September and October of 1787, but Russia's Black Sea Fleet was badly damaged in a storm. An attempt to transfer ships from Russia's northern waters was prevented by diplomatic complications. Though Austria joined Russia's war in early 1788, its dismal performance provided little concrete assistance. Sweden attacked Russia in summer 1788 with covert British and Prussian support, forcing Catherine to keep her ships in the Baltic for the defense of Petersburg. The Swedish war was more nuisance than threat, made dangerous only by the larger war against the Turks and the possibility of Anglo-Prussian intervention. While the Russian and Swedish fleets clashed repeatedly in the Baltic, Catherine stirred up antiroyal opposition within Sweden itself and achieved brief Danish intervention against Sweden.

Only in 1788 was Catherine able to bring her real advantage to bear against the Turks: a large and disciplined army. As in the previous war, Catherine split her forces in two west of the Black Sea. Rumiantsev, the most successful commander of 1768–1774, was forced to settle for a small auxiliary force of 40,000 well inland of the Black Sea to protect the right flank of the main army. That army of nearly 100,000 under Potemkin was tasked with the recurring problem of war against the Turks: capturing the many large and tenaciously defended fortresses studding the river barriers between Russia and the Turkish capital. Though Potemkin had great hopes, his push south stalled at its first obstacle: Ochakov and its garrison of 20,000. Though a naval campaign enabled Potemkin to cut Ochakov off from the sea, his poorly handled six-month siege achieved nothing. Desperate to take the fortress before the end of the year, Potemkin unleashed a costly but successful all-out storm on 6/17 December 1788. Since Potemkin's position was inviolable, Rumiantsev was sacrificed for the debacle—recalled from his command and retired from service.

For 1789, the Russian plan was to concentrate on capturing Turkish fortresses guarding the Dnestr River: Akkerman at its mouth on the Black Sea and Bender almost 100 miles upstream. To distract the Turks and provide a link to Russia's Austrian allies, a corps under Suvorov moved far south, past the Dnestr and Prut into Moldavia and Wallachia (present-day Romania). At the request of his Austrian allies, threatened by a much larger Turkish force, Suvorov led a forced march to unite the small allied detachments. Greatly outnumbered, Suvorov nonetheless went on the attack, using battalion squares similar to those Rumiantsev developed to attack a fortified Turkish encampment at Fokshani (eastern Romania) on 21 July/1 August 1789. Cooperating with the Austrians to attack from two directions, Suvorov sent 30,000 Turkish troops into panicked flight after a day-long struggle for the encampment.

Suvorov repeated his feat at Rymnik in September. Once again, superior Turkish forces attempted to catch an isolated Austrian detachment alone. Responding to pleas for aid, Suvorov rushed to create a combined army of 25,000 soldiers against 100,000 Turks. Suvorov's insistence on attack and decisive action led him to assault the Turkish army while it was encamped, counting on speed and audacity to defeat the enemy army in detail, destroying its individual parts before they could unite. The Turks were in three fortified encampments too far apart for mutual support in a line stretching west to east between the Rymna and Rymnik rivers. On the morning of 11/22 September 1789, the Russo-Austrian force crossed the Rymna River north of the Turkish camps, deploying into battalion squares in a checkerboard pattern. Suvorov's troops moved south alongside the Rymna to attack the westernmost Turkish camp, while the Austrians pushed southeast against the central one. Undeterred by a Turkish cavalry attack, Suvorov easily captured the western camp and sent its troops fleeing in disorder. He then turned east toward the central camp, clearing a small forest en route and eliminating a Turkish counterattack that had wedged itself between Suvorov and the Austrians to his northeast. He then joined the Austrian attack on the central camp. As his advance unhinged the left flank of the Turkish defense, Suvorov noticed the poorly constructed and incomplete fortifications of the camp and, in a violation of military orthodoxy, sent his cavalry to storm the position, followed by a bayonet charge. The broken Turkish troops fleeing east carried panic with them, and the allied forces captured the third, easternmost camp by the end of the day. A full day's fighting had inflicted nearly 20,000 casualties on the Turks at the cost of fewer than 1,000 from the allies.

Those two victories gained Suvorov both symbolic and financial rewards from Catherine and boosted his repute even further in the Russian army. From a military family, Suvorov was gaunt and eccentric, almost manic, but passionately loved by his soldiers. Following Rumiantsev's model, he emphasized the importance of hard and realistic training in peacetime, and speed, decisiveness, and shock in battle. Fighting the brave but fragile Ottoman army, these qualities of discipline and ruthlessness served him well. "The bullet's a fool," he remarked, "but the bayonet's a good lad."

The Russian main army was less audacious than Suvorov in 1789, but nevertheless won important successes. That autumn, the Dnestr River fortresses of Akkerman and Bender both surrendered, giving Russia control of the length of the river. Austria captured Belgrade and Bucharest, and the Ottoman hold on the Balkans seemed broken beyond repair.

In fact, Catherine's diplomatic position was growing increasingly precarious. In addition to the usual expenses in lives and money, Catherine faced a draining naval war with Sweden, and, worse, the prospect of war against a British-Prussian alliance, eager to limit Russian power, gain new sources of naval stores, and eliminate Russian influence from Poland. In early 1790, Catherine's ally Joseph II of Austria died, and his successor Francis II moved quickly to make peace. The strain began to ease in August 1790 when an exhausted Sweden agreed to end its war with Russia, but a British-Prussian-Polish attack against Russia was still possible. Frederick the Great had cheerfully proposed the partition of Poland, but his successor Frederick William II now affected sympathy for Polish concerns and support for Polish reforms.

The danger of general war and fear of a Turkish invasion of the Crimea delayed serious campaigning in 1790, and the only Russian effort that year was the siege of the Turkish fortress of Izmail, capture of which would give Russia a vital foothold on the Danube River. In late 1790, 35,000 Russian troops arrived outside Izmail. The brief campaigning season and the 30,000-strong Turkish garrison made the Russian commanders despair of capturing the fortress until Suvorov arrived and insisted on taking it immediately. Feigning preparations for a lengthy siege while secretly training his soldiers for assault, Suvorov launched a general storm on Izmail before dawn on 11/22 December 1790. This captured three gates, allowing the Russians inside the walls. Desperate house-to-house Turkish resistance continued the rest of the day, with the Russians hauling artillery in for point-blank fire against Turkish strongpoints. In the day's slaughter, two-thirds of the Turkish garrison was killed, and the rest captured.

The Turkish ability to resist was dwindling, but the prospect of foreign assistance kept the Ottomans in the war. Prussia and Britain insisted on the return of Russia's conquests, culminating in a March 1791 ultimatum to Russia to end the war on Turkish terms. Catherine stood her ground, and it became clear that the British government had badly overestimated its public's appetite for war. Catherine's ambassador to Britain helped with a masterful public relations campaign. And without British backing, Prussia had no appetite for a fight. Prussia began exploring other options: compensating for Russia's gains at the expense of Poland once again. Poland itself made matters much worse in spring 1791. Believing in Prussian protection, and inspired by the French Revolution, Poland established a new, centralized constitution. Once the Turkish war was over, Catherine could never allow Poland to build a functional government.

With growing urgency to end the war, Russian campaigns in 1791 extended south of the Danube. After a series of successful smaller engagements, Russian commander Nikolai Vasil'evich Repnin won the final major battle of the war at Machin. After a Danube crossing and a forced march through swamps, his 30,000 troops attacked a fortified Turkish encampment on 28 June/9 July 1791. The plan—to fix the Turks with a frontal attack while the main Russian forces circled left to make a decisive flanking blow—fell apart. Abandoning the passivity that too often characterized their fighting against the Russians, the Turks detected the Russian flanking maneuver and launched repeated counterattacks against it. Once again, Russian firepower and unbreakable squares repulsed the attacks, and the Turkish defense finally fell apart. Machin forced the Turks to accept defeat. A preliminary peace was reached immediately, and a final peace on 29 December 1791/9 January 1792, giving Catherine possession of the territory between the Bug and the Dnestr rivers, but returning to the Ottoman Empire many of the fortresses and much of the territory it had lost.

Catherine's former lover, possible husband, and chief political confidant Potemkin had died while negotiating with the Turks. Despite this, Catherine's room to maneuver had grown substantially, freed from war with Turkey and Sweden. In spring 1792, Prussia and Austria became embroiled in war with revolutionary France, giving Catherine the opening she needed to smash the Polish reforms. Using an invitation from pro-Russian Poles as political cover, Catherine's armies intervened in May 1792 to restore Poland's previous constitution. Though Poland's hastily assembled forces managed some initial victories, Russia's preponderant strength meant that Poland's position was hopeless. Poland's King Poniatowski lost his nerve and called off all resistance.

Catherine used her overwhelmingly dominant position to claim compensation from Poland for her efforts to crush revolution. Frederick William, with his war against revolutionary France going badly, comforted himself with Polish territory. By January 1793, Russia and Prussia had agreed on their territorial seizures. This second partition of Poland netted Russia the Lithuanian half of the Polish kingdom and right-bank Ukraine, almost 100,000 square miles of territory and 3 million new subjects. Poland itself was reduced to a vestigial and clearly nonviable fragment of its former territory.

What was left of Poland could not survive, giving Poles nothing to lose. Widespread passive resistance became open rebellion in spring 1794. Tadeusz Kosciuszko, who had assisted the American war for independence against Britain, became leader of the Polish national movement. This uprising seized control of Warsaw and even defeated initial Russian attempts to quash resistance. Overwhelming force, this time brought to bear by all three of Poland's great power neighbors, again meant that Poland's freedom was only temporary. Rumiantsev commanded the general suppression of the uprising, while Suvorov with his fearsome reputation was brought in to subdue Warsaw. Kosciuszko was wounded in battle and captured, and then on 24 October/4 November 1794, Suvorov stormed Praga, a suburb of Warsaw across the Vistula River. In full view of Warsaw's horrified citizens, Suvorov's troops massacred thousands, soldiers and civilians alike. Warsaw surrendered without a fight. Early in this uprising, Catherine had become convinced the time had come for the complete partition of Poland. Austria, Russia, and Prussia agreed on a settlement, the third and final partition, that ended Poland's existence as an independent state for over a century.

Throughout Russia's history, it has enjoyed an advantage in size and population over its rivals. Under Catherine, that advantage was applied more effectively than perhaps at any other time in Russia's history. The mechanisms of Catherine's absolutist state turned resources into practical power, power that eliminated Poland from the map of Europe and ended any hope that the Ottoman Empire might compete on equal terms with Russia. During Catherine's lifetime, though, Russian superiority was already being undermined. The French Revolution introduced new principles of government, principles that translated into new sources of military power. The French revolutionary governments, and the Napoleonic Empire that followed them, turned those new principles into mass armies driven by French nationalism and revolutionary fervor, armies that Russia would be hard-pressed to match.

CHAPTER **7**

The Napoleonic Wars

The wars of Catherine the Great's reign established Russia as the predominant power in central and eastern Europe. Poland had been wiped off the map, and Turkey decisively defeated. While Russia might fear a joint attack by Prussia and Austria, those powers had far more to fear from Russia. The greatest threat to Russia did not, however, come from eastern Europe at all. Out of the chaos of the French Revolution, Napoleon Bonaparte emerged as France's military dictator and self-crowned emperor. Bonaparte used his military skill and France's enormous resources in a nearly successful attempt to establish dominance over all Europe.

The French Revolution inspired fear by throwing every law and institution into question. If popular sovereignty trumped legitimacy, then no monarch or institution or law was safe. By elevating the nation above precedent, it also threw every border into question. Almost none of Europe's countries were nation-states, where the political borders neatly coincided with the ethnic nation. Either they contained substantial numbers from other nationalities, or (as in Germany and in Italy) the ethnic nation was divided among many petty states. Not only were Europe's monarchs willing to go to war to defeat the revolution and restore order, but the French revolutionary state was willing to go to war to consolidate its own successes at home and spread revolution abroad. The revolution also changed the way armies were built. It drove most of the French officer corps into exile, and France adapted its military to its revolutionary society. Short of trained officers, but with a nationalist and ideologically motivated population, the new French army made up in mass and fervor what it lacked in finesse. The French revolutionary state could and did ask more of its citizens than Europe's traditional monarchies could, including conscripting them *en masse*. French soldiers fought not for a French king, but for France, and that made all the difference.

Napoleon took the ideals and the army of the French Revolution and turned them into tools for territorial expansion, aimed at the complete

domination of Europe. Using the mass armies, meritocracy, and rational-
ized administration of the revolution, and justifying his campaigns with
the rhetoric of liberation, Napoleon embarked on conquests that terror-
ized Europe for almost 20 years. His unbounded ambition finally created
an unprecedented coalition of all the other European great powers to
destroy him and restore order.

Russia played a central role in the all-European coalition that ultimately
brought Napoleon down. Russia's wars with Napoleonic France can be
thought of as three rounds. In the first, under Tsar Paul I, Russia's armies
did not confront Napoleon himself, but handily defeated French armies in
northern Italy. In the second, lasting from 1805 to 1807 under Paul's son
Alexander I, Napoleon himself thoroughly defeated Russia's field armies.
The third, lasting from 1812 to 1815, was quite different. Napoleon's invasion of Russia in 1812 allowed Alexander to tap into the nationalism that
made French armies so powerful. While Russia had a *national* army, in
that it was predominantly made up of Russians, not foreigners, it did
not have a *nationalist* army. The year 1812 changed that, but only temporarily. The defeat of Napoleon marked a peak in Russian military power, a
point at which Russia was the dominant military power in all of Europe.
That power was, however, transitory. It depended on nationalist fervor
that could not be sustained without a mortal threat from a foreign invader.
Russia was in a way the personal property of a single individual, the tsar,
and that was in the long run incompatible with the ideal of a shared
national community.

Paul I

Paul, Catherine's only legitimate child, detested his mother. Catherine
raised Paul's sons and toyed with the idea of bypassing him for the
throne, but did nothing concrete before her death in 1796. Rightly paranoid over his mother's intentions, Paul had established his own court
and military units outside St. Petersburg. Though Catherine's husband
Peter III may not have been Paul's father, Paul shared his unstable personality and obsession with military discipline. Diagnosing mental disorders
in historical figures is a dangerous enterprise, but Paul displayed many
characteristics of an obsessive-compulsive. Convinced that everything
connected with his mother's regime was corrupt, he insisted on discipline, control, and rectitude. This did produce noteworthy improvements
in Russia's notoriously slow and venal bureaucracy. And Paul was correct
that late in Catherine's reign, discipline had slipped in the Russian army.
Almost everything Paul did, though, undermined his support among
Russian elites. He lowered the prestige of the influential guards regiments, relying instead on Prussian-style troops he trained and outfitted

while introducing German innovations to uniforms and drill. He emphasized meticulous parade-ground show over practical effectiveness. His capriciousness meant bureaucrats and officers might be exiled to Siberia or dispatched to the frontier for the least infraction. In a small matter that symbolized a larger shortcoming, he regulated building decoration and clothing colors in St. Petersburg.

Paul's arbitrary and unpredictable behavior extended to foreign policy at a time when European international relations were increasingly unstable. Soon after the French Revolution began in 1789, it generated serious pressures for war. The revolutionary regime was enraged by noble émigrés conspiring against it abroad and saw foreign war as a means to unite France behind the revolution. At the same time, other European governments feared their own populations might be infected by revolution. In April 1792 France declared war on Austria and was soon at war with Prussia as well.

Clumsy but massive French armies achieved striking successes. In 1792 they pushed France's borders outward, conquering the Austrian Netherlands (now Belgium), the west bank of the Rhine, and the small state of Savoy between France and Italy. Britain grew alarmed over the French danger and prepared for war. Revolutionary France, confident it could spread revolution by force of arms, declared war on Britain, Holland, and Spain, drawing most of Europe into war in 1793. French society moved toward total mobilization. By the end of 1794, Prussia tired of war and left the coalition to concentrate on partitioning Poland. While Catherine agreed with Britain in early 1795 to provide troops for the war against France, this achieved little result. French forces in northern Italy under the command of Napoleon Bonaparte, then only a rapidly rising general, decisively defeated the Austrians in 1796–1797. Austria had to surrender the Austrian Netherlands and accept a French puppet state in northern Italy. Thus by the time of Catherine's death and Paul's accession, the first coalition against revolutionary France was disintegrating. Paul ended Catherine's halfhearted intervention against France.

The First Round

France's growing power and Paul's odd obsessions brought Russia back into the epic 20-year struggle against revolutionary France. Paul wished to maintain a European balance of power, something incompatible with France's territorial conquests. Strangely, though, the final push into war seems to have been Napoleon's seizure of the island of Malta during his 1798 invasion of Egypt. Since childhood, Paul had been obsessed with the ancient order of the Knights of Malta. He took Napoleon's action as a personal affront, and Russia joined Austria and Britain in a loose second coalition against France. Though Napoleon was trapped in Egypt when the British destroyed his fleet in the August 1798 Battle of the Nile, the coalition partners did not establish common war aims, a matter that proved fatal to their cooperation. The Russo-Austrian cooperation was a particularly convoluted affair. Austria paid the expenses of Russian manpower: one army in northern Italy and another in Switzerland and along the upper Rhine. Command of the joint Russo-Austrian force in Italy went to Aleksandr Vasil'evich Suvorov, but he answered to the Austrian emperor. Worse, his speed and decisiveness, learned in years of warfare against the Ottomans, were utterly alien to the Austrians.

Suvorov conducted a brilliant campaign in northern Italy in summer 1799. Training Austrians and Russians alike in his aggressive methods, he did not waste time besieging French garrisons. Instead, he raced west along the southern slopes of the Alps, forcing the Adda River and capturing Milan in April. Sending detachments south to cut French supply lines to their isolated garrisons, he continued west to seize Turin. These successes created the first serious tensions in the Austro-Russian partnership. Suvorov's goal was defeating France. That meant restoring Italian governments and making Italian liberation an anti-French tool. Austria's priority, by contrast, was consolidating its dominion in Italy, and the Austrian government reined in Suvorov's initiatives.

Suvorov's priority was to keep French armies in central Italy and southeastern France separated. A French army advancing from the south caught an isolated Austrian detachment where the Trebbia River flows north into the Po. To rescue it, Suvorov's advance guard moved directly from a forced march into an attack on the French on 6/17 June 1799, forcing them to rally on the western bank of the Trebbia, with their backs to the river. The next day, Suvorov pushed forward with his reinforced right wing, attempting to turn the French southern flank. Bloody fighting pushed the French back across the Trebbia. On the third day, the French grabbed the initiative from the exhausted Russians, attempting to overwhelm the Russian southern flank. Suvorov personally rallied the counterattack that restored the Russian line. The French commander despaired of breaking through to his countrymen, and withdrew back south.

True to his decisive nature, Suvorov now wished to invade France as rapidly as possible. His French opponents were fleeing: south down the boot of Italy, and west toward France. There was no better time to topple the revolutionary regime. The Austrian government categorically forbade any such action. Instead, it ordered Suvorov to scatter his troops to liquidate French fortresses rather than concentrating to eliminate the remaining French field armies. A month of campaigning was lost before Suvorov could launch a new offensive.

By late July, Suvorov was ready to move south to the Mediterranean coast to eliminate the French foothold at Genoa in preparation for an invasion of France itself. The French acted first, moving north from Genoa to halt in the walled town of Novi, sitting on high ground above the northern Italian plains. Despite the strength of the French position, Suvorov insisted on attacking. On 4/15 August 1799, the Battle of Novi opened west of the town, as Austrian infantry hammered at French positions on the high ground. As the French left started to give way, reinforcements drawn from the right restored the position. Next, in the center, repeated Russian assaults on the walled town itself were repelled with heavy losses. All these unsuccessful attacks, however, drained French reserves and pulled troops from the French right, leaving their position vulnerable to the day's final attack. A final Austrian attack east of Novi broke the depleted French line and pushed through behind the town. In danger of being cut off entirely, the French orderly retreat became a rout as Suvorov ordered a general pursuit. Though Suvorov suffered terrible losses, the French army in Italy was shattered beyond repair.

Suvorov was now eager for an invasion of revolutionary France itself, but again Austrian political considerations removed that possibility. Fearing Suvorov might undermine Austrian control in northern Italy, the Austrian government insisted that he move north into Switzerland to campaign against the French there. This plan, however, put Suvorov in a terrible position. His 20,000 soldiers moving into Switzerland were separated from another 20,000 Russians and 20,000 Austrians around Zurich by 80,000 French in between. Suvorov thus needed to unite these scattered forces before the concentrated French could destroy them individually. While Suvorov fought his way north through tunnels, over narrow bridges, and past mountain passes, the French defeated the Russian and Austrian troops around Zurich in September 1799. This stranded Suvorov in central Switzerland, surrounded by superior French forces. Realizing his danger, Suvorov raced east to escape the tightening French net. He pushed aside French blocking forces while his rear guard kept French pursuers at bay. On reaching the town of Glarus, short of ammunition, Suvorov turned south toward the Rhine River, following it downstream to safety. He and the remnants of his army went into winter quarters to prepare for fighting in the spring. Though a defeat, Suvorov's campaign through the Alps and escape from certain destruction was a marvel of endurance.

Paul was furious over what he saw as the perfidy of his allies. Austria had led his troops to disaster in Switzerland, and Paul ordered Suvorov and his troops back home. To make matters worse, the British captured Malta from the French in September 1800, but refused to recognize Paul's prerogatives as master of the Knights of Malta. Paul organized a new, anti-British League of Armed Neutrality to cut off British access to vital naval stores and by early 1801 was secretly negotiating an alliance with

France. The British desperately needed a powerful continental ally against France; Paul wanted France contained, but not at the price of being a British or Austrian pawn.

Growing numbers among Russia's elite were convinced Paul's instability and capriciousness would ruin Russia, leading to his assassination in 1801. His eldest son, now Tsar Alexander I, had assented to the overthrow of his father, though not his murder. Complicit in his father's downfall, Alexander was tormented by guilt. His father's blood created in Alexander a deep ambivalence about power. Ruthless and autocratic at times, he harbored a deep romantic and a reformist, even revolutionary, streak. He swayed between the two extremes repeatedly over his reign. On taking the throne, Alexander strove to keep Russia neutral in the struggle against France.

Russia was therefore temporarily at peace. The rest of Europe followed. Napoleon had escaped from Egypt and returned to France in fall 1799, seizing control over the country in a coup. Without Russian aid, Austria lost northern Italy to Napoleon and in 1801 surrendered to France possession of Belgium, the left bank of the Rhine, and puppet states in Italy. Britain's naval power and France's land power could not effectively be brought to bear against one another, and the powers signed a peace in 1802 until they had some better opportunity to resume their struggle.

In this first round of Russia's wars against revolutionary France, Suvorov's victories, though impressive, had not been won against Napoleon himself. The Russian army had not yet been tested against Bonaparte's extraordinary talents for organizing armies and managing battles. In addition to inheriting mass armies and promotion based on talent, not birth, from the revolutionary regime, Napoleon added further innovations of his own. Strategically, Napoleon emphasized speed. He broke his armies into independent divisions and corps, each a mix of infantry, cavalry, and artillery and therefore able to fight independently. This in turn allowed him to disperse his armies to move separately and fight together in crucial battles. His fast-moving troops, not tied to slow-moving supply columns, lived effectively off the land, finding provisions over a wide swath of countryside, and covered ground more quickly than other armies. Napoleon was first an artillery officer, and tactically he employed massed artillery at the decisive point of a battle to blow holes for his infantry to exploit or to break squares for destruction by cavalry. He was adept at timing, finding the precise weak point in an opponent's line and the precise time to break it. For a decade, no European power, Russia included, caught up to Napoleon's skill. Only overwhelming material preponderance, and the slow internalization of Napoleon's innovations, allowed Russia and the European powers to match France's military power.

The Second Round

Peace in Europe was short-lived. Britain and France renewed their war in 1803, but it did not spread to the rest of Europe for another two years. In 1805, aided by British subsidies, Russia and Austria rejoined the struggle against France. As with Paul, Tsar Alexander was driven by a combination of strategic and personal interests. Russia was increasingly concerned about French power and the need to maintain a balance in Europe. In addition, though, in March 1804 Napoleon had kidnapped from Baden in Germany a member of the émigré opposition, executing him in a clear case of judicial murder. This was a personal affront to Alexander, whose wife was from Baden.

Fighting began in summer 1805. Napoleon canceled plans for an invasion of Britain and sent his armies into Germany. This campaign, more than any other, showed Napoleon's genius as a general and his enormous superiority over his competitors. The campaign moved far faster than the Austrians, in particular, were expecting. In southern Germany, Napoleon cut off and surrounded the main Austrian army at Ulm in October, then occupied Vienna without a shot in November. Despite these successes, Napoleon's victory was not complete. A Russian army under the aging Mikhail Illarionovich Kutuzov had withdrawn north into Moravia, accompanied by Tsar Alexander, Austrian Emperor Francis, and remaining Austrian troops. Faced with an allied army, the possibility of Prussian intervention, and Austrian reinforcements from Italy, Napoleon needed a battle to give him decisive victory.

Napoleon got his battle just west of the town of Austerlitz in Moravia. The joint Russo-Austrian force of 85,000 took the offensive as winter approached. Napoleon prepared his 70,000 troops to meet them on territory chosen to lure his enemies into reckless attack. Napoleon stretched his army along a series of streams and small lakes running north to south, allowing the Russo-Austrian force to occupy the Pratzen Heights, a plateau directly to his east. To provoke enemy attack, Napoleon deliberately weakened his right wing, concealing the bulk of his forces behind high ground to his left for a decisive counterattack. The Russians and Austrians fell into the trap. With Tsar Alexander and Emperor Francis looking on, the old and tired Kutuzov deferred to the Austrian commander Franz Weyrother. Weyrother advocated overloading the left (south) wing of the Russo-Austrian formation to overwhelm Napoleon's weakened right. After crushing the French right, the allied forces would then wheel right to smash the French center. The flaw was the weakness of the allied center from massing so many forces on the southern wing.

The Battle of Austerlitz opened early on 20 November/2 December 1805, with fog obscuring the field. The initial stages seemed to go well for the Russians; in confused fighting, they seized a pair of villages anchoring the French right. Napoleon saw, however, just how thin the Russo-Austrian center became as allied troops streamed south to complete the destruction of the French right. Napoleon sent his assault columns east up the Pratzen Heights, and within minutes they seized the high ground, stretching the Russo-Austrian line to the point of splitting in two. General Peter Ivanovich Bagration, a Georgian prince commanding the Russo-Austrian right wing, tried desperately to reconstruct a defensible line by reconnecting with his allies to the south.

At midday, Napoleon was ready to complete his victory by a decisive break of the enemy line, as he committed his final reserves to smash through. The Russo-Austrian center disintegrated, and Napoleon's troops turned south to encircle the enemy left wing, exhausted by hours of combat with the stubborn French right. Though Bagration extracted his right wing and escaped, the defeat was otherwise complete: one-third of the Russo-Austrian force was dead or captured, and Tsar Alexander almost fell into French hands. Austria immediately sought peace terms, while Alexander returned to Russia with his army, not surrendering but lacking good options for continuing the war.

Napoleon's spectacular victory at Austerlitz did not make up for terrible defeat elsewhere. At the Battle of Trafalgar in October 1805, the British navy had annihilated a joint French-Spanish fleet, eliminating any chance that Napoleon could invade Britain. Napoleon compensated for his failure against Britain by focusing on continental affairs, rearranging the petty states of Germany into a Confederation of the Rhine as an instrument of French control, and taking Austrian territory in Italy and on the Rhine. Alexander had not given up and negotiated Prussia's entrance to the war as an ally. In fall 1806, Prussia demanded French evacuation of Germany, and war followed immediately. Prussia, the weakest of the five European great powers, was doomed to defeat in any clash with Napoleon. In October 1806, at the twin battles of Jena and Auerstadt, Napoleon crushed Prussia's forces, followed by an effective and ruthless pursuit of fleeing stragglers. Berlin was occupied by French forces.

In addition to the blow of Prussia's defeat, Russia was distracted from the war against Napoleon by minor wars with Iran and the Ottoman Empire. The Iranian War (1804–1813) ultimately led to Iran's recognition of Russian hegemony over present-day Dagestan, much of Georgia, and Azerbaijan, but these several years of fighting took men and resources away from the greater struggle against France. Relations had been uncharacteristically good with the Ottomans before 1806, as both the Russians and the Turks feared French expansion in the Near East. By 1806, however, the Turks saw an opportunity to regain their losses at Russian hands with Napoleon's support. A dispute over the rulers of Moldavia and Wallachia (the so-called Danubian Principalities) led to Russian occupation of those provinces in late 1806; the Ottomans declared war in response. For the Turks, the course of this war was depressingly similar to previous Russo-Turkish wars: steady Russian expansion south along both the east and west coasts of the Black Sea. Russia took parts of Georgia and captured a host of Turkish forts in the Balkans over 1810 and 1811.

The last gasp of Turkish resistance began with an attack on the Russian fort of Rushchuk on the south bank of the Danube. Recognizing that war with France was imminent, Kutuzov wanted a quick resolution and sought battle in the open field. Outnumbered Russians formed in their typical squares south of the fort on 19 June/1 July 1811 and awaited Turkish attack. Repeated Ottoman cavalry attacks were easily repulsed on the Russian right and center. On the left, however, repeated battering allowed the Turkish cavalry to break into the Russian position and even move past the Russians to attack Rushchuk. Russian counterattacks restored the position, finally forcing the Turks to withdraw, but Kutuzov still had not achieved a decisive victory to end the war. Kutuzov then withdrew north across the Danube, hoping to draw the Turkish forces into pursuit and destruction. Taking the bait, the Ottoman Army crossed the Danube west of Rushchuk and built fortifications on both sides of the river. Kutuzov then sprung his trap, encircling and holding the main Turkish force on the north bank while sending troops across to the south bank. On 2/14 October 1811, this detachment took the southern Turkish fortifications, leaving the main force helpless and under artillery fire from all directions. The Turkish army finally surrendered on 23 November/5 December 1811. This Battle of Slobodzea (named for a nearby village) ended all hope of Turkish victory. Russia then settled with Turkey, winning western Georgia and Bessarabia (the territory between the Dnestr and the Prut), along with free passage for Russian commerce through the Turkish straits.

As mentioned, the Iranian and Turkish wars only distracted from the struggle against France. After Jena and Auerstadt, only Russian support and extortionary French terms kept Prussia fighting. Many in Russia had tired of war, but Napoleon's flirtations with Polish independence and his support of the Ottomans left Alexander little choice but to continue fighting. He moved additional forces into Poland, the key theater of the war.

Advance elements of the French and Russians clashed at Pultusk, just north of Warsaw, in December 1806. Indecisive fighting led to a Russian withdrawal east, and Napoleon's army maneuvered to stay between the Russians and their Prussian allies to the northwest. The main Russian army under Leontii Leont'evich Bennigsen, a Hanoverian German in Russian service, responded by shifting north, closer to the coast, and probing west after isolated French detachments. These raids west left the Russians vulnerable to a rapid French advance from the south; Napoleon accordingly moved north to sever communication and retreat back to Russia. Bennigsen escaped the trap and rallied at the East Prussian town of Eylau.

Napoleon's troops, strung out across the Baltic coastal plain by their pursuit of the Russians, gathered south and west of Eylau in bitter cold.

The Battle of Eylau opened on 26 January/7 February 1807 by chance, as Russian and French patrols stumbled into a battle inside the town itself in the midafternoon. Both sides fed newly arriving reinforcements into confused and bloody fighting through the streets of the town, producing heavy casualties on both sides before the Russians withdrew to a ridge northeast of Eylau, spending the night in the open. Napoleon's plan for the next day depended on the expected arrival of additional French troops from the northwest and southeast. One corps would attack northeast out of Eylau to pin the Russians in place. A subsequent attack by a newly arriving corps from the southeast would turn the Russian left flank while thinning and stretching the Russian line. A final attack would break the weakened Russian center while newly arriving troops from the northwest would cut off a Russian retreat.

After an artillery exchange on the morning of 27 January/8 February, the Russians disrupted Napoleon's plan with effective and damaging attacks on his center. Napoleon was forced to prematurely commit his reserves, originally intended for the final break in the Russian line, merely to preserve his position. Disorganized by a blizzard, a French attack blundered straight into massed Russian artillery. Bennigsen counterattacked, sending Russian infantry straight into Eylau itself. Only a spectacular massed charge by French cavalry won time and space to reconstruct the French center. Napoleon followed with his long-anticipated attack on the Russian left flank. Over the afternoon, the Russian left was steadily pressed back, bending the Russian line into a right angle, before the arrival of Prussian allies reinforced the beleaguered Russians and regained much of the lost ground. When darkness ended the battle, Bennigsen withdrew east to safety, 25,000 of his 75,000 men killed or wounded. French losses were equally bad.

Both sides used the spring thaw to rebuild their devastated armies. Napoleon had lost thousands of soldiers without inflicting a decisive defeat and thereby tarnished his reputation as an invincible field commander. Frustrated and anxious to force the Russians into a battle he could win, Napoleon split his army into separate corps in pursuit of Bennigsen. Bennigsen caught one of those corps isolated west of the town of Friedland and moved to destroy it before aid could arrive. The Battle of Friedland opened on 2/14 June 1807 with Bennigsen pushing slowly west from Friedland against much smaller French forces, unaware that Napoleon was rushing additional units to the battle. Bennigsen's slow-developing attack from within a bend in the Alle River allowed Napoleon to see a key weakness in the methodical Russian advance: a stream flowing perpendicular to the Russian line split its formation in half. Napoleon launched an all-out attack on the weaker Russian left late in the day, planning to drive the Russians into the river they had unwisely left at their backs. His troops drove steadily forward, despite the repeated coun- terattacks that Bennigsen threw at them, until a final French bayonet charge broke Bennigsen's final reserves, the imperial guard. As the south- ern wing of the Russian position collapsed, only a ford across the Alle Riv- er allowed Benningsen to pull the northern remnants of his troops to safety.

After this, Alexander had no choice but to admit defeat. Meeting alone with Napoleon on a raft in the Nieman River on 13/25 June 1807, Alexander was charmed and flattered into sacrificing Russian interests, and those of his unfortunate Prussian ally. The king of Prussia lost half his territory at Napoleon's hands. In this Peace of Tilsit, Alexander not only accepted Prussia's humiliation and the creation of a Grand Duchy of Warsaw on Polish territory, but secretly agreed to pressure Britain to end its war against France and if necessary join France. Napoleon and Alexander had become partners in the domination of Europe. With Rus- sia's tacit alliance, Napoleon widened the war against Britain, occupying Spain and intensifying a continent-wide embargo on British trade. Both moves were, in the long run, disasters for Napoleon. The Spanish occupa- tion turned into a lengthy and draining guerrilla war, worsened by British intervention. Napoleon's embargo, the Continental System, contributed to the collapse of the agreement Napoleon had negotiated with Alexander.

France and Russia's partnership had decidedly mixed results. Napo- leon encouraged Alexander to seize Finland from Sweden, an annoyingly persistent British ally. Alexander did just that in a short war in 1808–1809. Annexing Finland, Alexander retained the existing constitutional and legal order in Finland, as an island of constitutional monarchy in an auto- cratic empire. Generally, though, Russo-French cooperation showed increasing signs of strain. Tilsit provided for Russian evacuation of Mol- davia and Wallachia in return for peace with the Ottoman Empire. Alexander never did that, justifying this by Napoleon's failure to end his occupation of Prussia. Russian cooperation proved entirely worthless to Napoleon when Austria made another futile attempt to break Napoleon's hold in spring 1809. Napoleon again demonstrated his mastery over the Austrians, occupying Vienna, then smashing the Austrian army at the Battle of Wagram. Though Russia was obligated to participate as a French ally, it limited itself to halfhearted intervention to keep the Poles under control. Napoleon's Continental System also contradicted Russia's natu- ral economic interests, which had made it a long-standing trading partner of Great Britain. Finally, Napoleon's vision for Europe did not include sharing hegemony with any power, only his personal domination. An independent Russia was, in the end, intolerable, and Napoleon decided to invade.

The Third Round

Russia prepared itself for war with France by a series of reforms. Alexander had earlier replaced Peter the Great's colleges with European-style ministries, but the transition from War College to War Ministry made little practical difference. Real reform began under Barclay de Tolly, a Livonian of Scottish ancestry now in Russian service. Minister of War in 1810, Barclay de Tolly imported parts of Napoleon's organizational schemes into Russia, including the organization of stable corps incorporating all branches of arms—infantry divisions, cavalry, and artillery—and capable of independent action. In addition, he strengthened staff work and planning, while emphasizing marksmanship among the troops. He overhauled Russia's chaotic central military administration, divided into competing and overlapping fiefdoms. The War Ministry collected recruits, supplies, and money; distribution of those resources and command in the field lay with the field armies and their commanders. This divided system was designed for wartime, since Napoleon's hostile intentions were becoming clear. There was still little centralization; the individual commanders of Russia's field armies answered to no one but the tsar.

As war neared, Russia had three armies defending its western frontier. The 1st Army of 100,000 men under Barclay de Tolly covered the northern sector: the 2nd Army of 50,000 under Bagration was farther south. South of both lay the Pripiat Marshes, an enormous morass of wooded and swampy terrain, practically impossible to traverse. The 3rd Western Army held the frontier south of the marshes and played little role in the approaching campaign. Those forces were dwarfed by the invasion army Napoleon assembled, the largest in history to that time. The initial force was 400,000 men, later augmented to 600,000. Logistical requirements were correspondingly enormous. Napoleon pulled men, horses, and supplies from across his European empire to muster the necessary resources. Only a minority of the invasion force, in fact, was actually French, as Napoleon sacrificed his French national army to the requirements of invading Russia. Russia's size left Napoleon few strategic options. As there was nothing worth attacking south of the Pripiat Marshes, the only question was whether to push northeast to St. Petersburg or east to Moscow. Napoleon hoped to make the issue moot by crushing the Russian armies in a decisive battle at the border, enabling him to exact the kind of settlement he needed to make himself the clear master of Europe.

Napoleon's invasion began the night of 11–12/23–24 June 1812. He intended to push northeast through present-day Lithuania, then turn south to crush the defending Russian armies against the Pripiat Marshes, giving him victory within a month. His Russian opponents did not cooperate. Contrary to later beliefs, Russian strategy was not a deliberate attempt to draw Napoleon into the depths of Russia. Instead, Napoleon's

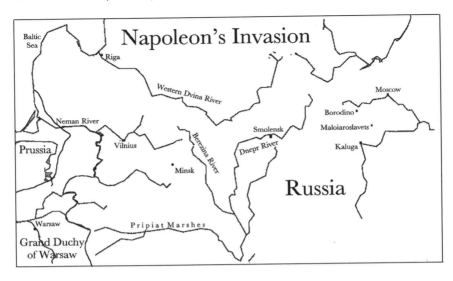

advance guard drove between Barclay de Tolly and Bagration. This prevented their uniting for a stand against Napoleon, who would almost certainly have annihilated them. Instead, Barclay de Tolly withdrew northeast, while Bagration skimmed east along the northern edge of the Pripiat Marshes. Napoleon first tried to catch Bagration's 2nd Army, but was unable to pin it in place and destroy it. He then moved north to cut off Barclay de Tolly's retreat toward Moscow, but his overloaded columns were again too slow. Both Russian armies escaped intact to rendezvous at Smolensk.

Even early in the campaign, there were alarming signs the invasion was in danger. The countryside was poorer than in western Europe and Napoleon's army larger, so his troops could not live off the land. Peasant partisans and roaming cossacks routinely picked off foraging parties, forcing the French to stay in tight columns and reducing Napoleon's knowledge of Russian dispositions. As Napoleon pushed east, the defense of his lengthening supply lines and open flanks drew still more men from his main force. By the time his troops reached Vitebsk, only halfway to Moscow, he had lost almost 100,000 men to heat, disease, desertion, or enemy action. At the same time, Napoleon refused to unleash a peasant uprising by proclaiming an end to serfdom, still hoping for a negotiated settlement with Alexander.

As July turned to August, Barclay de Tolly and Bagration rallied at Smolensk, the traditional invasion route to Moscow. Even here, they did not make a stand, despite pressure from the tsar and Russian public opinion to do just that. The two commanders despised each other and could not agree on a course of action. While Bagration remained at Smolensk,

Barclay de Tolly halfheartedly struck west in hopes of finding Napoleon's forces still dispersed on the march. While the Russians dithered, Napoleon's plan was clear: to force the Russians into a battle they would lose. He shifted his forces south, crossing the Dnepr River, then used the river as a screen to shield his move east along its southern bank, headed for Smolensk to cut off the Russian retreat. The river crossing was entirely successful, but Napoleon's swiftly moving advance guards ran into a sturdy and disciplined Russian division on 2/14 August 1812, at the village of Krasnoe, guarding against just such a maneuver. Repeated cavalry charges failed to break the division, which methodically withdrew along to the road to Smolensk. Napoleon was forced to halt and regroup, costing him surprise. Barclay de Tolly, north of the Dnepr, raced back to Smolensk to avoid the trap.

Smolensk was ringed by impressive fortifications, though they were not built to handle modern artillery and the city's suburbs had grown beyond them. Nonetheless, the city was still an imposing, well-garrisoned defensive obstacle on the south bank of the Dnepr. As the Russians on the north bank and French on the south raced east toward the city, the French advance guard assembled outside Smolensk on 4/16 August. The French assault on the southern suburbs began the next day. Bloody street-fighting left 10,000 killed and wounded on each side, but Smolensk remained in Russian hands and the retreat east was still open.

Rather than engage Napoleon's main force, Bagration and Barclay de Tolly, still barely speaking, continued east past Smolensk toward Moscow. After initial pursuit failed to catch the Russians, Napoleon halted in Smolensk to rest his troops and consider his options. There was an excellent case for wintering in Smolensk in warmth and safety, and then in the spring pushing east to Moscow or north to St. Petersburg. Napoleon's very presence that long on Russian soil might force Alexander into concessions.

The problem was that Alexander refused to negotiate so long as French troops were on Russian soil, and time worked in his favor. He ordered the mobilization of 300,000 peasants into a national militia. Russian opinion was solidly behind the tsar, leaving Napoleon no divisions to exploit. Napoleon's European empire was also not secure. His reluctant allies and resentful conquests might take advantage of his absence. In the end, Napoleon decided that taking Moscow would force Alexander to terms and that his generalship and the skill of his troops would guarantee victory. On 13/25 August, Napoleon's army, now 150,000 strong, resumed its march to Moscow.

Alexander replaced Barclay de Tolly, despite his skilled service, because Russian opinion resented him as a foreigner and blamed him for the lack of any stand against the French. Kutuzov, old but indisputably Russian, stepped in as commander in chief. As Napoleon neared Moscow, Kutuzov was as wary as his predecessor of meeting the French in open battle, but knew he could not abandon Moscow without a fight.

Kutuzov made his stand at the village of Borodino, 60 miles west of Moscow. Borodino stood amid broken terrain—small hills, streams, and woods—well suited to Russian light troops and difficult for any attacker. On 24 August/5 September 1812, Kutuzov's forces were in place, stretched southwest to northeast, with Borodino itself just in front of the center of the Russian line. The position was heavily reinforced with earthworks and redoubts, and its southwestern extremity was anchored at the village of Shevardino on a major redoubt. The initial French step was to clear Shevardino and dislocate the Russian line. Defended by an infantry division and several regiments of jägers, Shevardino's redoubt held almost a full day before Kutuzov ordered a withdrawal, rebuilding the southern end of the Russian line farther east. This left the Russian position slightly bent backward, with a shallow angle in the center of the line. At the apex of the line stood an enormous earthen fortification, the Great Redoubt.

The next day was quiet as the two armies, 130,000 French and 120,000 Russians, lined up along a five-mile frontage. Napoleon saw a key weakness in the Russian deployment. The northern half of the Russian line was well protected by terrain, behind a meandering stream with steep banks, but was more strongly manned than the comparatively vulnerable southern half. The sheer size of the opposing armies, however, left Napoleon little room for subtlety and maneuver. At Borodino, and at Leipzig the next year, Napoleonic armies outgrew the capacity of one man to command them. Napoleon decided on a frontal attack to drain Russian strength and showed listlessness and apathy through the battle. He was not the commander he had once been.

On 26 August/7 September 1812, the Battle of Borodino began well for the French. They quickly cleared Borodino and then mounted a full-scale attack along the southern half of the Russian line. Flanking forces on the French far right bogged down in inconclusive fighting. In the center, the French became embroiled in fierce hand-to-hand combat for a series of smaller redoubts on the Russian center-left, and then for the Great Redoubt at the hinge of the Russian line. Napoleon's reserves were rapidly consumed while Kutuzov shifted troops south from the overmanned northern half of his line. The Russian left flank wavered and nearly collapsed when Bagration was mortally wounded, but rallied along a new line farther east. By midday, the French left was almost bare from Napoleon's thirst for fresh troops. Russian cavalry raided across the dividing stream, panicking the French cavalry screen and forcing Napoleon to expend valuable infantry to restore his left flank.

All this delayed the final French assault on the Great Redoubt, which finally came in the early afternoon. A massive artillery bombardment, an infantry frontal assault, and cavalry sweeping around the redoubt to enter the earthworks from the rear finally captured it by 3:00 P.M., opening a yawning hole in the Russian center. French cavalry swept into that gap to exploit the break and complete the victory, but two Russian cavalry corps counterattacked to allow time to stabilize the Russian line. At sunset, a final French attempt to turn the Russian left flank only pushed it back, leaving the Russians in good order with intact lines, only a mile behind their original positions. At least 80,000 French and Russian soldiers lay dead or wounded on the field.

Kutuzov had made the stand Russian opinion demanded. Unwilling to repeat the experience and averse to risking his battered army, he withdrew through Moscow, then rallied south of the city. Napoleon could technically claim victory, but his army had been gutted by the horrific casualties of a day-long slugging match. Dubious triumphs like Borodino could not force Alexander to terms. Worse for Napoleon's prospects, Kutuzov still commanded an army somewhere beyond Moscow. A week after Borodino, Napoleon and his 100,000 remaining troops occupied Moscow. The city itself was deserted, evacuated by order of its governor. It burned to the ground shortly after French occupation, probably fired by retreating Russians. Napoleon hoped possession of Russia's ancient capital would force Alexander to recognize that he had been beaten. Instead, Alexander and Kutuzov played for time, with no intention of yielding.

After waiting six weeks for Alexander to see reason, and anxious over the approaching winter, Napoleon decided to cut his losses and return home. Upon abandoning Moscow, Napoleon's situation became increasingly desperate. He wished to retreat west along a route through Kaluga, south of his original road to Moscow. While his army would still suffer from cold, hunger, and partisan attacks, he would at least march through territory not picked clean by his soldiers on their way east. Kutuzov blocked Napoleon's advance guard on the way south at the town of Maloiaroslavets, on the Lusha River southwest of Moscow. French troops had taken the bridge over the Lusha and Maloiaroslavets itself, but on the night of 11–12/ 23–24 October 1812, a Russian corps infiltrated the town, recaptured the bridge, and fortified the crossing. This became a back-and-forth struggle for the town the next day as newly arriving French and Russian troops poured into the fray. Despite reinforcements from a second corps, the Russians were forced to abandon the town. Napoleon was unwilling to cross the Lusha River under Russian guns, however, and was nearly captured by cossacks while reconnoitering the situation. He abandoned the southern road and took his army north to return the way he had come.

Napoleon's army now began to disintegrate. The weather grew colder and food shorter. His troops marched past Borodino and thousands of rotting, unburied corpses. Russian cavalry harassed the marching columns, preventing French troops from foraging. At intervals, Kutuzov launched more serious attempts to divide and defeat in detail the long French column as it plodded west. To make matters worse, outlying Russian corps under Peter Khristianovich Wittgenstein (to the north) and the naval officer Pavel Vasil'evich Chichagov (to the south) closed in on Napoleon and threatened to cut off his escape entirely. Snow fell even before Napoleon's beleaguered army reached Smolensk. Without supplies sufficient to winter there, Napoleon's troops, now down to 40,000 organized troops and thousands more stragglers, evacuated the city at the beginning of November.

After battles around Krasnyi on 4–5/16–17 November, costing Napoleon another 20,000 casualties, the next barrier was the Berezina River, with Russian forces converging from all directions. Chichagov, moving up from the south, captured an enormous French supply depot at Minsk, destroyed the Berezina bridges at the town of Borisov, and stretched his forces along the Berezina's western bank to prevent any crossing. Napoleon learned of a ford in the river north of Borisov, and his engineers jury-rigged two bridges while skillful deception kept the Russians unaware of Napoleon's intent. From 14–17/26–29 November 1812, Napoleon got his army across the Berezina under constant Russian pressure, but at a cost of tens of thousands of combatants and stragglers killed, trampled in the press for the bridges, or frozen in the icy waters of the Berezina. Only Kutuzov's tacit cooperation made this possible. He saw no need to pursue the French vigorously when winter did his work for him. Over the Berezina, Napoleon left his army struggling toward the Russian border, prey to cold and Russian cavalry, while he sped to Paris to outdistance news of his disaster and ensure political stability at home. There was no way to conceal the scale of the defeat. Napoleon had invaded Russia with 600,000 men; perhaps 20,000 left Russia as an organized group. Including other formations, stragglers, and returned prisoners, only 100,000 ever saw their homes again.

The pursuit continued with multiple Russian armies crossing into Prussia and Napoleon's Grand Duchy of Warsaw. Napoleon's defeat created opportunities for a new coalition against him. Austria was deeply suspicious of Russian ambitions, but in Prussia, matters were quite different. A Prussian army accompanying Napoleon's retreat declared itself neutral. Resentment of French domination in Prussia produced an anti-French resistance movement in early 1813, forcing the Prussian king to join it or lose his throne. This culminated in a Russo-Prussian alliance, joined by Sweden and backed by British money, to maintain the pressure on Napoleon.

Napoleon himself spent the beginning of 1813 in a remarkable effort to rebuild his shattered forces. Scraping every available man from France, including wounded veterans, old men, and young boys, Napoleon assembled a serviceable force to contest the allies in central Germany. Since Napoleon's cavalry never recovered from the Russian debacle, taking longer to develop and train, his reconnaissance was never the same. After putting together an army, Napoleon moved east into Germany. Two battles at Lützen and Bautzen in April and May 1813 highlighted Napoleon's difficulties. In the first, a Russian army under Wittgenstein blundered into an attack against superior French forces and narrowly escaped destruction. The second, a two-day bloody slugging match, left Napoleon in command of the battlefield but without a clear victory to achieve a political settlement. Napoleon could ill afford his steady losses. The two nominal French victories cost Wittgenstein his post, and he was replaced by Barclay de Tolly. Austria, emboldened by Napoleon's losses, joined the alliance, aligning for the first time four of Europe's great powers against the fifth. The size of the coalition and the number of troops against him made Napoleon's task far more difficult. The allied coalition could threaten French control in Germany and northern Italy simultaneously, but Napoleon could be only in one place at a time. The allies fought the French only when Napoleon was not present to work his battlefield magic, grinding France down slowly and systematically. At Dresden, in August 1813, the pattern repeated itself. An unsuccessful allied attack on the city from the south was followed the next day by Napoleon's counterattack from the north. Once again, Napoleon had won a battle; once again he lost men he could not replace and was no closer to victory.

Napoleon's constant maneuvers to prevent an enemy concentration against him exhausted the legs of his inexperienced soldiers and the nerves of his overburdened marshals and never gained him the battle he needed to restore his fortunes. Running short on supplies in autumn 1813, Napoleon decided to withdraw west toward France. With his troops assembling around Leipzig in early October, he was caught by allied armies converging on his position from north and south. This created the largest battle of the Napoleonic Wars, with 500,000 men participating in a single engagement: the Battle of Leipzig, or the Battle of the Nations.

Napoleon's position at Leipzig was reasonably strong. He had 200,000 soldiers centered on Leipzig itself. The terrain around the city was channeled by rivers and marshes into separate avenues of approach, preventing the allies from moving their troops from sector to sector, while Napoleon's base in the city let him shift units easily. Nonetheless, the odds were against him. A force equal to Napoleon's was closing on Leipzig from the south, while unbeknown to him, another 130,000 approached from the northwest. Of those 330,000 allied troops, 125,000 were Russian. The combination of 500,000 soldiers and a vast battlefield made meaningful control of the battle impossible. Ignorant of the danger from the northwest, Napoleon planned on taking the offensive, pushing south from

Leipzig with three full corps, while additional troops looped left to envelop the right flank of the allied drive north. Allied plans envisaged an attack from the south, one that would run straight into the teeth of the planned French attack, but their effort was dispersed across a very large field of battle. In addition, the allies planned subsidiary attacks from the southwest and the northwest, separated from each other and from the main attack by marshy rivers running through Leipzig.

As the battle opened on 4/16 October 1813, Napoleon summoned troops from north of Leipzig to join the southern push, unaware of the allied approach. His subordinate commanders canceled those orders. Fierce fighting erupted north, west, and south of Leipzig. In the north and the west, the French fought desperately to hold advancing allied troops out of Leipzig, employing corps that Napoleon badly needed for his main attack south. In that sector, the enormous size of the battlefield and the number of troops involved meant the allied attack was disorganized and piecemeal. After it spent its force, Napoleon began his counteroffensive at midday. Though he succeeded in driving back allied forces all along the southern front, Napoleon could not break the allied line or send them into general retreat before darkness fell. The first day inflicted a toll of between 25,000 and 30,000 killed or wounded on each side, but Napoleon's smaller force could not afford those losses, and the allies received additional reinforcements that night. The next day was quiet. The allies prepared a general offensive to crush the French, while Napoleon weighed the worsening odds against him and prepared for evacuation west to the Rhine.

The renewed battle on 6/18 October 1813 involved allied attacks on a reduced French perimeter, but no major gains for either side, only continued attrition Napoleon could not sustain. He began pulling his troops out of Leipzig early on 7/19 October, without serious pressure from the allies. In a fateful error, though, the lone bridge across the marshes west of Leipzig was blown up with 30,000 French troops still on the wrong side. They surrendered, adding to the 40,000 killed and wounded Napoleon's troops had already lost. Though the size of the battlefield and difficulties controlling and coordinating troops prevented the destruction of Napoleon's army, Germany was entirely lost to him, and the question was whether he could build a defense to protect France itself.

Napoleon's retreat to the Rhine only delayed the inevitable, as France no longer had the soldiers and resources to sustain the war. Napoleon's increasingly shaky political grasp at home forced him to spend valuable time in Paris rather than at the front. His only hope was discord among the allies, increasingly at odds over the shape of the final peace settlement. As allied armies closed in on Paris, however, the key members of the coalition—Austria, Britain, Prussia, and Russia—agreed in a formal alliance to fight as long as necessary and to accept no separate peace with France.

They even offered Napoleon a chance to retain the throne and France's frontiers of 1791; he refused. In March 1814, allied troops entered Paris. Though Napoleon wished to continue the fight, his marshals agreed that the war was over and refused to go on. Napoleon resigned himself to abdication, and the allies exiled him to Elba in the Mediterranean. Louis XVIII, the new king of France and nephew of the deposed Louis XVI, accepted a reversion to the frontiers of November 1792, retaining some of France's gains since the revolution.

Napoleon's career had one final act. Escaping Elba in February 1815, he returned to France, taking back his throne as Louis XVIII fled the country. The allies hardly interrupted their ongoing negotiations at Vienna over a final peace and reaffirmed their commitment to Napoleon's downfall. Russian troops did not take a direct role in the final destruction of Napoleon. At Waterloo in June 1815, British and Prussian troops ended this brief encore. Napoleon was dispatched to a more secure exile on the remote island of St. Helena in the south Atlantic.

Russian soldiers, mobilized by resistance to a foreign invader, had chased Napoleon the length of Europe, from Moscow to Paris. Now occupying France, Russian officers (often more at home in French than Russian) read the political philosophy produced by revolutionary France and pondered its application to their own country. Russian soldiers gave French bistros their name; demanding fast service, they would shout, *"bystro!"* (quickly!) at cafe owners. Tsar Alexander, triumphant, had enormous power. His army, at the dawn of the industrial age, was more powerful than any in Europe. The question was, how would he use it?

CHAPTER 8

Repression and Defeat

Napoleon's defeat made Alexander I the arbiter of European affairs. Russian military power lacked any counter with Napoleon safely exiled to the south Atlantic. Luckily for the stability of Europe, Alexander approached post-Napoleonic foreign policy with a profound distaste for revolution, upheaval, and conflict. In common with many other statesmen, he imagined a concert of Europe to settle international disputes amicably, through compromise and negotiation. While certainly a positive vision, Alexander's ideal had a darker side. It entailed suppression of both revolution abroad and political reform at home. The Russian officers who occupied France after the Napoleonic wars brought home French ideas of political liberty and constitutional monarchy. Neither Alexander I nor his brother and successor Nicholas I wanted any part of that. Under Nicholas, in fact, Russia's political atmosphere became even more repressive. While some military reforms did take place, the social stagnation imposed from above kept Russia from modernizing itself or its army. When faced with war against Western powers, the illusion of Russian military power disintegrated ignominiously.

Congress of Vienna

The political issues raised by 20 years of war were settled by the European powers at the Congress of Vienna. While dozens of European states were represented, important decisions were made by the great powers alone: Britain, Prussia, Austria, and Russia. An initial clash showed the dangers of confrontation. Prussia and Russia had worked out a territorial settlement between them: Prussia would keep Saxony, which had unfortunately sided with Napoleon, while Russia took Poland. Britain and Austria were deeply disturbed by this side deal. Their need for support to block it gave France an opportunity to reenter the discussions, allying itself with Britain and Austria. This threat of renewed war, and the general sense among the European powers that competitive approaches to international politics brought war, revolution, and disaster, produced a compromise on this issue and a generally conciliatory approach to all issues. Prussia received only part of Saxony, and Russia only part of Poland. The Congress then functioned by two basic principles. The first was legitimacy, that rightful rulers should return to their thrones, as Louis XVIII returned to France. Legitimacy did not prevail everywhere. The hundreds of petty states that made up Germany were consolidated into three dozen larger and more formidable governments. The second principle was compensation. The great powers should be kept reasonably balanced, if need be by granting them territory from smaller states less important to the system.

The final settlement restrained France, which even without Napoleon was a country of immense potential power. France was returned to its 1790 frontiers and hemmed in with buffer states. Piedmont in northern Italy was enlarged and the Dutch Republic was granted present-day Belgium. Prussia received additional territory on the Rhine. In addition to paying an indemnity, France was saddled with foreign occupation until 1818. The Quadruple Alliance, the wartime alliance against France, continued as insurance against French belligerence.

Given the general consensus among the great powers that war was too dangerous a tool for resolving differences, the greatest danger to the Congress of Vienna system was revolution. Those revolutions might be political, for constitutional reform or greater liberties. They might just as easily be nationalist, where national boundaries clashed with political ones. In Germany and Italy, the ethnic nation was divided among many states; in Austria, a single state encompassed many nations. In each case, changing regimes or borders threatened legitimacy and stability. The problem was that Britain was fundamentally indifferent to the political regimes of European states, and the rest of the great powers had only a limited ability to control revolution outside their own borders. Alexander I feared and hated revolution and saw Russian might as a bulwark against any recurrence of the nightmares of the French Revolution and Napoleon. He gave this concrete form through the creation of the Holy Alliance in 1815. This was a joint pledge by the monarchs of Austria, Prussia, and Russia to adhere to Christian principles; Alexander took it very seriously.

Alexander had by 1815 abandoned his youthful revolutionary ideals. He committed himself instead to rigid conservatism, represented in the army by his chief military advisor Aleksei Andreevich Arakcheev. To reduce the expense of Russia's army and demonstrate for Russia the advantages of order and discipline, Arakcheev experimented with "military settlements." He drew upon ancient traditions of Russian military policy. For centuries, as Russia pushed south into the steppe north of the Black Sea, it manned its defenses with military homesteaders: men given farmland in return for border defense. Impressed with the order and discipline on Arakcheev's own estates, in 1810 Alexander had authorized him to create military settlements in which soldiers farmed with soldierly diligence and precision. The end of the Napoleonic Wars sped implementation. Peasants were uprooted from their lands and replaced by soldiers. These soldiers wore uniforms in daily life, lived in regimented villages, were subject to military discipline, and combined military drill with farming and labor on public works. By the time of Alexander's death in 1825, 750,000 people lived in these settlements. They were deeply unpopular among soldiers and peasants alike. Recurring mutinies and uprisings meant they were gradually deemphasized after Alexander's death. Though they were intended to reduce Russia's expenditures on the military, they failed, leaving Russian finances in ruins. Russia simply could not support Alexander's army of 800,000 men.

The Decembrists

In most of Europe, military officers were the foremost supporters of established order. It was a mark of Russia's political backwardness that officers formed the earliest and, for a time, the only revolutionary groups. Exposed through campaigns abroad and the occupation of France to European political concepts and culture, Russian officers returned with conceptions of liberty and reform ill suited to an autocratic system. Alexander bore some responsibility for the spread of these ideas, having toyed with them himself early in his reign. As part of a Europe-wide fashion of secret societies, revolutionary and otherwise, Russian officers formed groups dedicated to political change. The first was the Union of Salvation, organized in 1816 by a number of noble officers who later became leading figures in the Decembrist movement. Over time, the secret societies became two groups, a northern society in St. Petersburg and a southern society in Tulchin, a military headquarters in Bessarabia. The two groups had substantially different programs. The northern society envisaged Russia as an equal and free society without serfdom, but with nobles maintaining their landed estates. Its draft constitution was based on the United States, with a federal structure and formal separation of powers. It was quite vague on how to achieve this end. The southern society was more radical, imagining immediate emancipation, land guaranteed to peasants, and a centralized state. It was committed to violent revolution, even plotting to assassinate the tsar.

Both societies were taken off guard by Alexander's sudden death at Taganrog in southern Russia in November 1825. This unleashed a succession crisis. Alexander left no children, leading to the popular belief his successor would be his younger brother Constantine. Constantine had, however, married a Polish Catholic, leading Alexander (with

Constantine's knowledge) to secretly name their third brother Nicholas as heir. While Nicholas understood Alexander's intentions, he was ambivalent about taking the throne, and upon receiving word of Alexander's death, swore allegiance to Constantine as the new tsar. Constantine was out of the capital in Poland and refused the throne. Word of conspiracies against him finally forced Nicholas to proclaim himself emperor.

The northern society recognized this confusion over the succession as its best opportunity for seizing power, and its officers led their soldiers into the center of St. Petersburg on 14/26 December 1825 to proclaim that Nicholas was a usurper and that the absent Constantine was the rightful tsar. Only a small proportion of officers in the capital joined the uprising, and their soldiers were utterly baffled. Some thought their rallying cry of "Constantine and Constitution" referred to Constantine and his wife. Once Nicholas had rallied loyal troops and determined that he was not in immediate danger, he attempted to convince the mutineers to end their defiance peacefully. When they refused, a few artillery blasts scattered the soldiers, ending the uprising the day it began. Subsequent investigations broke up both the northern and southern societies, culminating in five executions and over 100 persons being exiled to Siberia.

The Decembrists, named for the month of their uprising, failed completely and inspired no later military revolutionaries. They were, however, the first Russian revolutionaries motivated by and promulgating an ideology, a particular way of thinking about the world and how it ought to change. Russia had seen many rebels, but never a serious political program. For the next two centuries, such ideological revolutionaries, drawn from Russia's small but volatile educated classes, were central to Russian history.

Nicholas I, the new tsar, was a military man by training and avocation, with German sympathies by upbringing and marriage. All his life, he was preoccupied with discipline, order, responsibility, and law. The Decembrist uprising only solidified his opposition to anything smacking of revolution, liberty, or political change. His 30 years in power were marked by deadening censorship of subversive ideas and repression of all political opposition. Though remarkably gentle by the standards of the twentieth century, Nicholas's regime was perceived at home and throughout Europe as the height of tyranny. Nicholas developed an extensive system of political police (small by modern standards) to monitor developments in Russia. He greatly expanded Russia's gendarmes, militarized police for maintaining social order. He experimented with thought control through his sponsorship of "official nationality," an ideology of "Orthodoxy, Autocracy, Nationality." This was designed to inculcate an understanding and acceptance of strict hierarchy: of God above all, of the tsar and his autocratic power put in place by God, and the unity and coherence of the Russian nation under the tsar.

Previous Russian tsars had all employed military officers extensively in civil government, but Nicholas took it further. A majority of provincial governors and government ministers were military men. Given that military officers made up a substantial proportion of Russia's educated class, this was to some degree unavoidable. Nicholas's preoccupation, however, with surface appearances and parade ground drill as opposed to flexibility, initiative, and military effectiveness had pernicious effects on the Russian military and Russian society as a whole. While western Europe was transformed by the Industrial Revolution, Russia remained stagnant. It avoided the social tensions industrialization created, but did not develop the railroads and modern factories essential for waging war in the industrial era.

Imperial Warfare

Over the late 1820s and early 1830s, a series of minor wars along Russia's periphery revealed major problems in the Russian military behind a facade of overwhelming power. Russia's immense army, with manpower of 800,000 on paper, was run by a wasteful, bloated bureaucracy, stretched thin around Russia's lengthy frontier, and could not move quickly to respond to a crisis. The army was too large to afford, but too small to defend the frontiers. First came the Russo-Iranian War (1826–1828). After Islamic clergy in Iran declared a holy war against Russia, Iranian forces invaded in summer 1826. The invasion penetrated temporarily into the Russian-controlled Caucasus as far as Baku and Tbilisi. As a result of the war, Russia won Erevan and Nakhichevan, much of present-day Armenia. Though Russia's eventual victory was assured, it could muster only small forces and the war took far longer than it should have.

Next came another Russo-Turkish War. In 1821, Greece had rebelled against Ottoman rule, backed by popular sympathy in western Europe and in Russia. In 1827, Britain, France, and Russia agreed to intervene as a peacekeeping force. While carrying out this vague mission, their combined fleets confronted a Turkish fleet in Navarino Bay on 8/20 October 1827. A Turkish vessel opened fire, provoking a short but decisive naval engagement. The Turkish fleet was annihilated, a key step toward Greek independence. Seeing Russia as the most pressing threat, the Ottoman sultan declared war at the end of 1827 and closed the Turkish Straits to Russian exports. Though Russia responded with a declaration of war on 14/26 April 1828, Nicholas was cautious. He naturally wished to restore Russian exports and boost Russian power in the Black Sea, but had to be careful. If Russia were too successful, Britain and France might intervene against Russia, and complete Ottoman collapse might allow British or French control of the straits.

As in the Russo-Iranian War, Russia found itself unable to employ its manpower effectively. Only about 100,000 of Russia's 800,000 soldiers could be spared. As a result, three Russian corps easily cleared Moldavia and Wallachia, but did not push south far past the Danube River. They did capture Varna on the Black Sea, opening the coast for the next year's campaign. Turkish fortresses between the Danube and the Black Sea had as many troops as the Russians, hindering further progress. To make matters worse, Nicholas joined the campaign, distracting his commanders. Poor planning and shoddy logistics crippled the Russian war effort, as did an outbreak of plague. The costs of war undermined Russian finances, already under strain from the expense of Russia's army. The only good news came from the Caucasus, where Russian troops made impressive gains against the Turks. Those successes, though welcome, could not decide the war.

After the winter, the Russian plan was to push along the Black Sea coast toward Constantinople to pressure the Turks to settle. After a slow Russian start in the spring, a Turkish army met the Russians at Kulevcha, west of Varna, on 30 May/11 June 1829. The resulting Russian victory opened the road south through the Balkan Mountains. A quick Russian push toward Constantinople forced the Turks to make peace. The September 1829 Treaty of Adrianople awarded Russia relatively little: access to the mouth of the Danube and Turkish recognition of Russia's Caucasus acquisitions. Its greater result was a substantial step forward in the disintegration of the Turkish Empire in Europe and a false impression of Russian might.

The next conflict grew out of an 1830 European revolutionary wave. French king Charles X provoked revolution by his aggressive promotion of the thoroughly discredited notion of divine right. After his overthrow, disorder spread north, where Belgium revolted against Dutch rule. The king of the Netherlands appealed to Nicholas for aid. Though Nicholas prepared to send the Russian army west, Britain and France were unwilling to see Russian troops on the English Channel, threatening general war in Europe.

This danger was preempted by revolution closer to home. Poland sat uneasily under Russian rule. The revolutions of 1830 provided inspiration for Polish revolutionaries, and a ticking clock. Poland would soon be occupied by massive numbers of Russian troops preparing for foreign intervention, meaning revolution had to come quickly or not at all. In November 1830, Polish cadets and junior officers launched a coup in Warsaw. They occupied public buildings, Warsaw crowds seized weapons from a government arsenal, and Russian authority evaporated. Nicholas's brother Constantine, governor of Poland, escaped capture but begged Nicholas to show restraint. Constantine's hopes for moderation were dashed. The Polish insurgents grew increasingly radical, formally deposing Nicholas as king of Poland at the beginning of 1831. Nicholas in turn resolved to crush this by force.

As in the two preceding wars, Russia found it difficult to employ its potential strength effectively. Nicholas's troops invaded Poland in February 1831, and the early clashes were inconclusive enough to give Poles some hope of success. The spring thaw of 1831 turned roads to mud and delayed Russian progress, along with supply problems, a cholera epidemic, and harassment by Polish partisans. Finally, at the end of May, the Poles suffered a major defeat at Ostroleka, and the cohesion of Polish resistance broke down. A Russian army reached Warsaw in September 1831, and resistance collapsed. Thousands of Poles went into exile in western Europe, boosting an already-burgeoning wave of Russophobia. Nicholas was restrained in his reimposition of order in Poland, though the separate Polish army was abolished and its troops integrated into Russian forces.

Nicholas's three wars exposed two fundamental problems with Russia's military. One was solvable; one was not. The correctable problem was the bureaucratic chaos of Russia's military administration. From the Napoleonic Wars, Russia inherited a division of military administration between the War Minister and the Chief of the Main Staff. The Staff was intended to oversee planning and fighting wars, leaving the War Ministry to handle supplies and logistics. While that made some sense in wartime, in peacetime it only divided and confused authority, while generating mountains of paperwork. After the Napoleonic Wars, there had been no attempt to clarify the division of labor, only budget cuts to reduce the military burden. From 1827, one man, Aleksandr Ivanovich Chernyshev, held both posts. While this did at least prevent conflicting policies, it still left two large bureaucracies working independently. To make matters worse, there had never been any systematic codification of the thousands of individual decrees and regulations making up Russian military law, creating a morass of contradictory and confusing dictates.

The result in the early 1830s was a program of conservative bureaucratic reform. In addition to sorting out Russia's convoluted military law, and humanizing the conscription and training of soldiers, it unified military authority under the War Ministry. Staff work was handled by a new Department of the General Staff, subordinate and answerable to the War Ministry. In 1832, to augment staff work and raise the intellectual level of the Russian army, a new educational institution was founded, ultimately named the Imperial Nikolaev Military Academy after the tsar. In 1855, artillery and engineering academies were added.

Though the Nikolaev Academy created an intellectual elite within the military, it did nothing to solve the other fundamental contradiction of Russian military policy. The country's far-flung borders required a huge army for effective defense. Railroads might allow a smaller, more mobile army, but railroads required industrial development Russia did not possess and brought social and economic dislocation Nicholas did not want. Likewise, Russia could not reduce the peacetime burden of its immense army by creating a trained reserve for wartime call-up. Russia conscripted its soldiers from serfs. As long as the norm was essentially lifelong service, that presented no particular problems. But turning to a small peacetime army supplemented by reserves meant training serfs in the use of arms, then returning them to the countryside and, in effect, slavery. So long as serfdom persisted, Russia was doomed to an unsustainable military burden.

Nicholas's reign was also marked by a lengthy struggle for control of the North Caucasus. The Caucasus had always been a zone of conflict between the Russian, Ottoman, and Iranian empires. In the wake of Nicholas's foreign wars, he faced the challenge of the Caucasus's indigenous inhabitants. In 1801, Russia had annexed the Christian kingdom of Georgia on the south side of the Caucasus Mountains. That left a band of territory on the north slope of the Caucasus between Russia and Georgia in limbo. Between Russia proper to the north and the crest of the Caucasus lay Muslim hill peoples. Until the 1830s, Russia's chief priority was containment: keeping mountain tribes from raiding Russian and Georgian villages. Co-optation of tribal elites and punitive measures kept the north Caucasus quiet until the nature of the threat shifted in the 1820s and 1830s. Muridism, a new religious movement among Caucasus Muslims, turned those fractious peoples into a serious threat. In 1834, an imam named Shamil emerged as leader of a confederation of mountain peoples and a much greater threat to Russian rule. Shamil led a 25-year campaign of resistance to Russian domination.

From the earliest conflicts with the hill peoples, perceptive observers agreed on the basic problem. Russia lacked the manpower to protect peaceful territory and at the same time carry the war into the mountains. Security required garrisons scattered around the north Caucasus, but because there were so many, they were small enough to be overrun and destroyed. The natural protection of forests and hills prevented Russian expeditions from inflicting serious damage on the insurgents. Russian campaigns developed an unfortunate pattern. Russian columns fought their way into the mountains to take a particular stronghold. The mountain fighters, skilled in guerrilla warfare, took a heavy toll on Russian troops, then melted away into the forested hills. The Russians failed to capture Shamil or to make any lasting gains. In 1843, Shamil even turned the table and went on the offensive to seize the region of Avaria and capture Russian strongpoints there.

Mikhail Semyonovich Vorontsov took over as viceroy of the Caucasus in 1844. After initial failures using old tactics, Vorontsov turned to the slow, systematic strangulation of Muslim resistance. His troops cleared forests and built roads to tame the terrain. A systematic policy of resettlement forced hundreds of thousands to relocate to the plains north of the mountains or flee into the Ottoman Empire. Vorontsov's successor Aleksandr Ivanovich Bariantinskii continued the process, consolidating small, vulnerable garrisons into stronger fortresses and freeing troops for campaigns into the mountains. It took years, but the patient counterinsurgency chipped away at Shamil's support. His movement was finally destroyed in 1859, and Shamil himself was captured and sent into internal exile in Russia. The long and costly campaign could only have been managed by an autocratic government, indifferent to its expense in money and lives. The war for the Caucasus did, however, have compensations, providing a ready school for combat even in peacetime. Russian officers regularly rotated through the Caucasus for training.

The Crimean War

The wave of revolutions that swept Europe in 1848 further convinced Nicholas of the danger of instability, leading him to crack down domestically. This succeeded: Russia and Britain were the only two powers to escape upheaval in 1848. He had limited opportunities to use Russian military power against the 1848 revolutions, but did assist the Turks in suppressing revolution in the Danubian Principalities. The most important Russian intervention came in assisting Austria to crush a Hungarian uprising that took half the empire out of Vienna's control. Deeply humiliated by his failure to defeat Hungary himself, Emperor Franz Joseph finally agreed to Russian assistance in spring 1849; 350,000 Russian troops poured into Hungary, restoring the Austrian Empire and withdrawing without incident. Nicholas clearly believed he had accumulated some moral capital. On the contrary, as Austrian chancellor Felix Schwarzenberg correctly predicted, Austria would shock the world with the extent of her ingratitude.

The Crimean War exhibits an extraordinary contrast between the deep forces pushing for war and the comical superficial causes. The long-term problem remained the Ottoman Empire's long, steady decline, a decline that Russia promoted while enjoying its territorial benefits. For a brief time in the 1830s, Russia treated the Ottoman Empire as a protectorate instead of a target, but by the 1840s Nicholas again saw the Ottoman Empire as an arena for expansion. British mistrust over Russian expansionism in the Near East and in central Asia, threatening Britain's colonial empire, grew and flourished, especially after Nicholas broached the subject of a partition of the Ottoman Empire. Turkey's previous wars made it abundantly clear the Turks could not resist Russia alone. Britain, however, feared Russia's march south toward its Indian Empire and the

Mediterranean sea-lanes. In France, the 1848 revolution had concluded with Napoleon's nephew, Louis Napoleon, elected French president. Eager to emulate his uncle's prestige while building support among French Catholics, Louis Napoleon pressured the Turks to allow France a special position as protector of Catholics in the Holy Land, at the expense of Orthodox Christians.

The Holy Land gave ample opportunity for Catholic-Orthodox conflict. Communities of Catholic and Orthodox monks had disputed control of Christian sites for decades, disputes often degenerating into fistfights. Wrestling monks had little to do with power politics, but symbolized a larger question of French or Russian predominance in the Near East. The Ottoman government was caught in-between. Given Russian determination to expand, Turkish determination to resist, and British and French determination to knock back Russian power, any pretext might start a war.

That pretext came in spring 1853 when Aleksandr Sergeevich Menshikov, Russian envoy to the Turks, demanded concessions from the Ottomans, including expanded Orthodox rights in the Holy Land and recognition of Russia as protector for all Orthodox under Ottoman rule. These demands were on their face religious, but had a deeper political meaning: was the Ottoman Empire an independent state or a Russian puppet? Nicholas miscalculated badly, expecting French opposition but British and Austrian neutrality. With British and French backing, the Turks refused these demands. Russia responded on 21 June/3 July 1853 by sending its troops into Moldavia and Wallachia, nominally under Ottoman suzerainty.

The Turks did not immediately declare war in response, instead temporizing while awaiting British and French support. In autumn 1853, the British and French fleets sailed into Turkish waters in preparation for a move into the Black Sea, and the reassured Turks declared war on Russia on 4/16 October 1853. Hoping to avoid European intervention and already in possession of the Danubian Principalities, Nicholas assured the other powers that Russia would avoid offensive action. The Turks had no such scruples and crossed the Danube to attack the Russians occupying Moldavia and Wallachia. The Turks went on the offensive in Transcaucasia, also without success. In the Black Sea, the initial fighting produced the first battle of steamships in history on 5/17 November 1853 when the Russian vessel *Vladimir* captured a Turkish ship.

As indecisive combat on land continued, more important developments took place at sea. A Russian squadron under Pavel Stepanovich Nakhimov trapped a Turkish fleet sheltering under the guns of Sinope, an Ottoman city on the Black Sea. On 18/30 November 1853, Nakhimov attacked the fleet at anchor. Russian exploding shells wreaked havoc on the wooden Turkish ships, sinking or grounding over a dozen. This victory, raising the possibility of complete Russian domination of the Black Sea, provoked the British and French fleets to move into the Black Sea. After Russia rejected an ultimatum to evacuate from Moldavia and Wallachia, Britain and France declared war in March 1854. As in previous Russo-Turkish wars, the greatest danger to Russia was not failure but excessive success.

By May, Russian troops under Ivan Fyodorovich Paskevich were besieging the Turkish fortress of Silistria on the Danube. Paskevich was, however, losing his nerve. His lines of supply and retreat back through Moldavia were long and vulnerable, especially as Austria massed troops along its border. Under pressure from Austria, Russia evacuated the Principalities and, by arrangement with the Turks, Austria occupied them instead. Russian evacuation should have provided an opening to resolve the conflict, for Russian occupation of the Principalities had provoked the Turkish declaration of war in the first place. Instead, Britain and France alike did not want to waste an opportunity to limit Russian power, while Russia saw no need to settle when it had not been defeated on the battlefield.

Britain and France faced a basic strategic problem: from the opposite end of Europe, how could they inflict sufficient pain on Russia to force Nicholas into meaningful concessions? One option was the Baltic Sea. British and French fleets attacked Russian shipping and bombarded ports and fortresses, and the Russian fleet was too weak to leave harbor and resist. While these actions did not induce Sweden to join the war as Britain and France had hoped, they did prove humiliating and forced Nicholas to maintain substantial forces in the north to prevent an amphibious landing. The other option was the Black Sea, where overwhelming British and French naval superiority meant invasion was a possibility anywhere. Britain and France chose to invade the Crimean Peninsula, giving the war its name. Command in the south went to Menshikov, an arrogant and overconfident blowhard whose obnoxious diplomacy helped provoke the war in the first place. Reacting passively to the growing British and French naval presence in the Black Sea, Menshikov failed to improve Crimean fortifications, particularly at the main Russian base of Sevastopol. Though Nicholas attempted to move reinforcements into the Crimea, lack of railroads meant that all troops and supplies inched south at marching speed. It was easier and faster for Britain and France to move troops from London and Paris to the Crimea than for Nicholas to move troops within his own country. By September 1854, Russia had 70,000 soldiers and sailors in the Crimea.

Those 70,000 reveal the extent of the Russian crisis. With potential armed forces of nearly a million men, Russia could spare only 30,000 troops for the Caucasus and 80,000 for the Balkans. Defending Russia's western border against possible Prussian or Austrian intervention while protecting the Russian coast from British naval attack meant Russia simply lacked men. That was only the beginning of Russian problems. Staff work had been neglected for decades, and there were no coherent war plans. Conscripts still served 25–year terms, reduced to 15 under good conditions. Few soldiers who survived even 15 years were in condition to be brought back in wartime, meaning there were few reserves. Russian infantry were armed with muzzleloading smoothbore muskets, not the much more accurate rifles the British and French had available. Russian tactics were still Napoleonic, relying on dense columns that took no account of rapid advances in the lethality of fire. The Russian navy had not rebuilt for steam power and so could not contest possession of the Black Sea. The war on land was primed for Russian disaster.

On 1/13 September 1854, 60,000 British and French troops and some Turkish contingents landed at Evpatoria, north of Sevastopol. Menshikov did not contest these vulnerable landings, contenting himself with concentrating his troops behind the Alma River, midway between Sevastopol and Evpatoria. This was a strong defensive position, with high ground on its southern bank. That defense still required competent command. Menshikov instead left a mile-long gap between the seacoast and the start of his lines, trusting the cliffs on the riverbank to prevent an enemy attack. He placed his 35,000 Russian troops in dense formations close to the river, not on the higher ground close behind. No effort was made to dig trenches or construct earthworks, and Menshikov left his chain of command vague and disordered. He complacently expected to defeat the British and French by counterattacking as they were hit by defensive fire and thrown into disorder crossing the Alma.

On 8/20 September, the Battle of Alma began with a slow, methodical morning advance by 55,000 allies, the French to the west, the British inland. As British and French naval vessels bombarded Russian positions, French troops speedily worked their way along the seacoast, crossed the Alma, and scaled the undefended cliffs on the south bank. By the time Menshikov knew what had happened, the French were firmly in place on high ground overlooking the Russian left flank and pushing artillery pieces up ravines from the river to enfilade the entire Russian position. Russian troops found themselves under immense pressure all along their front, as their muskets were outranged by more modern allied rifles. Russian troops took casualties from allied rifle fire at distances of more than half a mile, outdistancing even Russian artillery. The entire Russian left caved in, swinging back away from the seacoast and French high ground. On the Russian right, the slowly advancing British took heavy losses from Russian artillery until British riflemen creeping through vineyards along the river silenced Russian guns by long-range fire at their crews. By mid-afternoon, the Russian right wing had collapsed under repeated British assaults, though it withdrew in reasonably good order. A lack of British and French cavalry prevented the defeat from turning into a rout. An energetic pursuit could have captured Sevastopol, for the Russians lacked any organized troops between the Alma and their base.

The Siege of Sevastopol

Sevastopol lay on the south bank of an inlet from the Black Sea, clustered around a small bay and defended from seaborne attack by 500 guns on both sides of the inlet. Its landward defenses were much shoddier. The city had been left undefended during the battle of the Alma, but the defeated Russians flooded back into it. Panicked at the thought of a seaborne attack, Menshikov scuttled ships to block the inlet's entrance. He then, however, decided to abandon the base, moving the army inland on 12/24 September and leaving the city's defense to half-completed fortifications, a small garrison, and sailors of the Black Sea Fleet. With Menshikov's flight, command went to the inspired leadership of Vladimir Alekseevich Kornilov, ably seconded by Nakhimov.

The British and French were unsure how to attack Sevastopol, whether to move directly south from the Alma to seize the northern shore of the inlet first, to circle east to attack Sevastopol from the south, or to take the city from the sea. Deciding on the southern approach, British forces skirted around Sevastopol to the east to seize the inlet of Balaklava, several miles south of Sevastopol, as an advance base.

Kornilov had only days between Menshikov's exit and the arrival of the British and French, but the allies did not press their advantage with an immediate attack on Sevastopol. Together with the base's small civilian population and 25,000 soldiers and sailors left behind, Kornilov improvised a remarkable network of fortifications ringing the city. Bombardment from land and sea began on 5/17 October, with 100,000 shells flying in a single day. The ferocity of the artillery died down over the next few days, and allied efforts to pound the city into submission failed. Kornilov was killed by a cannon ball, and command of the defense went to Nakhimov. The allies sapped trenches closer to the bastions defending Sevastopol's southern, landward side to take by assault what they did not destroy by bombardment. At the same time, and for the remainder of the siege, the Russian defenders constantly repaired ongoing damage to their siegeworks from artillery bombardment and expanded their network of trenches, foxholes, and strongpoints. Losing hundreds of men every day of the bombardment, the Russian garrison received reinforcements and shipped out wounded while maintaining an active defense.

The feckless Menshikov attempted to relieve beleaguered Sevastopol through an attack on Balaklava, the British base south of Sevastopol. Without waiting to concentrate his forces, on 13/25 October Menshikov threw three columns of troops against the redoubts protecting the approaches to Balaklava. Routing the Turks holding those works, the Russians then ran up against British infantry and cavalry holding a second line of defenses and failed to make further progress. Through miscommunication, British light cavalry were drawn into a hopeless attack, the fabled "Charge of the Light Brigade." Russian artillery and infantry fire slaughtered them. This tactical success, however, did not enable Menshikov's men to reach the British base or break the siege.

The allies split their 70,000 troops in two. One half concentrated on Sevastopol, keeping up a periodic bombardment while digging mines under the Russian position. The other half screened the city from Menshikov's relief troops. Russian reinforcements trickling into the Crimea gave Menshikov a substantial edge in numbers over the allies, an edge he needed to use before the British and French besiegers took Sevastopol's defending bastions and captured the city. Forced into action by Nicholas despite his own deep reluctance, Menshikov decided to attack a British-held ridge east of Sevastopol, just south of the end of the inlet on which the fortress sat. Menshikov's goal, though he doubted his chances, was to grab high ground east of Sevastopol to lever the British and French out of their positions ringing the base.

In the Battle of Inkerman on 24 October/5 November 1854, 60,000 Russian troops rushed the high ground east of Sevastopol in uncoordinated masses from the northwest and the northeast. Though enjoying surprise, the attacks ran into accurate British rifle fire and took heavy casualties, made worse by organizational chaos. Though the British were under heavy pressure, French reinforcements from the south restored the situation. The bloody fighting achieved nothing except demoralizing Menshikov and his hapless field force. After this, there seemed little hope of saving Sevastopol. In February 1855, well aware that his bungling was winning him political enemies with every passing day, Menshikov tried to salvage the situation by another offensive. On 5/17 February 1855 he attacked Evpatoria, the initial allied landing site. Though it was defended by Turks, who had not performed well at Balaklava, the Russian attack failed miserably.

To make matters worse, Russia's diplomatic position was declining rapidly. At the end of 1854 Austria joined the anti-Russian coalition, though it did not intervene militarily. At the beginning of 1855, tiny Piedmont-Sardinia joined the alliance, though in pursuit of European influence, not from antipathy toward Russia. Confronted by defeat after defeat, and worn down by the strain of his responsibilities as autocrat, Nicholas died on 18 February/2 March 1855. Before his death, he directed his son and heir Alexander II to dismiss Menshikov. Mikhail Dmitrievich Gorchakov, an aged veteran of the Napoleonic Wars, took over as commander in chief in the Crimea. He continued to funnel soldiers into Sevastopol, as the Anglo-French net around the base was never complete.

By June 1855, allied trenches were close enough to Russian bastions to make an assault conceivable. The French and British planned a major attack on Sevastopol's eastern perimeter for 6/18 June 1855, the anniversary of Waterloo. The predawn attack was detected by Russian outposts and defeated by morning. Only one bastion was temporarily captured by the French, and it was recaptured just as quickly. The boost to Russian morale proved counterproductive and temporary. It raised false hopes the war might still be won, and only days later Nakhimov was mortally wounded by a sniper's bullet.

Though Alexander harbored little hope for victory, he did not wish to begin his reign with ignominious surrender. With deep misgivings, Gorchakov and his commanders agreed to another attack on the allied ring east of Sevastopol. This assault was directed at the Fediukhin Heights, an isolated mass of high ground physically separate from the plateau on which the British and French shielded Sevastopol, so even Russian success would be pointless. Gorchakov's ambivalence extended to his organization of the attack, which was extraordinarily indecisive and timid. On the morning of 4/16 August 1855, four Russian infantry divisions in succession and under fire crossed swamps, a river, a canal, and assaulted dug-in French troops on the heights. Predictably, they were shot down with no discernible result, losing 8,000 killed or wounded.

This desperate Russian attack convinced the allies victory was close, and the bombardment of Sevastopol intensified. Ammunition shortages meant that the Russian defenders could not respond. Expecting an epic final assault at night, the Russians were taken by surprise by the massive French storm at midday on 27 August/8 September 1855. On the southeastern side, using surprise, the French fought their way into a key bastion on the Malakhov Heights, from which repeated and bloody Russian attacks could not expel them. Other French assaults on the southwestern defenses achieved little, as did British attacks on the southern defenses. Those failures were irrelevant, for French possession of the Malakhov bastion made the entire defense of Sevastopol untenable. After a day that left 25,000 killed or wounded on both sides, though, the allies were in no position to press their advantage. This allowed Gorchakov to evacuate the remainder of the Sevastopol garrison by boat and pontoon bridge across to the northern side of the inlet. The yearlong siege of Sevastopol killed and wounded 170,000 men, not including the tens of thousands the British and French lost to disease.

With Sevastopol fallen, there was no longer any way of denying Russia's utter defeat, but peace negotiations seemed hopeless. Only substantial victories against the Turks in the Caucasus gave any leverage at the bargaining table. On-and-off negotiations since mid-1854 had made no progress. An Austrian ultimatum at the end of 1855 warning of war unless Russia capitulated finally forced Alexander to accept terms. The settlement was not unduly harsh on Russia itself, though it produced a substantial setback in Russian influence over the Ottoman Empire and in the Balkans. The demilitarization of the Black Sea deprived Russia of its Black Sea Fleet and prevented any naval defense against future interventions like the invasion of the Crimea. Far more serious than the penalties of the peace settlement was the destruction, for Russians and foreigners alike, of the illusion of Russian military power. Something had to change.

CHAPTER 9

Reform and Recovery

Russia's defeat created a clear understanding among its elites that the empire required reform to survive. Russia's inability to defend its own territory, despite having the largest army in Europe, made economic, political, and military modernization a necessity. By nature conservative, Tsar Alexander II was a reluctant reformer, but reality left him no choice. In the aftermath of the Crimean War, he began far-reaching efforts known collectively as the Great Reforms. Among other things, Russia's vulnerability required careful and restrained diplomacy. Despite France's participation in the Crimean coalition, Russia generally cooperated with France in foreign policy, reserving its real enmity for Britain and especially Austria, given what Russia saw as Austria's lack of gratitude for Russian assistance in pacifying Hungary. In 1859, France and Austria became embroiled in war in northern Italy. Russia's attempt to mobilize its troops to pressure the Austrians was a failure, deepening commitment to military reform.

The most fundamental of the Great Reforms was the emancipation of the serfs. A growing consensus among Russia's elites recognized the moral wrong of holding people as property, but more material considerations forced action. The new tsar Alexander II alluded to the possibility of serfdom abolishing itself from below—by bloody revolt. Russia's economic modernization required a free and mobile labor force, incompatible with half of Russia's rural population being bound to the land. In 1861, without a shot being fired and two years before Abraham Lincoln's Emancipation Proclamation, Alexander freed Russia's serfs. Other reforms followed over the next two decades: notably, elected local governments and an overhaul of the court system.

In addition to social backwardness, the Crimean War revealed a concrete problem of infrastructure: Russia's inadequate railroad net. This forced Russia to garrison all its vulnerable frontiers, since it could not react to crises with transporting troops by rail. It was nearly impossible to provision and reinforce forces in the field. While the Russian government recognized the need for railroads, precarious finances made this difficult to achieve. Moreover, rail lines that made strategic sense (running from population centers to frontiers) conflicted with rail lines that made economic sense (from grain-growing regions to ports).

Miliutin's Reforms

Military defeat required military reform, and emancipation made it possible. Informed observers agreed Russia's antiquated system of conscription was incompatible with military effectiveness. Other European armies had moved to a system of universal short service with large reserves. Under this, most men served for a period of two or three years, followed by reserve service with periodic refresher training and call-up in wartime. This provided a smaller and less expensive peacetime army, but a mass army when needed. In Russia, by contrast, service for conscripted peasants was long: initially for life, later reduced to 25 years, and by the Crimean War, in practice, to 15 years. This meant a large, expensive peacetime establishment and few able-bodied veterans in reserve. Until emancipation, however, there was no alternative. No Russian regime could train large numbers of serfs in the use of weaponry and subsequently return them to the countryside, or alternatively, free huge numbers of serfs as they cycled through a universal-service army. Once the decision to free the serfs had been made, though, new possibilities opened.

Alexander II entrusted his military reforms to Dmitrii Alekseevich Miliutin. Born into an impoverished noble family and trained as an artillery officer, Miliutin enjoyed a distinguished career even before his 1861 appointment as War Minister. He was an early graduate of the Nikolaev General Staff Academy and taught there, served on a politically delicate investigative commission dealing with the Crimean War, and fought in the Caucasus. Miliutin also had a well-developed professional interest in military statistics, a field that became a key conduit for science and rational planning into Russian military affairs. His Caucasus experience of unconventional warfare honed his appreciation of decentralization, flexibility, and initiative, qualities notably lacking in the Crimea.

In the five years before Miliutin's appointment, little had been done to repair the broken Russian army. Russia's bankruptcy from the Crimean War had trimmed the army's size, but that was liquidation, not reform. Soldiers were simply discharged and sent home. The only signs of hope came from the military press, beginning with the navy. Konstantin Nikolaevich, Naval Minister and younger brother of Alexander II, created an atmosphere of free and open discussion of reform, using the navy's official journal as an arena for debate. Even before his appointment, Miliutin promoted a similar forum for the army. As a result, ideas were plentiful; only implementation was lacking. One difficulty was the association of reform with revolution. Indeed, Miliutin's key associate Nikolai Nikolaevich Obruchev, a central figure in the military press and later in Russian war planning, had extensive revolutionary ties.

In January 1862, two months after taking office, Miliutin presented the tsar an ambitious reform agenda. Though Alexander was uneasy with many specifics of Miliutin's program, he trusted his subordinate. Miliutin enjoyed 20 years of backing as War Minister to push through his reforms against substantial conservative opposition. His military reforms were temporarily derailed by another Polish uprising in 1863. This was less serious than the 1830 rebellion, but still required substantial effort to quell. The Crimean coalition of France, Britain, and Austria did not unite to aid the Poles, in part because Britain was preoccupied with the consequences of the American Civil War, and France with intervention in Mexico. Prussia cooperated in suppression of the uprising, a favor repaid later in the decade.

The Polish insurrection did give a boost to military reform by proving the worth of military districts (*voennye okrugi*), an experiment introduced in western frontier provinces in 1862. In August 1864, additional military districts were created in central Russia. Before this reform, Russia's armies and corps carried large administrative bureaucracies with them. Indeed, the Field Army on the western frontier had acted as a separate War Ministry of its own, directly subordinate to the tsar. The new military districts removed the burden of administration from field commanders. Instead, the reform handed mundane administrative duties to the military district, which acted as a war ministry in miniature. Field formations received supplies and personnel from the district and focused their attention on training and preparation for war. Armies and corps, which previously handled this administrative burden, were simply dissolved, leaving the division as the key tactical unit. In event of war, armies and corps would be reconstituted from the military district staff.

Miliutin's initial reforms thus centralized control in the War Ministry. In addition to removing the separate authority of the Field Army, Miliutin firmly subordinated all staff work to himself. Instead of a separate and independent General Staff for war planning, he created a Main Staff under himself, dealing with personnel questions and containing within it a General Staff for war planning. Miliutin's motivation here was political: he wanted a single person, the War Minister, as the conduit for all information to the tsar and all decisions from the tsar. At the same time, he decentralized the administrative burden by passing it from the War Ministry in St. Petersburg to the military districts. The net result was a substantial reduction in administrative personnel. Eliminating the armies and corps with their duplicated functions released hundreds of officers, many of whom resented their displacement. Efficiency increased greatly, as mundane questions no longer routinely went to St. Petersburg for resolution. The military districts proved so effective that their essential function remained intact through the final decades of the imperial and the Soviet period as well.

Miliutin sought to improve Russian equipment, which had been so poor in the Crimea. This faced two serious obstacles. First, funding was short in light of Russia's ongoing financial crisis. Second, technology was evolving quickly, making arms obsolete as soon as they reached the troops. In 1857, the Russian army began replacing its antiquated muskets with muzzle-loading rifled weapons, then converted to a series of breech-loading rifles from the end of the 1860s. The slow conversion meant that by the Russo-Turkish War, Russia had multiple models of rifles in service. Matters were just as complicated in the slow transition to rifled, breech-loading artillery.

In 1866, Prussia defeated Austria in a quick war and then in 1870–1871 defeated France in the Franco-Prussian War, creating a unified German Empire. Russia repaid Prussian assistance in the Polish insurrection by pressuring Austria to keep out of the Franco-Prussian War. Russia took advantage of the upheaval to reassert its right to a navy in the Black Sea, regaining what it had lost after the Crimean War. Prussia's victory not only demonstrated the importance of Russia's continuing shift to rifled, breech-loading weaponry, but also the superiority of Prussia's short-service army backed by substantial reserves. Miliutin's reforms gained additional political traction as a result.

It took 12 years for this central element of Miliutin's reforms to overcome political resistance. On New Year's Day 1874, Alexander II promulgated a new universal service law. Ever since Aleksei Mikhailovich began conscription in the 1600s, military service had been a collective responsibility, with a given community of peasant households obligated to produce a recruit. The new system made military service the personal obligation of every male. Purchasing exemptions or producing substitutes was no longer an option. Though the state might not have every individual serve, the responsibility to serve remained: six years of active duty, followed by nine years in the reserves, though in practice the active term was much shorter. Russia's privileged classes had fought this tooth and nail, and only Prussia's victory finally overcame opposition. The ostensibly universal obligation had many loopholes. There were substantial premiums for education: university graduates had their term reduced to a mere six months. Certain ethnic groups, particularly Muslims, were excused from service altogether. Even more, the army could not afford to feed or train an entire year's class. It was lucky to manage a quarter of the age cohort actually serving.

As elsewhere in Europe, universal military service had important political consequences. If all men were equally obliged to serve the state, then the state had a commensurate obligation to serve all men equally. While this did not bring universal suffrage to Russia, it did reduce the prevalence of corporal punishment. It also produced widespread education in basic literacy for soldiers with clear benefits for training and military effectiveness. Literacy rates among Russian soldiers went from 10 percent before the Great Reforms to nearly 33 percent afterward. The Russian army, like its Soviet successor, deserves much of the credit for teaching Russia to read.

A larger and a better-trained army required more officers, and the Russian army was desperately short. Miliutin overcame noble resistance to expand the pool of officers. Before Miliutin's reforms, a majority of the army's officer corps, short-staffed as it was, lacked formal military education. A quarter to a third came through technical schools or cadet corps (better at training etiquette than military subjects). Many of the rest were junior officers (*iunkery*) who had simply passed an exam. While Miliutin wished to abolish the aristocratic cadet corps, he settled for limiting their influence, converting most into military gymnasia. He built a network of junker schools for those already possessing civilian education. These soon produced the bulk of Russia's officer corps. Though many of their students were noble, the junker schools provided a pathway to advancement for non-nobles, who swamped the noble element with sheer numbers by World War I.

As a military intellectual himself, Miliutin tried to invigorate the intellectual life of the officer corps. He strengthened the rigor of the Nikolaev General Staff Academy, introducing research projects and military debates. Though the academy developed an unfortunate tendency to overtheoretization, it undoubtedly improved the officer corps and became a vital means of mobility. By 1914, a majority of corps and division commanders were academy graduates. The danger, though, was that General Staff officers were a small fraction of the whole—perhaps one thousand in an overall officer corps of almost 40,000. Staff work built grandiose war plans, but neglected practical improvements to the army's performance in the field. Indeed, line officers resented General Staff officers for their intellectual pretensions and lack of practical experience. In addition, the Staff's preoccupation with technical aspects of war planning tended to blind it to the political realities of warfare, something more apparent when Miliutin's reforms were put to the test.

The Russo-Turkish War, 1877–1878

The test of Miliutin's reforms came in the Russo-Turkish War of 1877–1878. That grew out of an 1875 Balkan rebellion against Turkish rule. Some

European powers wished to impose reforms on the Ottomans to halt the violence, but the British government opposed interference in Ottoman affairs. In 1876, Serbia and Montenegro went to war against Turkey in defense of their fellow Slavs. Russian nationalism in the late 1800s emphasized pan-Slavic themes of ethnic solidarity under Russian leadership, and the developing popular press recounted Turkish crimes and heroic Slavic resistance, boosting sympathy for the Balkan rebels. Large numbers of Russians (including military officers) volunteered for Serbian service during the war, but the Serbs were soundly defeated nonetheless. Widespread reports of Ottoman atrocities soured European opinion on the Turks, even in Britain. In Russia, the tsar's government came under increasing pressure to do what it wished to do anyway: aid fellow Orthodox Slavs. Austria and Russia, freed by the British public's antipathy to Turkey, came to a secret understanding. Austria would stand aside while Russia went to war against Turkey, receiving in return Russia's permission to occupy Bosnia-Herzegovina.

Russia declared war on the Ottomans on 12/24 April 1877. The basic conceptions of the war, drawn up by Miliutin's collaborator Obruchev, envisaged a rapid drive south through Romania, across the Danube, through the Balkan Mountains, finishing in Constantinople. Speed was key. A quick victory was the only way to prevent a repetition of the Crimean debacle: a coalition of European powers protecting the Ottomans against Russia. That in turn meant Russia had to devote its main effort to the Balkans; Transcaucasia offered little chance of rapid success, though it might tie down Turkish troops. As in the Crimean War, Russia's manpower on paper far exceeded what it could effectively employ. As a result of Miliutin's reforms, Russia had 700,000 soldiers on active duty and 500,000 ready reserves. It conducted two partial mobilizations before the declaration of war and secured agreement with Romania for Russian deployment on and through its territory. Despite this, garrisoning Russia's vast spaces meant it could muster only 250,000 for the Balkan theater. The Ottomans had 400,000 troops on active duty or ready reserve, but mustered only 200,000 for the Balkans.

Like the American Civil War and the Franco-Prussian War before it, the Russo-Turkish War illustrated the problem created by increased firepower. Modern artillery and breech-loading rifles meant frontal attacks were suicidal. While attacks by massed infantry across open ground had been costly in the Napoleonic Wars, they often succeeded. Troops with breech-loading rifles, however, could fire a dozen rounds a minute with reasonable accuracy to distances of up to a kilometer. This created a terrible problem. Wars still needed to be fought, but it was unclear how to achieve any result besides mass slaughter when attacking troops with modern weapons.

Geography dictated the Russian plan. Since the Crimean War had crippled Russia's Black Sea Fleet, Russian troops had to stay well inland. Reaching Constantinople required first crossing the Danube, then penetrating the Balkan Mountains. The Turkish plan was essentially passive, relying on those natural obstacles, its troops' skill in positional defense, and a cluster of four fort complexes between the Black Sea, the Danube River, and the Balkan Mountains. The Russian high command, led by the tsar's brother Grand Duke Nikolai Nikolaevich, decided to outflank those fortresses inland.

The crossing of the Danube was a triumph. A reinforced infantry division under military theorist and educator Mikhail Ivanovich Dragomirov carried out a rapid crossing at Svishtov on the night of 14–15/26–27 June 1877. After the first of three waves of assault boats made the crossing, Dragomirov's small unit commanders quickly expanded their beachhead, keeping the Ottoman defenders off-balance while the balance of the division landed, followed by the better part of a corps. Once two pontoon bridges were built, the Russian army poured across to the southern bank. Pushing south as rapidly as possible, a small detachment under Iosif Vladimirovich Gurko slipped through a narrow, unguarded pass in the Balkan Mountains. Gurko then moved west behind the Balkan range to attack a Turkish blocking position at the much more important Shipka Pass. After Russian assaults from both the north and the south, the Turks abandoned their defenses. The Russians were now past the best barriers the Turks had, 200 miles from Constantinople with months of good campaigning weather left.

Russia failed to take advantage of this. While Russian detachments raided south of the Balkan Mountains, the Ottoman government rushed reinforcements into Thrace to block approaches to the capital. The Russian high command also feared that an immediate drive south might be cut off by Turkish pincers converging between the Danube and the Balkan Mountains. The Russian army thus focused its attention on consolidating its position south of the Danube, preparing for a later exploitation of the breach it had forced in the Balkan Mountains. Some troops were tied down defending the mountain pass at Shipka against vigorous Turkish attacks. To the east, an eventual total of four Russian corps were delegated to screen or eliminate the Turkish fortifications threatening the Russian left flank. The eternal Russian problem of geography had reappeared. Operating far from home, any Russian push south to the Ottoman capital might be isolated by Turkish forces still operating north of the Balkan Mountains on the Russian left and right flanks.

Protecting the Russian right flank proved far more difficult and bogged down the Russian advance for months. After taking the Turkish stronghold of Nikopol on the Danube, the Russians moved southwest to occupy the road junction of Plevna. Unknown to the Russians, 30,000 Turkish troops had left the Serbian border to push east toward the Russians. On 7/19 July 1877, Turkish lead elements moved into Plevna with just hours to spare. The Turks dug in on a line of hills northeast of the town to prepare for the Russian advance. The Russian brigade sent to Plevna marched straight into Turkish artillery fire and deployed to prepare for an attack the next morning. The Russian brigade attacked at dawn on 8/20 July without artillery preparation. Reconnaissance might have discovered the lack of Turkish defenses south and west of Plevna. Instead, three Russian regiments launched frontal assaults across open ground, two from the north, one from the east. The Russian attackers took terrible losses, reaching 50 percent casualties, and failed to crack the Turkish defenses, demonstrating just how deadly modern firepower could be.

The Russian command responded by sending a full corps to Plevna and repeated the assault ten days later. The Turks made good use of the delay to turn their improvised positions into elaborate earthworks, but still only north and east of Plevna. As in the first battle, Russian attacks failed to take advantage of the incomplete Turkish defenses. While the Russians did employ artillery to prepare their assaults, it was ineffective. The Russian main attack fell on a series of redoubts east of Plevna, with a secondary assault on a hilltop artillery battery southeast of the town. In a comedy of errors, the commanders of the two Russian detachments each believed the other to be attacking and rushed to the assault before preparations were complete. As in the first battle, Russian infantrymen were slaughtered as they advanced across open ground toward prepared positions and achieved nothing. These twin defeats at Plevna forced a halt on demoralized Russian troops. The Turks were lodged west of the Russians at Plevna, in effect an improvised fortress. Four Turkish fortresses remained to the east. Ferocious Turkish pressure continued against Russian defenders of the Balkan passes. Until Plevna was reduced, the Russian advance south stalled.

Romanian troops joined the Russians in the third battle of Plevna, bringing the total allied forces to 80,000 against 35,000 defenders, though creating serious political disputes over command of the combined forces. The allies began a lengthy bombardment on 26 August/7 September, hoping the damage inflicted would make up for the lack of surprise. The culminating assault, hindered by mud and heavy fog, came on 30 August/ 11 September. The Romanians massed east of Plevna, supported by a Russian brigade, and attacked the redoubts that had been the focus of the second battle. They had learned less than the Russians and took enormous casualties. Despite heavy loss of life, the joint force temporarily wedged itself into the Turkish fortifications, but was eventually forced out. To the south of Plevna, a Russian push failed to breach the Turkish defenses. Only a diversionary attack had much success. The charismatic and dashing General Mikhail Dmitrievich Skobelev attacked from the south-

southwest, feeding additional regiments whenever his attack faltered. Though his troops managed to reach Plevna itself, the general failure in the other sectors forced them to withdraw.

After three failures, the Russian command decided on a siege. Throughout the first three battles, the Turks pushed supplies and reinforcements into Plevna, but the Russians now cut off all access. After four months, running short of ammunition, the Plevna garrison made a desperate attempt to break out through Russian lines at dawn on 28 November/ 10 December. After the breakout failed, the wounded Turkish commander surrendered his 40,000 soldiers.

The prolonged struggle for Plevna cost Russia five months, though it did lead Serbia to rejoin the war. While the right flank of a Russian push through the Balkan Mountains was now secure, conventional military thinking held it was folly to force a mountain passage in the depths of winter. With 500,000 soldiers now in the theater, however, the Russian command believed that a winter offensive, though risky, offered surprise and the possibility of quick victory before European intervention on behalf of the Turks.

The winter offensive opened on 13/25 December 1877 at the western end of the Balkan Mountains stretching across Bulgaria. By contrast to the narrower passes farther east, a substantial stretch of easier terrain northeast of Sofia allowed Russian troops to pour through. A small detachment liberated Sofia while the remainder turned east, unhinging Turkish defenses all along the southern slopes of the Balkans. A second Russian column pushed through the Troian Pass farther east on 23 December/4 January. Finally, in fierce fighting from 24–29 December/ 5–10 January, the Russians broke out of the foothold at the south end of Shipka Pass. With 165,000 troops across the Balkans, the Russians pursued the Turks southeast toward Constantinople. Snow prevented the Russians from catching the Turks before they rallied at Philippopolis (now Plovdiv). Three days of battle (3–5/15–17 January 1878) destroyed the last Turkish troops before Constantinople.

With exhausted troops and a British fleet in the Turkish Straits, the Russians did not risk a wider war by entering Constantinople. The Turks were still decisively beaten and had to accept harsh terms. While direct Russian gains from the Treaty of San Stefano were limited, Russia gained a great deal indirectly. San Stefano created a huge Bulgarian state, extending even to the Aegean Sea, while granting additional territory to Serbia and Montenegro. Russia's Slavic allies would dominate the Balkans and wall off Austrian influence. Austria had not signed off on Russian aggrandizement on this scale, and the British government was equally unwilling to see Russian power so close to the Mediterranean. Rather than going to war, the European powers settled the dispute at the Congress of Berlin, using Germany as a neutral arbitrator. The Congress cut Bulgaria down to a fraction of its San Stefano size and granted Austria the right to occupy and administer Bosnia-Herzegovina. This maintained the Austrian-Russian balance in the Balkans, while substantially weakening the Ottomans. Russian overreaching produced political gains far smaller than it had hoped.

Despite diplomatic defeat, the Russian military had reason to be pleased with the outcome of the war. Its overall performance had been quite good. The most fundamental problem the war revealed was not a particularly Russian one, but one of warfare in the industrial age. Battle after battle revealed the lethality of modern weaponry, particularly when employed from fortified positions against infantry in the open. Russia had fought the war with a doctrine that encouraged tight formations and bayonet charges, and, in a way, Russia's successes prevented it from addressing the problem. In smaller actions around Plevna, clearing towns and outposts to carry out the siege, Russian troops had in fact taken Turkish fortifications by frontal attack. The lesson drawn was that even in the modern age, men could overcome technology with valor. Less attention was paid to artillery preparation, covering fire, concealing terrain, and field entrenching, just as useful as raw bravery to successful assaults. These failings should not be overdrawn. Russian doctrine did accept the need for open, dispersed formations and firepower. Still, the emphasis was mastering Napoleonic warfare, not understanding how technology made that warfare obsolete.

Imperial Warfare

Russian imperial expansion east through Siberia to the Pacific had begun under Ivan the Terrible. In the nineteenth century, that expansion changed direction, moving south into Central Asia. First to come under Russian control were the nomadic hordes of what is now Kazakhstan. By the 1840s, Russia had solidified its control over the Kazakh steppe and was in regular contact with the settled oasis societies of Turkestan farther south: Kokand, Bukhara, and Khiva. Protecting trade and preempting British moves into central Asia from India led to the establishment of Russian forts in the region. From the beginnings of Russian expansion in central Asia, Russian troops were never seriously challenged by the relatively primitive and poorly organized central Asian opposition, nomadic or settled. The problem instead was getting Russian troops to central Asia at all, given the region's formidable natural defenses.

Though the Crimean War temporarily delayed Russian advance, the American Civil War (1861–1865) raised the stakes. By interrupting the supply of cotton to textile manufacturers around the world, the Civil War made central Asian cotton especially vital. When the British protested Russian pressure on the northern approaches to their colonial empire in India, Russian Foreign Minister Alexander Mikhailovich Gorchakov argued that a civilized society like Russia had no choice when faced with barbarian raids from beyond its frontier but to push that frontier outward, bringing order with it. Diplomatic cover or not, Russian expansion was quick. The Russian commander Mikhail Grigorevich Cherniaev, acting under secret orders, took Tashkent in 1865. In 1867, Russia established Konstantin Petrovich Kaufman as governor-general in Turkestan, with his capital at Tashkent. By 1868, he had taken Samarkand and established Bukhara and Kokand alike as Russian protectorates. Khiva, surrounded by protective deserts, followed in 1873. Conquest did not mean pacification. An anti-Russian uprising in Kokand in 1875 met a crushing defeat, ending in the abolition of the Kokand khanate and its full incorporation into the Russian Empire. Skobelev led the ruthless suppression.

The only remaining independent people in central Asia, the Turcomans, lived east of the Caspian Sea and south of the Aral Sea. Skobelev, returned from the Russo-Turkish War, led their conquest. After a carefully planned expedition, he besieged the Turcoman fortress of Geok-Tepe, just north of the Iranian border, with 7,000 men. After his two attacking columns stormed into Geok-Tepe through holes blown in the walls, the Turcoman defense collapsed and the slaughter began. Thousands of Turcomans, combatant or not, were killed in storm and pursuit. The conquest of central Asia was complete.

In military terms, Alexander II's reign was a qualified success. The Russian army was in far better shape to defend Russia and promote Russian interests than it had been after the Crimean War. Though the Russo-Turkish War revealed substantial remaining shortcomings, it had nonetheless been a victory, and central Asia was conquered with relative ease. Alexander's general reforms must be judged the same way. In moral terms alone, his abolition of serfdom without a shot fired is a remarkable achievement. It still left many social problems unsolved, and much of Russia's intelligentsia remained alienated from the Russian state. Russia was still an autocracy, there was no mechanism for Russian society to participate in national government, and the peasants were still desperately poor. Some alienated intelligentsia turned to revolution, and some of those to terrorism. People's Will, one terrorist organization, succeeded in 1881 in killing Alexander in St. Petersburg with a bomb. Russia's era of reform was over.

CHAPTER 10

The Russo-Japanese War

After Alexander II's 1881 assassination, he was succeeded by his son Alexander III, and then in 1894 by his grandson Nicholas II. A conservative reformer was followed by a strong reactionary then, worst of all, a weak reactionary. After his father's assassination, Alexander III oversaw the annihilation, albeit temporary, of revolutionary parties in Russia. An enormously strong bear of a man, with an imposing physical presence, Alexander stopped reform in its tracks. While he left most of his father's reforms intact, he reversed the tentative opening of intellectual life that had been a key component. Alexander III died relatively young in 1894 and, as a result, had not trained his much weaker son Nicholas II in statecraft. Though Nicholas was pious and decent, he was wavering and indecisive. Indeed, his chief commitment, other than to his family and God, was to maintaining inviolate the autocratic power he inherited from his father. As a result, he was unable to formulate and impose a coherent political program, and at the same time he was unwilling to allow a prime minister or cabinet to do it for him.

After the relative success of the Russian army in the Russo-Turkish War of 1877–1878, the Russo-Japanese War of 1904–1905 showed how much further it had to go. It combined remarkable examples of individual endurance and heroism with staggering levels of official incompetence. As in the Russo-Turkish War, Russia's failings were in part the result of the changing nature of warfare, not Russian shortcomings. All powers wrestled with the problems created by technology. The war saw the large-scale introduction of the technologies that brought World War I to a stalemate and stymied every European army's efforts to manage modern war. Rifles with multishot magazines, machine guns, barbed wire, and quick-firing artillery made the battlefield a deadlier place for Russians and Japanese alike. The growing scale of warfare in time, space, and manpower presented challenges the Japanese mastered only marginally better than the Russians. The war brought with it revolution, presenting Russia in 1905 with dual challenges: rebuilding domestic order and reforming its army to deal with the manifest failures revealed by the war.

Origins

The long-term origins of the war lay in Russia's expansion east and Japan's expansion on the Asian mainland. Russia had crossed the Pacific to establish a presence in Alaska and down the west coast of North America, but had long abandoned those projects by the end of the 1800s. It had, however, won Chinese acquiescence in 1860 to extending Russian control in Asia south to the mouth of the Amur River, where the city of Vladivostok ("Rule the East") was founded. Painful negotiations with Japan awarded Sakhalin Island to Russia and the Kuriles to Japan.

The chief remaining Russo-Japanese dispute was over Manchuria, resource-rich northeastern China. In 1894–1895, Japan won a crushing victory in a brief war with China. In addition to winning Taiwan and establishing a protectorate over Korea, Japan claimed the Liaodong Peninsula, northwest of Korea. Diplomatic pressure, led by Russia, forced Japan to surrender the peninsula. Russia later established Port Arthur at its tip as the main base for its Pacific Fleet. Russia then compounded this insult by building its Trans-Siberian Railway, begun in 1891, through Manchuria. This railway, linking Moscow to Vladivostok, was a direct challenge to Japanese influence. The fact that it went through Manchuria, rather than skirting Manchuria on Russian territory, only made matters worse.

Japan attempted to head off confrontation by negotiating a deal establishing mutual spheres of influence. These attempts failed, in large part through the Russian government's mismanagement. Russian elites had deeply conflicted views of Asia, seeing it simultaneously as a terrible threat, the "yellow peril," and at the same time as an extraordinary opportunity for Russian expansion. Tsar Nicholas II himself dismissed any possibility that Japanese "monkeys," as he termed them, threatened Russia or deserved to be dealt with as equals. In fact, Japan had obtained the best advice in the world in building a modern army and navy: Britain at sea, Germany on land. After Japan established an alliance with Britain in 1902, it felt it had diplomatic cover for a showdown with Russia.

On 24 January/6 February 1904, Japan broke off negotiations with Russia and prepared a surprise attack on Port Arthur. The Japanese plan was well conceived and aggressive. Simultaneous attacks on the Russian Pacific Fleet and Japanese landings in Korea and southern Manchuria would establish a mainland foothold, permitting reinforcement for a final battle to expel the Russians from Manchuria altogether. Despite Nicholas's dismissal of the Japanese, his Far Eastern defenses were in no condition for war. The Russian Pacific Fleet at Port Arthur, seven battleships

The Russo-Japanese War

and supporting vessels, was utterly unprepared. On the night of 26–27 January/8–9 February 1904, a squadron of Japanese ships launched a torpedo attack on the battleships at anchor. Enormously fortunate, the Russian fleet had only two battleships damaged. The main Japanese fleet continued the next day with an ineffective exchange of gunfire. Despite indecisive results, the Japanese were able to blockade Russia's Pacific Fleet inside Port Arthur, leaving it unable to interfere with Japanese landings in Korea. After the Russian flagship was sunk by a mine in a brief sortie, further attempts to escape had no success.

Russia's strategic position was dismal. The Trans-Siberian Railway linking Russia's heartland to the Far East was broken at Lake Baikal. In the interests of economy, the railroad had not been extended around the shores of the lake, meaning troops and supplies traveling east either had to be ferried across the lake in summer, shipped across thick ice in winter, or halted entirely in spring and fall. Though a crash building program completed the southern route around Baikal by fall 1904, the Russian buildup in the Far East was slowed in the first crucial months of the war. On the other hand, Port Arthur was a formidable defensive position, with the guns of its fleet available for defense, a garrison of over 40,000 soldiers, and large stocks of supplies. Even bottled up in Port Arthur, the Russian fleet presented a grave danger to the Japanese war effort. Furthermore, the garrison was a substantial threat to Japanese supply lines north to Manchuria. Winning the war and expelling Russia from Manchuria required eliminating Port Arthur. Since its guns and mine fields meant that the fleet could not be destroyed from the sea, the Japanese had to eliminate it by land. The land war thus had two components. The first was the Japanese effort to besiege and capture Port Arthur, and with it the Russian Pacific Fleet. The second was the Russian attempt to mass troops in Manchuria to relieve Port Arthur, and the concurrent Japanese effort to prevent that.

Command of the Russian ground forces went to War Minister Aleksei Nikolaevich Kuropatkin, a close associate of the dashing Mikhail Dmitrievich Skobelev, hero of Russia's last war. Unlike his mentor, Kuropatkin was cautious and passive to a fault, believing he needed months to build up troops necessary for offensive operations. To make matters worse, Kuropatkin was nominally under the authority of Russia's aggressive and bombastic Far Eastern viceroy Evgenii Ivanovich Alekseev. Kuropatkin deployed his forces around Liaoyang, a town on the railroad line 200 miles northeast of Port Arthur. He split his forces into three parts, with the main body of 35,000 at Liaoyang, a southern detachment of 30,000 closer to Port Arthur, and, finally, an eastern detachment of 25,000 to block any Japanese crossing of the Yalu River from Korea into Manchuria. This force, under the command of Mikhail Ivanovich Zasulich (the brother of a noted revolutionary), deployed just inland from the mouth of the Yalu.

Zasulich's eastern detachment saw the first serious land combat of the war. Though Zasulich had correctly surmised the location of the Japanese crossing, he failed to prepare to meet them. He left his troops, particularly his artillery, unprotected in open terrain. On 18 April/1 May 1904, Japanese infantry pinned his forces with an attack across the Yalu. Two additional divisions crossed upriver, sweeping around the Russian left flank, and forcing Zasulich to withdraw. Though Russian rifle and machine-gun fire inflicted heavy losses, Zasulich showed himself incapable of managing the demands of a modern battle, a failure Russian commanders repeated throughout the war.

Another Japanese army landed on the southern shore of the Liaodong Peninsula, 80 miles east of Port Arthur. It sent troops north to sever the railroad to Port Arthur, and others west down the peninsula toward Port Arthur itself. Anatolii Mikhailovich Stessel', commander of the Port Arthur garrison, enjoyed an enviable defensive position. The Liaodong Peninsula narrowed sharply to an hourglass three miles across only 30 miles outside Port Arthur. A substantial hill commanded the surrounding terrain. Stessel', however, garrisoned the neck with a single regiment of 4,000 men. On 13/26 May, the Japanese attacked with 35,000. Though another entire Russian division was nearby, the single regiment fought alone an entire day, resisting repeated Japanese assaults and infiltration by Japanese infantry wading through shallow waters off the peninsula. Only at nightfall, out of ammunition and stranded by a general withdrawal, did the Russians abandon their position. The precipitous Russian withdrawal into Port Arthur allowed the Japanese to seize without a fight the port of Dalnii, only 30 miles from Port Arthur. With Port Arthur under siege, the Japanese landed two additional armies, one to take over at Port Arthur and the other to join in pushing the Russians out of Manchuria.

Kuropatkin attempted to relieve Port Arthur by sending his Southern Detachment along the railroad to break the Japanese siege. This detachment, moving south slowly, met the Japanese just north of Wafangdian on 1/14 July 1904. Just as at the Yalu, the Russians had major failures of intelligence and deployment. A single Russian corps was unknowingly taking on an entire Japanese army and left its artillery in open, exposed positions. In a day of fierce but indecisive fighting, a Japanese division worked its way around the Russian right flank into the rear, forcing a precipitate retreat back north to the main Russian staging area at Liaoyang. Port Arthur was left to defend itself as best it could.

By August, the Japanese had three armies in Manchuria and were ready to attack Kuropatkin's main force at Liaoyang. Though 130,000 Japanese were outnumbered by 150,000 Russians, the Japanese conceived an ambitious plan for the double envelopment of Liaoyang, aiming at the complete destruction of the Russians. The Japanese First Army would attack the city from the east, the Second from the west, and the Fourth from the south. Unaware of his own numerical superiority, Kuropatkin was convinced he needed reinforcements before any offensive action. Kuropatkin's forces were strongly entrenched in three semicircular bands south of Liaoyang, with the outermost nearly 20 miles outside the city. The ends of that semicircle, the Russian flanks, hung dangerously in mid-air, leaving the entire position in danger of being outflanked and destroyed. Kuropatkin's passivity made the threat much graver.

The Battle of Liaoyang opened on 11/24 August with the Japanese First Army attacking the Russian left flank. Though two days of attacks made little headway, Kuropatkin feared Japanese infiltration through wide gaps in his outer defenses and ordered his left wing to retreat to its second line of defense. Two days later, the Second and Fourth Armies began their own push south of Liaoyang. Again, Kuropatkin ordered his troops to retreat to their second line despite limited Japanese progress. Kuropatkin intended to ride out the next set of Japanese attacks and then go on the offensive with his cavalry-heavy right flank. Fearing encirclement, he withdrew half his forces into reserve in Liaoyang itself, leaving his forward lines of defense weak. Ominously, it was already becoming clear that the battle was too large and too complicated for a single commander, especially one of Kuropatkin's limited gifts, to command effectively.

The Japanese resumed their general onslaught on 17/30 August. This time, the Russians had learned from their earlier experience, firing their artillery indirectly from concealed or covered positions to break up Japanese infantry attacks. Russian defensive positions remained intact. That night, the Japanese shifted their right wing even farther right to get behind the Russian left. This opened a gap in the Japanese line. Rather than counterattacking into it, Kuropatkin lost his nerve and late the next day ordered a general withdrawal into the third and final line of defenses just outside Liaoyang itself. The Russians had abandoned two of their three lines of fortifications without being forced out of either of them.

The final clashes took place 19–21 August/1–3 September. Having withdrawn to his final line of fortifications, Kuropatkin prepared a counterattack on his left flank, intended to crush elements of the overextended Japanese First Army that had crossed to the Russian side of the Taizi River. Instead, the Japanese seized the initiative, grabbing high ground on the Russian left and preempting the Russian attack. Any grand Russian plans for cutting off and eliminating the Japanese right flank were abandoned in the back-and-forth struggle for a commanding hill. Kuropatkin's subordinates, infected by his passivity, reported that their positions were rapidly becoming untenable. He accordingly ordered a general withdrawal north, abandoning Liaoyang altogether, on 21 August/3 September.

Liaoyang, even more than the war's previous battles, highlighted the essential weakness of the Russian war effort. Russian troops had fought bravely and tenaciously, inflicting terrible losses on the Japanese. Russian commanders, however, abandoned strong position after strong position while failing to take advantage of numerous opportunities to counterattack their overextended and outnumbered enemy. Just as at the Yalu, Russian passivity and poor intelligence allowed Japanese commanders to outflank and envelop Russian defenses repeatedly, winning even with inferior numbers.

The ongoing siege of Port Arthur told the same story as Liaoyang: individual courage and official incompetence. After the Japanese had forced the neck of the peninsula and taken the port of Dalnii, the front lines stabilized 15–20 miles outside Port Arthur while the Japanese brought in reinforcements. After accumulating the necessary strength, the Japanese attacked Russian outer defenses on 13/26 July 1904. Despite heavy losses, within a week the Japanese had pushed Russian positions through and past the Volchi Hills, the last major natural barrier outside of Port Arthur. This brought the Japanese within 3–5 miles of Port Arthur itself. Though Port Arthur had a substantial network of fortresses, they were not far enough from the port to protect it from Japanese artillery.

The initial attempt by the Japanese Third Army to take Port Arthur began 6/19 August and continued until 11/24 August 1904. After preparatory bombardment, the Japanese attacked the port's perimeter. The main effort against the northeastern sector of the line culminated in a final night attack. Heavy casualties and the lack of significant gains forced the Japanese to halt and prepare for a longer siege, including bringing in siege artillery and constructing trench parallels to press closer to Russian lines. The Russians continued feverish efforts to improve their own fortifications.

The second storm of Port Arthur shifted direction, focusing on Russian fortifications farther west. Opening on 6/19 September with a lengthy artillery barrage to level Russian redoubts, the Japanese followed with a rush at Russian fortifications. Despite terrible losses to Russian machine-gun fire, the Japanese captured two redoubts and a hill as their defenders ran out of ammunition and reserves. The Russians nevertheless held on to their key defensive positions, using improvised hand grenades to recapture lost trenches. Again, the Japanese storm was stopped, but with significant Russian losses that could not be replaced. The Japanese besiegers reverted to pounding Port Arthur with siege artillery and digging closer to Russian lines and began a third storm on 17/30 October after a four-day bombardment. The focus returned to the northeast section of Port Arthur's perimeter. Though Japanese infantry penetrated Russian fortifications, vigorous Russian counterattacks drove them back.

A fourth general storm in the northwest followed on 13/26 November, initially producing the same bloody failure as before. This time, though, the Japanese shifted immediately from the failed attack in the northwest to High Hill, northeast of Port Arthur. Artillery bombardments began the next day, alternating with infantry attacks. As the siege artillery pulverized Russian trenches and dugouts, the defenders took unsustainable losses. There were no reserves to replenish them. On 22 November/ 5 December, the Russians decided to abandon the hill.

The Japanese capture of High Hill doomed Port Arthur. It provided an observation post from which to direct the fire of siege guns onto the Pacific Fleet in the harbor and onto Port Arthur's inner defenses. The ships were pounded into oblivion. Even worse, the chief organizer and spiritual bulwark of Port Arthur's defenses, General Roman Isidorovich Kondratenko, was killed by a Japanese shell on 2/15 December. With Kondratenko's death, the only remaining authority in Port Arthur was Stessel', who had had enough of death and destruction. He surrendered on 20 December 1904/2 January 1905, when the Russian garrison had 20,000 defenders still fighting or only lightly wounded, along with substantial stores of ammunition and over a month's supply of food. Stessel' was sentenced to death (later commuted) for his capitulation when resistance was still possible. At a cost of 30,000 killed or wounded, the Russian defenders had inflicted 100,000 casualties on the Japanese.

Mukden

While one Japanese army attacked Port Arthur, three more pushed north into Manchuria. For the Japanese, the goal was defeating the Russians before reinforcements along the Trans-Siberian gave Russia overwhelming material superiority. For the Russians, some success, *any* success, was vital to restore the declining prestige of the monarchy and the Russian government. Though Kuropatkin had retreated north after Liaoyang, his nearly 200,000 troops no longer gave him any reason to avoid taking the offensive. On 22 September/5 October 1904, Kuropatkin pushed south along the railroad from Mukden to Liaoyang, intending this frontal attack to fix the Japanese in place while a second detachment skirted through hills to the east to attack the Japanese right flank and rear.

Kuropatkin's limitations again came to the fore in these operations along the Sha River. He insisted on close control over his subordinates, scattered across miles of difficult terrain. Russian maneuvers were agonizingly slow, in part because of the hills and in part Kuropatkin's micromanagement. As at Liaoyang, his poor intelligence and paranoia at being encircled by the more active Japanese meant Russian numerical advantage was squandered in huge reserves held out of the fighting.

Kuropatkin inched south along the railway, halting at any sign of Japanese resistance and thereby enabling the Japanese to take rapid countermeasures. On the Japanese right, the Russian flanking attack was stopped in the hills, while the Japanese counterattacked in the center and on their own left. Kuropatkin was forced to throw troops in to plug gaps in Russian lines. Over several days of meeting engagements, the Russian advantage in numbers was lost in Kuropatkin's failure to manage his far-flung battlefield effectively. After a week of fighting in September and October, both armies were exhausted. Combat ended by 5/17 October, and the troops dug in to extensive trench systems to recuperate.

By February 1905, Kuropatkin had almost 300,000 men in three armies dug in along a 60-mile front running east-west south of Mukden. With cavalry screening the open flanks, the breadth of the Russian position was nearly 100 miles. Reinforced by the conquerors of Port Arthur, five Japanese armies had 270,000 men. Predictably, Kuropatkin's lethargic offensive preparations were preempted by an aggressive and ambitious Japanese plan to encircle and annihilate Kuropatkin's entire force. After the newly created 5th Army attacked the Russian left flank, and the 1st, 2nd, and 4th armies engaged the Russians along their front, the newly arrived 3rd Army would move around the Russian right to capture the railroad link through Mukden, cutting off Russian retreat.

The Battle of Mukden began on 6/19 February 1905 with a Japanese attack on the eastern cavalry screen protecting the Russian left flank, followed by a full-scale attack on 10/23 February against the Russian left wing itself. Kuropatkin responded precisely as the Japanese hoped, calling off his plans for a western offensive and instead moving his reserves to shore up his left wing. Once those reserves began shifting east, the Japanese 2nd Army launched a frontal attack on the Russian right wing to pin it in place, while the 3rd Army swung west around the Russian right to cut off its retreat. Kuropatkin's troops detected this flanking maneuver on 14/27 February, but could not stop it. The Russian right wing was deployed too far forward and engaged too heavily to turn right and protect itself against encirclement, and Kuropatkin had depleted his reserves shoring up the Russian left.

By the time Kuropatkin recognized his danger, it was almost too late. His troops were engaged all along the line, and his surplus forces were on his left, 60 miles east of where he needed them. He frantically pulled units out of the line wherever possible to march them west to stop the Japanese 3rd Army, swinging like a hammer toward Mukden. Kuropatkin hoped to rupture the overextended Japanese line where it bent around Mukden, but that required commanders with more initiative and better morale. Late on 22 February/7 March, Kuropatkin opted to withdraw his troops to the northern bank of the Hun River, flowing through Mukden.

The Japanese maintained pressure on the withdrawing Russians, and found a critical weak point. In the disorganization as the Russian left crossed the Hun River, Japanese probing attacks found a weakly held sector and blasted through it on 24 February/9 March. Kuropatkin had already decided to pull out of the city of Mukden itself, and the Japanese breakthrough made it impossible to hold the Hun River line. To Kuropatkin's credit, he managed to hold a coherent defense together and protect the railroad out of Mukden long enough to enable the bulk of his forces to retreat north, with heavy losses nonetheless. Of the nearly 600,000 total soldiers engaged on both sides for three weeks of fighting, the Russians had suffered 90,000 killed, wounded, or captured to the Japanese 70,000.

Though Kuropatkin's performance was dismal, enough to get him relieved of command, there were extenuating circumstances. Mukden, and Liaoyang which preceded it, marked a qualitative shift in warfare. Military theorists before the Russo-Japanese War had thought of warfare in Napoleonic terms, divided into strategy and tactics. Strategy governed the large-scale movement of armies across territory, and tactics governed the conduct of battle. There was a clear distinction between the two. While strategy dealt with long periods of time and large spaces, tactics covered battles, lasting only a single day, taking place over a few square miles, and within the competency of a single commander to understand and manage. By the end of the Napoleonic Wars, this sharp distinction was beginning to break down. Borodino and Leipzig were larger, bloodier, and more complicated battles than what had come before, and Napoleon's mastery of smaller engagements was pushed to its limits by larger ones. In the 90 years between Waterloo and Mukden, the lack of general war in Europe masked how changing technology blurred the sharp distinction between strategy and tactics. Modern states drew more men from larger populations. The increasing deadliness of rifles, machine guns, and artillery meant that soldiers had to disperse and entrench to survive. This expanded the size of battlefields and reduced officers' ability to control their soldiers closely. The wars that did take place—the American Civil War, the Franco-Prussian War, and the Russo-Turkish War—amply demonstrated the deadly effects of modern firepower, but did not produce a clear verdict that the Napoleonic distinction between tactics and strategy was dead.

The Russo-Japanese War was different. Liaoyang and Mukden had hundreds of thousands of soldiers fighting across dozens of miles of fronts for a week or more. Commanders had to think in *operational* terms: narrower than strategy, broader than tactics. They had to coordinate movements of large bodies of soldiers across large spaces to fix, outflank, break, and destroy opposing forces. Unlike the Napoleonic Wars, campaigns did not culminate in single battles that decided wars. Instead, large modern armies sustained defeats and continued to fight. This operational revolution required innovations in command structures as well. In traditional Napoleonic armies, battalions made up regiments, regiments made up brigades and divisions, brigades and divisions made up corps, and several corps united to form an army. There was no need for a larger formation, and almost by definition there could not be anything larger: an army was what fought a battle. But with battles now extended in numbers, time, and space, the increasing strain of managing this complexity required an additional level of command. Mukden, for example, was fought by three Russian and five Japanese armies. The innovation was what Westerners called an "army group," and Russians called a "front." When, during the approach to Mukden, Kuropatkin organized his troops into three armies under his joint command, he created the organizational scheme of a front that would carry through the Russian experience in World War I and the Soviet experience in World War II.

Tsushima

Despite the Russian defeat at Mukden, the war was not over. Russia slowly built superior manpower in Manchuria. Japan was nearing exhaustion and was in no position to exploit its Mukden victory. Most importantly, Russia still had a fleet to attempt to even the scales. Almost as soon as the war began, Nicholas's government prepared to send its Baltic Fleet around the world to the Far East. It departed in October 1904 and spent the winter of 1904–1905 circling the globe in a comedy of maritime errors. It nearly managed to start a war with Britain when it shelled fishing boats, taking them for a Japanese fleet, and learned while refitting at Madagascar that Port Arthur, its ostensible destination, had fallen to the Japanese. With Port Arthur gone, the fleet's sole remaining haven was Vladivostok. It prepared for a run through the Tsushima Strait between Japan and Korea into the Sea of Japan and north to Vladivostok.

Japanese cruisers spotted the Russian fleet early on 14/27 May 1905 as it passed through the Tsushima Strait. Shortly after midday, Japanese main elements caught the disorganized Russian formation from the west, to the left of the Russian course, and focused concentrated and accurate gunfire on its lead elements before a textbook "crossing of the T." As the Japanese steamed across the head of the Russian formation, they poured shells into the helpless Russian ships. In less than an hour, the Russian flagship was disabled and its admiral, Zinovii Petrovich Rozhestvenskii, seriously wounded. Rozhestvenskii had not prepared for the orderly transfer of command, and his fleet fought without a leader until early evening. The ships that survived Japanese gunfire continued their run north to Vladivostok, but were harried all night by Japanese torpedo boats. The next day, the remnants of the Russian fleet surrendered. The Japanese had sunk six Russian battleships and captured two. Five thousand Russian sailors were dead, and another 6,000 captured. One cruiser and two torpedo boats made it to Vladivostok.

The staggering defeat at Tsushima left Nicholas with no alternative to peace, but his situation was not as desperate as it seemed. Despite Japan's run of victories, it was running low on manpower. To make matters worse, the now-complete Trans-Siberian Railway was moving Russian reinforcements to the Far East with growing speed. Both sides were eager for peace. Talks opened in Portsmouth, New Hampshire, on 27 July / 9 August 1905 with U.S. President Theodore Roosevelt as mediator. Thanks to Japan's sense of urgency, and Roosevelt's Russian sympathies, the final settlement was lenient. Russia lost its base at Port Arthur and surrendered the South Manchuria Railway and the southern half of Sakhalin Island to the Japanese.

As the Russo-Japanese War ended, Russian domestic discontent was spiraling out of control. Mounting social, economic, and political discontent had culminated in Bloody Sunday, 9/22 January 1905, when a delegation of workers carrying icons and portraits of the tsar was shot down by troops in the center of St. Petersburg. Over 1905, assassinations, peasant uprisings, and strikes mounted steadily. This had relatively little effect on the war against Japan for, in a pattern repeated in 1917, mutinies were absent from the field forces and limited to rear areas. By October 1905, a massive general strike brought Russia to a standstill. Told that his plans for martial law were unworkable with his army strung out across the Trans-Siberian, Nicholas was forced to issue the October Manifesto, granting an elected legislature, universal (but unequal) manhood suffrage, and civil liberties.

The October Manifesto was enough to let Nicholas's police and military regain control in late 1905 and 1906 through forcible repression. Thousands were killed by left-wing terrorism, right-wing reprisals, and forcible suppression of revolution. Nicholas delivered on his promise of an elected legislature, the Duma, though the votes of social elites were weighted to skew its makeup rightward. Even this was not enough to produce a workable Duma, and Nicholas dissolved the first two Dumas before his chief minister Peter Arkad'evich Stolypin changed the electoral laws in June 1907 to engineer a reliable progovernment majority in the third set of Duma elections. The rebuilding of a shattered Russia now began.

Aftermath of the Russo-Japanese War

Well before the Russo-Japanese War, Russian foreign policy in Europe had centered around an alliance with France, emerging from the wars of

German unification. When in 1871 German Chancellor Otto von Bismarck created the new unified German Empire out of a patchwork of German states, he did it through the defeat of France, including the annexation of Alsace and Lorraine. This ensured French hostility, but Bismarck removed France's ability to act by taking away all possible French alliances. By consciously avoiding efforts to build a navy and empire, Bismarck kept Britain friendly. He established a Triple Alliance in 1881 with Austria-Hungary and Italy. As a former ambassador to Russia, he never underestimated Russia's potential power, and he saw no inherent reason why Germany and Russia should be hostile. He accordingly supplemented the Triple Alliance with a 1887 Reinsurance Treaty with Russia to keep France isolated and Germany safe.

When Wilhelm II inherited the German throne in 1888, however, Bismarck was dismissed and the Reinsurance Treaty lapsed in 1890. Russia was forced to look elsewhere for security. Russia's chief geopolitical rival was Austria, tied irrevocably to Germany by the Triple Alliance. British and Russian interests clashed in central Asia. That left France, so a Franco-Russian alliance was formed in 1892. The alliance gave Russia welcome security from European war, even more when Russia and Austria agreed in 1897 to put the Balkans on ice, postponing any conflict over southeastern Europe. The European diplomatic landscape at the turn of the century was thus clear: Germany and Austria, together with reluctant Italy on one side—Russia and France on the other. Britain remained a neutral and disinterested party, though with persistent concerns about Russian expansion in Central Asia and French ambitions for an African empire. The Russo-Japanese War and German pretensions to world power changed that dramatically.

By 1907, Russia's loss to Japan and subsequent revolution meant that Russia had to be more cautious and realistic about its foreign policy. Devoid of a navy thanks to Port Arthur and Tsushima, Russia presented less of a threat to Britain. At the same time, Germany was becoming a greater threat to both Britain and Russia. German pretensions to *weltpolitik*, to becoming a world power with global interests and influence, were a direct challenge to the British Empire. At the same time, expanding German commercial and political influence in the Ottoman Empire and Iran threatened Russian interests. With France as a willing broker, Britain and Russia settled their differences in Asia, demarcating spheres of interest to focus on the greater threat in Europe. Though tensions and conflicts remained sharp, they were temporarily outweighed by the common German threat. This created the Triple Entente—France, Britain, and Russia—to oppose the German-led Triple Alliance.

Tensions mounted in 1908. Austria-Hungary had *occupied* Bosnia-Herzegovina in the wake of the Russo-Turkish War (1877–1878), but this did not mean that the province was formally part of Austria-Hungary.

Russia negotiated with Austria to exchange Russian approval of Austria's full legal possession of Bosnia-Herzegovina for Austrian support of Russia's effort to obtain passage for its warships through the Turkish Straits. These talks were preempted by a 1908 coup inside the Ottoman Empire. Austria then annexed Bosnia-Herzegovina unilaterally, leaving Russia humiliated and devoid of compensation. Austria's annexation, together with Germany's belligerent support of her ally, convinced the Triple Entente that Germany was a dangerous power, intent on hegemony in Europe.

Since the expiration of the Reinsurance Treaty in 1890, Russia had to prepare for the possibility of war against a German-Austrian coalition, a possibility that seemed much more likely after 1908. For much of the 1890s, war planning fell to Dmitrii Alekseevich Miliutin's associate Nikolai Nikolaevich Obruchev, who had drawn up the plans for the Russo-Turkish War. Obruchev had to wrestle with a number of unpleasant strategic realities, including facing two great powers alone which made him a key advocate of the French alliance. After the alliance, the dilemma was over Russia's proper target. Russia's Balkan interests clashed with Austria-Hungary, not Germany, suggesting a southern focus, while France's priority was clearly Germany.

Russia's manpower advantages were undercut by its slow mobilization. Not only was it larger than any European state, but its population centers were far from the western frontier. To make matters worse, it could not efficiently employ the population it did have. In Poland, for example, Russian fears about Polish reliability meant no more than 25 percent to 30 percent of any unit could be made up of Poles. Mobilization plans thus shipped Poles out of Poland and Russians in. Russia's railroad net was terribly underdeveloped compared to the rest of Europe, so Russia would be slower to fight. Precise figures varied over time, but at the turn of the century Germany and Austria could mobilize, deploy troops at the frontier, and be ready to fight in about two weeks. Russia would take at least twice as long. Given the general assumption the next war would be short, since no European state could sustain the burden of war for more than a few months, Russia's delay was critical.

While French investors underwrote Russian railroad construction, Russia's response was to make its war plans defensive, at least for the early stages of the next war. That meant using fortress complexes in Poland, massively expanded in the 1890s to counter improvements in artillery, to hold back German attacks. Once mobilization was complete, Russia's eventual offensive would be directed against Austria. Russia's slow mobilization meant that its standing army was disproportionately stationed in the west, to hold the borders until full mobilization.

The Russo-Japanese War brought Russia's complete military collapse. The country was simply unable to wage major war, and some in Germany and Austria argued for preventive war to settle matters before Russian recovery. The results of the Russo-Japanese War were reflected in 1910's Schedule 19 war plan. Cautious to a fault, it shifted Russia's deployments east, away from the frontier, to prevent destruction by a sudden German attack while easing troop transfers east in the event of renewed war with Japan. Schedule 19's timidity ran into a number of political objections. Its defensive orientation directly contradicted Russia's alliance commitments to France, something French officials emphasized repeatedly. In addition, Russian planners understood Germany's war plan involved concentrating against France to knock it out of the war quickly. If Russia did nothing to stop that, it faced the unwelcome prospect of a war against Germany and Austria with its French ally lost. Finally, Schedule 19 wrote off most of Poland as lost and delayed indefinitely the offensive against Austria-Hungary that Russian generals thirsted for. As Russia recovered from the disasters of 1904–1905, Russian generals pushed for a more aggressive strategy.

After tumultuous debate in early 1912, Schedule 19 was revised and split into two variant war plans. Both were more aggressive, moving quickly to offensives. Indeed, in 1913 the Russians promised the French to begin offensive operations 15 days after the start of mobilization, long before it would be complete. Variant A, the default option, projected directing the bulk of Russian forces—45 infantry divisions, 18.5 cavalry divisions, and 3 rifle brigades—against Austria, leaving 29 infantry divisions, 9.5 cavalry divisions, and 2 rifle brigades against Germany. Variant G reversed the proportions, sending 41 infantry divisions, 13.5 cavalry divisions, and 2 rifle brigades against Germany and 33 infantry divisions, 14.5 cavalry divisions, and 3 rifle brigades against Austria. Even Variant A, the one employed in 1914, provided for a two-pronged invasion of East Prussia to take pressure off the French. In neither variant did the Russians employ overwhelming force against either Germany or Austria, leaving them vulnerable to launching two offensives, each just weak enough to fail.

The 1905 Revolution also reshaped the workings of Russian government, though less in foreign and military policy than in other areas. Though the Duma had legislative power, the tsar retained exclusive control over war, peace, and foreign relations. A Council of Ministers existed to coordinate policy, but in practice Nicholas granted the Foreign Ministry great latitude to conduct foreign affairs. Defense policy, by contrast, was subject to Duma scrutiny because it was, above all, expensive. The Duma's budgetary powers meant military policy was a matter of public debate. The Duma was not opposed to military spending, only to Nicholas's mismanagement. Indeed, in 1914 it approved a "Great Program" to boost Russia's peacetime strength to 1.6 million men, as well as a major expansion of the Russian artillery park. Together with French loans for railway construction, this promised a qualitative leap in Russian military capacity.

Nicholas created a new State Defense Council in 1905 to coordinate foreign policy and, in addition, a new Main Directorate of the General Staff. This reflected a desire to do something, *anything,* after the Japanese debacle, not any real reform program. The State Defense Council had a president who centralized authority by serving as a superminister over the War and Navy ministries. On the other hand, Nicholas decentralized authority by splitting the General Staff from the War Ministry. In both cases, Nicholas sacrificed these reforms in the interests of political expediency. He dissolved the State Defense Council in 1908 for opposing his costly initiative to rebuild the destroyed capital ship fleet. He returned the General Staff to the War Ministry in 1909 to promote his own control over military affairs. As this makes clear, Nicholas's meddling in defense policy, as in the rest of the Russian state machinery, was the central obstacle to effective administration. Nicholas felt compelled to maintain autocracy, his own personal and undivided authority. That meant the management of an empire spanning one-sixth of the earth's surface was inordinately centralized in the hands of a single individual. Nicholas was neither stupid nor ignorant, but completely incapable of handling the governmental burdens he refused to share.

Beginning in 1909 Nicholas relied on Vladimir Aleksandrovich Sukhomlinov as War Minister and ensured that no Chief of Staff challenged him. Though Sukhomlinov was not the monster he was often portrayed as being, he was venal and consummately political. At the tsar's behest, he made every effort to prevent Duma interference, so the Duma detested him in return. Sukhomlinov did push through some reforms, but was handicapped by a lack of funding for his initiatives and opposition from high-placed aristocrats. To reduce the peacetime expense of the army and increase available reserves, the standard service term was reduced to three years in the army (five in the navy), while exemptions and deferments were reduced. He attempted to reduce Russia's reliance on its Polish fortresses, but was blocked by political opposition. Sukhomlinov failed to improve Russia's industrial infrastructure for war by resisting the integration of private enterprise into munitions production, and he failed to acquire the heavy artillery required to deal with fortifications and earthworks.

Finally, the Russian army itself had to incorporate the consequences of the Russo-Japanese War. The war's lessons, however, were complex and ambiguous, and the Russian official history of the war was not critical enough. Though some thinkers groped toward an operational understanding, Russian doctrine was still too committed to a Napoleonic view of warfare, with a clean divide between tactics and strategy, and the idea that wars were decided by single great battles, not extended campaigns.

As shown in a new 1912 field manual, Russian tacticians understood the power of modern firearms, but this did not mean rejecting the offensive. Indeed, firepower promoted the offensive, since attacks should be launched quickly, before defenders had time to entrench. While frontal assaults, even bayonet charges, were costly and to be avoided if possible, Russian doctrine held they were sometimes necessary and could be successful. Russia's theory and training doomed its soldiers to costly and futile attacks in the next war, but in that it was like every other European power.

The Russian officer corps charged with implementing new doctrines in the wake of the Russo-Japanese War was deeply divided. For many, their privileged upbringing and conservative outlook combined to produce a deep distaste for politics and intellectual life. The Russian intelligentsia as a class was viscerally opposed to the regime and the army. Many officers in response rejected anything that smacked of a critical analysis of the regime, or even of scientific research. They remained convinced that will and discipline could overcome any material deficits. For others, however, the Russo-Japanese War meant Russian society had to change for Russia to survive. Individual Japanese were simply better soldiers than their Russian counterparts. This was not a racial judgment, but a political and cultural one. Russians needed to be taught to be committed citizen-soldiers, conscientious and dedicated. While training peasant automata might have sufficed in the nineteenth century, it was not enough for the twentieth. Accordingly, the tsarist government introduced systematic military education in schools and supported paramilitary youth groups. Elaborate celebrations commemorated Russia's military triumphs, including the 200th anniversary of Poltava (1909), the 100th anniversary of Napoleon's invasion (1912), and the 300th anniversary of the Romanov dynasty itself (1913). For other officers, Russia's key failing was technological. They turned to the new science of aviation as both a tool for increasing Russia's military power and sparking Russian development.

In many cases, though by no means all, this traditionalist-reformist split was between Guards and General Staff officers. The aristocratic guards regiments served as finishing schools for the high nobility, who disdained formal military education and cherished their elevated rank and status. On the other hand, the General Staff officers, graduates of the Nikolaev Academy, saw themselves as an intellectual elite, superior in technical skill to the dilettante guards. At the beginning of World War I, there were only about 1,000 General Staff officers among the 40,000 in the officer corps, but they exerted a disproportionate influence. Russia's officers, like Russia itself, were caught between tradition and modernity with little understanding of how to balance their competing demands.

Pernicious divides were not limited to the military. After the Russo-Japanese War, Russia enjoyed an unprecedented economic boom, characterized by rapid industrial growth. While this boosted Russia's potential power, it enlarged the alienated urban working class, which saw little concrete improvement in its living standards from Russian economic growth. At the same time, Russia's educated elites were not only alienated from the urban poor, but from their own government as well. The tsar consistently and resolutely opposed meaningful participation by Russian society in the government of the empire. All this would have terrible consequences when the next war came.

CHAPTER 11

World War I

Russia recovered remarkably quickly from the twin catastrophes of the Russo-Japanese War and the 1905 Revolution. It had, however, little time before an even more daunting task: fighting in the First World War. Russia's recovery took place at a time of growing international tension. Imperial Germany's burgeoning power alarmed Russia, Britain, and France, but Germany regarded its position as precarious and fraught with danger. Its ally Austria-Hungary was hobbled by interethnic tension, and Italy was more likely to fight against Austria than beside it. To make matters worse, the breathing space Germany gained from Russia's defeat quickly disappeared, while Russia's internal reforms, economic growth, and railroad construction made Germany's long-term prospects for victorious war increasingly dim. Russia and France were more confident in their chances, while Germany and Austria feared that unless they fought a war soon, any hope of victory would be lost. In particular, the German-speaking elite of Austria feared the future, given the rise of nationalism among its dozen non-German nationalities.

The rivalry between Russia and Austria for dominance in the Balkans was dangerous enough in normal circumstances, but it became critical as the Ottoman Empire declined. The long, slow retreat of Ottoman power left behind a number of small Balkan states, eager for territorial expansion. In early 1912, Serbia, Bulgaria, Greece, and Montenegro agreed to partition the remaining Ottoman possessions in Europe. The great powers failed to dissuade them from war. In October 1912 the First Balkan War began. The Ottoman Empire was powerless to resist its four smaller neighbors, which collectively swallowed up Ottoman Europe. This local war threatened general war. Austria was terrified at the prospect of its smaller neighbors becoming more powerful and came close to war in November 1912. Russia, on the other hand, could not let another power control the Turkish Straits if the Ottomans collapsed and so prepared to seize them itself. No other power wished to see Constantinople in Russian hands. In the final success of European cooperation, the Great Powers

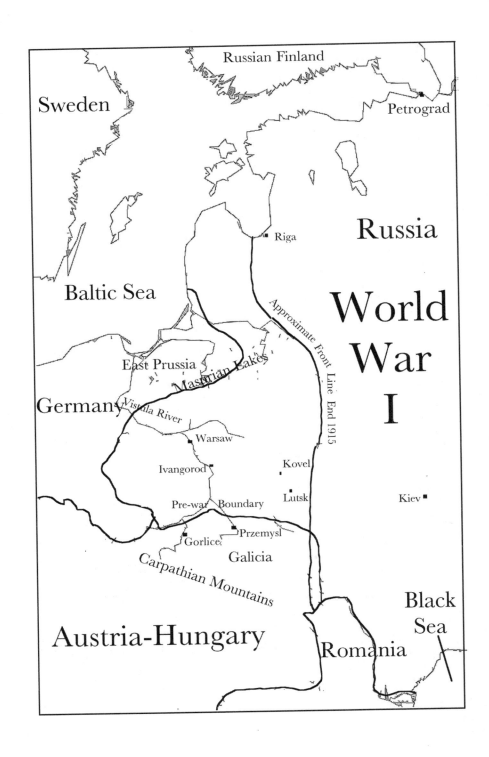

averted general war by obtaining a May 1913 peace settlement that cost the Ottomans all of their possessions in Europe except a small foothold on the European side of the Turkish Straits. The victors of the First Balkan War immediately fell out over division of the spoils. Bulgaria insisted on the lion's share of Macedonia, and in June 1913 attacked Serbia to obtain it, beginning the Second Balkan War. The Serbs and Greeks easily defeated the Bulgarian offensive, while Romania and the resurgent Ottomans joined the war against Bulgaria, bringing it total defeat.

The Balkan Wars were a disaster for Austria-Hungary. Its tiny rival Serbia had doubled its territory, making it more than ever before a magnet to discontented south Slavs inside Austria-Hungary. An already intractable nationalities problem became worse. Devoid of options, Austria-Hungary saw war against Serbia as the only solution to its internal problems. War with Serbia, however, risked war with Russia, so Austria needed German backing. Germany was willing, seeing a closing window of opportunity for war. If war with Russia and France were coming, better it come soon.

The July Crisis

The spark that brought war is well-known: on 15/28 June 1914, Franz Ferdinand, heir to the Austrian throne, was assassinated in Sarajevo. His killer, part of a Serbian nationalist group, was apprehended on the spot. For the Austrian government, the assassination was a perfect pretext for war to punish Serbia. Fearful of Russian intervention, the Austrians first made sure of German backing, which Kaiser Wilhelm II gave enthusiastically. Nearly a month after the assassination, on 10/23 July, Austria issued Serbia a deliberately provocative ultimatum, demanding suppression of nationalist groups and Austrian participation in the investigation of the conspiracy. This ultimatum was based on two assumptions: first, that the Serbs would reject it, and, second, that Russia would be deterred by Germany's stand.

Neither happened. Serbia's response was conciliatory, accepting almost all of Austria's terms. This, together with the passage of time, allowed passions to cool and drained the righteousness from the Austrian cause. At the same time, Tsar Nicholas and his government agreed Russian honor, future Balkan expansion, and indeed Nicholas's domestic credibility required Russia to protect Serbia. Consultations with the French were difficult: the French president and prime minister had just left St. Petersburg after a state visit, and the Austrian ultimatum had been deliberately delayed until they were on a ship home. Nonetheless, the French ambassador to Russia passionately assured Nicholas of French loyalty. Early on the morning of 13/26 July, Russia began preparations for mobilization. Just as Austria hoped German backing might keep Russia from war, the tsar and his government hoped their demonstration of support for Serbia might keep Austria from war.

Events spiraled out of control. German war plans depended on attacking France as quickly as possible, so French survival depended on Russia attacking Germany as quickly as possible. These war plans meant there was no time for negotiation. On 15/28 July, Austria declared war on Serbia and the next day bombarded Belgrade. Disregarding German threats to halt preparations for war, Russia moved to full mobilization on 17/30 July 1914. Nicholas toyed with limiting the conflict by mobilizing against Austria alone, not Germany, but his advisors convinced him this was madness. In any event, Germany could never have permitted a war limited to Austria and Russia, ending in certain Russian victory and leaving Germany without an ally. In response to Russian mobilization, Germany declared war on Russia on 19 July/1 August. Since German war plans entailed an attack on France, not Russia, Germany declared war on France on 21 July/3 August, invading neutral Belgium the next day as the quickest route to Paris. Britain was committed to the defense of Belgium, but more importantly could not tolerate a German presence on the English Channel coast or a German-dominated Europe. It declared war that night.

The 1914 Campaigns

The Russian army that marched to war in 1914 reflected Russian society. Russia's population of 170 million was twice as large as Germany's, but had less than half its per capita gross domestic product. Its railroads, war production, and educational level all reflected that basic fact. Economic backwardness meant Russia could not use its manpower effectively. It mobilized less of its population than the other major powers. In 1914, Russia called up 4.5 million men to supplement the 1.4 million already serving, and over the course of the war, Russia mobilized some 15 million men, slightly more than Germany did with half the population. Russia's low levels of education meant that it had a shortage of officers and noncommissioned officers. This was, indeed, one reason for its relatively low conscription. The army, though aiming at universal service, could not induct and train more than a quarter or third of the annual cohort of men reaching the service age of 21. During the war, the Russian government was slow to extend conscription to the majority of men who had escaped service earlier in life, fearing its political repercussions and the greater training they needed.

Russia's relative poverty also affected its soldiers' equipment. All powers wrestled with poor preparedness to some degree. Russian officials, like all others in Europe, assumed the next war would be short and planned accordingly. No state was ready for a long war, and all had to improvise. That said, Russian policies worsened matters. Nicholas's prewar insistence on rebuilding a navy starved the army of resources. Vladimir Aleksandrovich Sukhomlinov had tried and failed to reduce Russia's dependence on Polish fortresses, leaving thousands of artillery pieces and millions of shells in useless installations. Russia had only 4.5 million rifles at the outbreak of war, not enough to equip the initial contingents, and the problem worsened as the war lengthened. The country had stockpiled a thousand rounds per artillery piece, but that proved woefully insufficient. The Russian aristocracy's distaste for businessmen meant domestic production was concentrated in state armories. Russia's booming private industry thus lacked experience and expertise in military orders. The assumption had been that foreign purchases would make up any shortfalls, but this neglected the time lag for such deliveries, and, more importantly, the simultaneous rush of orders from other belligerents.

Though World War I is often regarded as destroying tsarist Russia, it initially improved the tsar's domestic standing. In a strong but brief outburst of patriotism, a strike wave building since 1912 dissipated. Russian educated society, alienated from the tsar's government, rallied around national defense. Even Russia's revolutionary left regarded war in defense of Russia as legitimate, and, importantly, the Duma's socialist parties abstained from voting for war credits, rather than opposing those credits altogether. After voting, the Duma dissolved, granting its government a free hand in the conduct of the war. Mobilization went remarkably smoothly, with draft resistance acceptably low. Even St. Petersburg's German-sounding name was changed to the more Russian Petrograd.

Russia's war plan in summer 1914 was Schedule 19(A). Unlike any other state, Russia envisaged simultaneous offensives against two great powers. In the north, the Northwestern Front's two armies (9 corps) would drive into East Prussia from the east and the south. In the south, the Southwestern Front's four armies (16 corps) would invade Galicia from the north and the east. In this division of effort, however, neither attack enjoyed overwhelming predominance. In the Russo-Japanese War, War Minister Aleksei Nikolaevich Kuropatkin had taken over field command against the Japanese. In 1914, though, overall command went not to Sukhomlinov, who stayed at the War Ministry as a glorified supply officer, but instead to the Grand Duke Nicholas, Tsar Nicholas's first cousin once removed, who hated Sukhomlinov. He operated through a new high command, *Stavka,* created from the Main Directorate of the General Staff and based in a central location at Baranovichi. His chief of staff was Nikolai Nikolaevich Yanushkevich, a thoroughgoing mediocrity distinguished by high-placed friends, an addiction to pornography, and pathological anti-Semitism. The Main Directorate of the General Staff remained to handle mobilization, manning, training, and administration, leaving war planning and operations to *Stavka*. Government of extensive territory behind the front lines was handed to the two Fronts.

The first campaigns of the war illustrated Russia's awkward position. Against Germany, high-level incompetence brought disaster, but against Austria-Hungary, hard fighting won impressive successes. In East Prussia, the Northwestern Front attacked with two armies: the 1st Army pushing west, while the 2nd Army moved from Poland in the south. Geography worked against them. The invading Russian armies were separated by the Masurian Lakes and fighting essentially independently. The Russians had few radios for communication. Those they did possess, lacking trained operators, broadcast without codes. Iakov Grigor'evich Zhilinskii, the Northwestern Front's commander, made no effort to coordinate his subordinates. Still, Germany defended East Prussia with only a tenth of its available manpower, sending everyone possible against France. That left Germany's 8th Army defending East Prussia with 14 divisions against more than double that number.

The Germans first blunted the Russian eastern pincer by moving against the 1st Army. The Russians crossed the border to East Prussia on 4/17 August, and after initial skirmishing, the Germans struck back in force on 7/20 August. The Russians proved remarkably resilient, sending their German attackers retreating in disarray. The 8th Army's commander lost his nerve and was replaced by Paul von Hindenburg, who later used his successes to take control of the German war effort. Fatally, the 1st Army failed to exploit its success, halting instead. This gave the German 8th Army a free hand to turn from the 1st Army's eastern invasion to the 2nd Army's southern invasion. The 2nd Army had crossed the border on 7/20 August, pushing north into a vacuum. The German divisions then shifted, either marching southwest behind the screen of the Masurian Lakes to attack the 2nd Army's right flank or circling by rail to attack its left flank. The 2nd Army marched forward blindly into a trap. German units linked up behind it on 16/29 August, cutting off communications, supplies, and reinforcements. More vigorous action might have permitted a breakout—there were more Russians in the pocket than Germans surrounding it. Instead, devoid of leadership, 100,000 Russians surrendered. The 2nd Army's commander shot himself.

After the disastrous end of the 2nd Army (labeled the Battle of Tannenberg by the Germans), the German 8th Army returned east to expel the stalled Russian 1st Army from East Prussia. Without the Russians walking into a trap, however, they did not move quickly or decisively enough to encircle and destroy the 2nd Army wholesale. The front stabilized along the prewar frontier. Zhilinskii, the Northwestern Front's commander, was removed and later posted as liaison to France.

At terrible cost, the Russians had achieved precisely what they promised the French. They drew the attention of the German high command,

and more importantly German troops, east to the defense of the frontier, away from Paris. On 12/25 August, the German high command had ordered three corps to the Eastern Front, where they arrived too late to make any difference. This critically weakened the German sweep through Belgium and south to Paris, which just failed to take the French capital and end the war.

While much attention, then and now, has been devoted to the defeat in East Prussia, Russia devoted more men and resources to its initial campaign against Galicia, an Austrian-ruled arc of Ukraine extending northeast from the Carpathian Mountains. Austria-Hungary's war began with traditional Habsburg incompetence. Austrian military planners understood the need to prepare for three contingencies: war against Russia, against Serbia, or against both. Accordingly, the Austrian army was split into three groups for mobilization. Minimal-group Balkan was intended for Serbia, Group A for Russia, and Group B, delaying its deployment, for whichever sector the high command directed. When Austria declared war on Serbia, Franz Conrad von Hötzendorf, chief of the Austrian General Staff, sent Group B south. After Russian intervention, Conrad needed those troops in Galicia. Reversing them en route would have thrown the Austrian railway system into chaos, so instead seven Austrian corps traveled south to Serbia, got back on their trains, and rolled back north to Galicia. As a result, despite Austria's superior speed of mobilization, the Galician campaign was fought on Austrian soil.

The battles for Galicia involved 1.5 million soldiers on a 250-mile front. In an epic clash, an Austrian invasion north into Russia's Polish salient collided with a two-pronged Russian invasion of Galicia in August and September 1914. The commander of Russia's Southwestern Front, Nikolai Iudovich Ivanov, was not particularly talented, but not the manifest incompetent Zhilinskii was. Austria had four armies in Galicia, totaling around 40 infantry and 10 cavalry divisions. The 1st and 4th Armies, to the west, planned to move northeast toward Lublin and the southern flank of the Polish salient. The 3rd and 2nd Armies, farther east, were tasked with limited advances to protect Lvov and shield the right flank of the first two armies as they moved north. Russia's Southwestern Front ultimately had five armies, with over 50 infantry and 18 cavalry divisions. The Russian plan for Galicia, like East Prussia, was a pincer attack. The 4th and 5th Armies (and later the 9th) were to push south into western Galicia, putting them on a collision course with the Austrian offensive. The 3rd and 8th Armies planned to move west into eastern Galicia along the north slopes of the Carpathians, threatening a double envelopment of the entire Austrian force.

The campaign opened with meeting engagements as Russian and Austrian divisions collided in eastern and in western Galicia. The Russian armies moving south had the worst of it, and withdrew back north. The

Russian advance from the east, however, smashed the Austrian armies moving to stop it and took Lvov on 21 August/3 September. Conrad decided to retreat his eastern armies directly west, bringing them under the shelter of his western armies. As the exhausted 4th Army turned to stop the Russian advance from the east, it was likewise defeated. Worse, by weakening his northern push, Conrad enabled a renewed Russian offensive that erased Austria's previous gains. With his armies collapsing under the Russian onslaught, Conrad ordered a retreat west on the night of 29–30 August/11–12 September 1914, abandoning Galicia and leaving the fortress of Przemysl with its garrison of 120,000 to Russian encirclement. The Austrians lost 400,000 killed, wounded, or captured, compared to the Russians' 250,000.

After the Austrian retreat, the Russians were in a position to force the Carpathian Mountain passes into the Hungarian plain. Instead, the Russian command attacked west out of central Poland. Massing the 5th, 4th, and 9th Armies on the Vistula River southeast of Warsaw, the Russians crossing the river met a German offensive aimed at breaking through to Warsaw from the south. The Germans made some progress, but failed to cross the Vistula in force and had to withdraw back southwest. Following this German failure, the Russians prepared an offensive from the northern side of the Polish salient. The German 9th Army, operating from northwest of Warsaw, preempted that attack on 29 October/11 November, wedging itself between the 1st and 2nd Armies and threatening to turn south behind the 2nd Army and cut off its retreat. Only a hasty withdrawal toward its supply base at Lodz, Poland, saved the 2nd Army from a second encirclement and destruction. Growing Russian pressure on the buckling Austrian army in the Carpathians led to German assistance in limited counteroffensives and a seesaw struggle for western Galicia.

The vast bloody campaigns of 1914 took a terrible toll on Russia, inflicting 1.2 million casualties. The six months had been even harder on Austria. Little was left of the army with which Austria began the war. It had called up 3.5 million men at the outbreak of war, and (discounting rear echelon troops) had only 250,000 left by December 1914. It had suffered as many casualties as Russia from a much smaller population, and those losses exacerbated its ethnic tensions. Austria-Hungary's dual structure, split between Austrian and Hungarian halves, made it impossible to centralize government and rationalize the economy for total war. Already over the winter of 1914–1915, it was clear only massive German assistance, including the growing integration of German officers into the Austrian army, could sustain Austria's war effort

The 1914 fighting illustrates key characteristics of World War I on the Eastern Front. The first battles of World War I, on both the Eastern and the Western Front, were far more mobile and more deadly than later western campaigns. Soldiers moved and fought as their doctrine taught: in groups, in the open. They were killed by the hundreds of thousands before bitter experience taught them to spread out, go to ground, and dig trenches to survive. Unlike the west, though, the Eastern Front never stagnated into immobile trench warfare. First, the front was twice as long as in the west. The Eastern Front stretched 600 miles from the Romanian border to the Baltic Sea, farther after Romania's entry in 1916, compared to 300 miles from Switzerland to the English Channel. Unit densities were much lower, making defenses fragile. A dearth of roads and railways made it difficult to shift reserves and halt breakthroughs.

Late 1914 and early 1915 clarified Russian war aims. In September 1914, Russia had agreed with Britain and France to make no separate peace with Germany and Austria. What Russia wanted out of the war, and demanded from its alliance partners, was the Turkish Straits. There were other goals, including the unification of German- and Austrian-controlled Poland with Russian Poland. Poland's precise future status was a touchy subject. No power wished to alienate Polish soldiers (fighting for all three powers in eastern Europe) by denying a sovereign Polish state, and Russia shifted toward endorsing Polish autonomy over the course of the war. Though the Ottoman Empire had not initially been part of the war, it tipped into the German camp. A German officer, Liman von Sanders, had rebuilt the Ottoman army after the Balkan Wars, and two German cruisers took refuge in Ottoman waters in the first days of the war. After those cruisers passed into the Black Sea and shelled Odessa, the Allies declared war on the Turks in October 1914. Once the Ottoman Empire was in the war, neither Britain, France, nor Russia had any qualms about partitioning it. They apportioned Ottoman territory among themselves, and in March 1915 Britain and France explicitly endorsed Russian possession of the Turkish Straits after the war. Russia in return accepted that substantial sections of the Ottoman Empire would fall to Britain and France. As part of the negotiations to bring Italy into the war on the Allied side, in April 1915 Russia acquiesced in Italian possession of Austrian territory populated by South Slavs. This payment was sufficient to produce Italian participation. On 10/23 May 1915, Italy joined the war against Austria-Hungary.

Russia's war against the Ottoman Empire provided it with its only unqualified success of the war. In late 1914, an Ottoman invasion of Transcaucasia was annihilated by outnumbered Russian troops, who by early 1915 pushed into Ottoman territory. Through 1915 and 1916, the Russians pressed farther, even moving south into Iran, through Tehran, to link up with the British in Mesopotamia. Difficult terrain prevented further exploitation into the Ottoman heartland, but Russia's Caucasus frontier was secure.

The 1915 Campaign

Despite impressive victories, Germany's strategy had failed. Russia had mobilized faster than expected, and Germany failed to knock France out of the war. New thinking was required. Over the winter of 1914–1915, the German high command turned its resources against the weakest link in the Allied coalition: Russia in the east, rather than the combined forces of Britain and France in the west. Some in the German high command were deeply skeptical of the wisdom of throwing troops into Russia's trackless spaces, but the Western Front did not offer better opportunities. The weight of the German military machine would be brought to bear on a Russian army ill prepared to cope.

The Russian high command in early 1915, as in much of the rest of the war, bungled its responsibility to produce a clear and coherent strategy. Russia had over 100 infantry divisions on the Eastern Front at the beginning of 1915, compared to 80 German and Austrian, but the high command failed to establish priorities, choose a decisive point, and mass forces there. Instead, those divisions were split between the Northwest and Southwest Fronts, and each Front developed its own offensive. The Northwestern Front prepared an offensive by its 10th and 12th Armies to clear East Prussia, set to begin 10/23 February. It was instead preempted by a German offensive to take the pressure off Austria in the Carpathians. Four carefully assembled German corps struck both flanks of the Russian 10th Army in an effort to surround and destroy it. Negligent intelligence and reconnaissance led the 10th Army's command to misjudge the seriousness of the attack. Only when its northern flank had completely collapsed did the army retreat. The 10th Army's XX Corps failed to withdraw in time and was encircled and destroyed.

In the south, the besieged Austrian fortress of Przemysl finally fell on 9/22 March, freeing the Russian 11th Army and allowing the Southwestern Front to expand its struggle for the Carpathian Mountain passes. Though the Austrians took terrible casualties, they blocked the Russian advance through the Carpathians into Hungary. By the time fighting halted in April, Russian troops were exhausted, and stocks of ammunition were dangerously low. Russia still threatened a Hungarian invasion, and Erich von Falkenhayn, chief of the German General Staff, was finally convinced the situation warranted substantial German intervention to keep Austria in the war. The Russians were in no condition to withstand the coming offensive. The Germans enjoyed a marked superiority in artillery, particularly heavy artillery. This was worsened by Russia's rudimentary trench systems, which lacked depth: they were neither deep enough vertically to withstand bombardment nor extensive enough horizontally to provide defense in depth. Russian deployments put too many troops in the front lines, vulnerable to artillery fire, and left insufficient reserves to plug inevitable holes. Finally, Germans transferred from the Western Front brought experience in advanced techniques of trench warfare.

As a result, the German 11th Army's offensive on 19 April/2 May 1915 obliterated Russian positional defenses, blowing open a major gap near Gorlice, Poland. Russia lacked the heavy artillery and shells to counter Germany's ability to blast Russian positions into oblivion. The breach forced Russian troops in neighboring sectors to withdraw or be encircled. Once they left their trenches, however primitive, they became more vulnerable to enemy fire and could retreat no faster than German and Austrian infantry could pursue. The Russian 8th Army, bearing the brunt of the attack, fed inadequate reserves into the gap piecemeal, achieving little. Despite this success, the German advance through Galicia was slow. The Russians took advantage of north-south rivers as defensive positions, making a final stand at the San River, 40 miles behind their initial lines. The Germans did not clear the San River line and retake Przemysl until a month after their offensive began, and Lvov, chief city of western Ukraine, two weeks later. The price the Russians paid for this delay was terrible losses among soldiers who stood and fought instead of retreating to safety.

The losses meant that Russia was in no position to rebuild sound defenses. The southern flank of Russia's immense Polish salient was collapsing, but political considerations prevented a judicious retreat to a shorter front. By July, Germany was ready for a second major offensive. From the south, the Germans and Austrians attacked north to Lublin. From the north, another German offensive pushed out southeast from East Prussia. As in Galicia, the advance was slow, but Russian failure to abandon lost positions meant Russian troops were wiped out in place.

Despite slow German progress, losses on the flanks and continuing German pressure from the east meant Poland could no longer be defended and the Russian high command approved a retreat. Warsaw was abandoned along with major fort complexes, stuffed with artillery and ammunition. Once the retreat began, it carried its own momentum, and over August and September all of Poland and much of Belorussia were given up. Despite the huge territory and hundreds of thousands of prisoners lost, this "great retreat" was conducted reasonably well. Slow German progress meant that the retreating Russians were not cut off and destroyed. The front line stabilized in the fall, running from Riga to the Romanian border. The shortening of the front meant Russian manpower was sufficient to hold the line. The Germans were exhausted by the chase across eastern Europe and thinly stretched at the end of tenuous supply lines.

The defeats of 1915 had profound domestic consequences. Political opposition to the tsar grew. Popular patriotism, fragile but real in 1914, was gone by 1915. A burgeoning strike wave protested the rising cost of living and mismanagement of the war, while draft dodging increased. The rapid German advance created swarms of refugees, some 6 million people by the end of the war. This burden surpassed the government's ability to cope, breeding nongovernmental charitable organizations and with them a model of popular participation in the work of managing society. Most refugees were not ethnically Russian—Jews, Poles, Lithuanians, Latvians—and their alien presence bred resentment in Russia's heartland and increased ethnic consciousness among the displaced. German successes triggered substantial riots against Moscow's German community. Among political elites, the moderate parties in the Duma formed a Progressive Bloc in the summer of 1915. Opposed to the tsarist government's manifest bungling, the Bloc nonetheless endorsed fighting the war until victory. It saw that victory as requiring political reform, particularly a government acceptable to the nation, not just the tsar. Growing numbers of reformist military officers agreed, seeing Nicholas not as a leader but an obstacle to victory. Tsar Nicholas simply stonewalled these demands, while making personnel changes to appease popular discontent.

As the Germans marched across Poland, Nicholas dismissed Sukhomlinov as Minister of War, appointing instead Aleksei Andreevich Polivanov. Sukhomlinov was held responsible for shortages of artillery and shells, particularly because of his failure to involve Russian industry in war production. He was also embroiled in a trumped-up spy scandal involving a close associate and was arrested soon after his removal. Polivanov was an improvement on Sukhomlinov and certainly was more amenable to the modernization of the Russian war machine by involving private enterprise. The high command was also overhauled by splitting the overburdened Northwestern Front into a Northern Front and a Western Front. In a disastrous decision, Nicholas also responded by dismissing his cousin Nicholas as commander in chief. Against all advice, he took over himself. He employed the reasonably competent Mikhail Vasil'evich Alekseev as his chief of staff, replacing the odious and incompetent Yanushkevich. Alekseev had fought in the Russo-Turkish and Russo-Japanese wars, taught at the Nikolaev Academy, and served as Chief of Staff of the Southwestern Front. Nicholas was not foolish enough to intrude on military decisions, making Alekseev a *de facto* commander in chief. Nonetheless, Nicholas's presence at *Stavka* near the front took him out of touch with politics in the capital and made him personally responsible for future failures. His absence gave his German-born wife and her crazed monk companion Rasputin pernicious influence over the Russian government.

The crisis of 1915 galvanized efforts by Russia's nascent civil society to organize for war. Russian war production from late 1915 is one of the few examples in Russian history of active and successful cooperation between the government and the public. Numerous private committees and boards managed industrial production and the war economy. The

Russian government set up a Special Commission for State Defense in May 1915 to coordinate industry and government. Expanded by the addition of representatives of Russian small business, this further evolved in August into four special councils. Combining representatives of industry, government, and the Duma, these committees boosted industrial production substantially while also handling food, fuel, and transport. Russia's *zemstvos*, local government councils, organized a network of hospitals as well as a national effort to cope with refugees. Though industrial reorganization eliminated shortages of ammunition and weaponry, this new productivity had serious repercussions. Without experience in production or the economies of scale of large government arsenals, private firms produced war material at prices much higher than state suppliers. Integrating private industry into war production meant lucrative contracts and windfall profits for industrialists and financiers. Industrial workers, by contrast, dealt with doubled wages and quadrupled prices.

The defeats of 1915 also produced a manpower crisis. Russia quickly ran through its 1914 standing army and recently discharged reservists. It then tapped those who had never done military service and advanced its call-up schedule, bringing in men younger than 21. It extended conscription to central Asians, provoking a massive native uprising in 1916. Pushing further meant drafting the sole male supporters of families and stripping the countryside even further of the labor needed to feed the country. Even worse was the shortage of capable officers. The 40,000 serving in 1914 were whittled down by casualties. As Russia's expanding officer corps suffered well over 100,000 killed, wounded, or captured over the course of the war, by 1917 only 10 percent of the officer corps consisted of prewar regulars. At the same time, the officer corps was diluted by an influx of hastily trained novices. In addition, Russia had a structural shortage of noncommissioned officers, the sergeants who did much practical training and small-unit leadership. With a social structure split between peasants and nobles, Russia had few of the educated lower middle class who were noncommissioned officers in other armies.

War, as always, brought inflation. In a well-meaning but disastrous move, the Russian government halted production of vodka (a state monopoly) at the outbreak of war. Whatever its benefits for sobriety, this devastated state finances, already strained by the expense of war. Russia was able to borrow some funds abroad and introduced an income tax in 1916, but covered most of its deficit by printing money. Peasants withdrew from the cash economy into subsistence agriculture. Urban workers had no such luxury. This explained Russia's biggest crisis: food production. The problem was not a shortage of manpower; Russia drafted less of its population than the other great powers. Instead, the war's inflation reduced the amount of food available to Russia's population. The railroads were strained to their limits moving soldiers and war material, leaving little spare capacity for moving food to cities. Since military production had crowded out civilian goods, peasants had no use for worthless cash and no incentive to sell their grain. Peasant households had ready uses for their surplus grain. In time-honored Russian tradition, they could happily convert it into meat or vodka for their own consumption. That left urban workers scrambling to feed their families, while peasants and industrialists grew rich.

The 1916 Campaign

The winter of 1915–1916, much as that of 1914–1915, left the Germans in a quandary. Their western strategy had failed in 1914, and their eastern strategy in 1915 brought them territory but not victory. Falkenhayn saw no future in pursuing the Russian army into the endless steppe and in 1916 turned back west. His plan was to attack Verdun, a fortress complex the French could not abandon, and use firepower to bleed France of soldiers until its war effort collapsed. Germany's Verdun Offensive began on 8/21 February 1916. Though Germany sustained as many casualties as France in the slaughter, the French requested a Russian offensive to relieve the pressure. In late 1915, the four allies—Britain, France, Italy, and Russia—had conferred at Chantilly on their strategy for the next year, marking the first attempt at real coordination. All had agreed on simultaneous offensives to prevent the Central Powers from shifting reserves between theaters and that, in principle, if one of them were subject to a concerted offensive, the others would attack.

The question was whether Russia was prepared. Materially, the Russian army was ready. The overhaul of Russian industry had paid great dividends, and no Russian commander could reasonably complain of shortages of rifles, artillery, or ammunition. Manpower was not bad either. The combined Northern, Western, and Southwestern Fronts had 1.7 million combatants available, compared to just over 1 million for the Austrians and Germans. Reaching that figure meant borrowing against the future by bringing in conscripts ahead of schedule, but for 1916 at least, manpower was sufficient. Even Russian intelligence had improved greatly from its failures in the first two years of the war. By contrast, doctrine and training were still poor. The prewar officer corps had been eliminated by the fighting of 1914 and 1915, leaving behind superannuated generals devoid of any understanding of modern warfare. The Russian army was short of competent officers, while its rank-and-file soldiers were demoralized. Under pressure from the French, the Western Front attacked near Lake Naroch. Despite almost double the manpower of the opposing Germans, its 5/18 March offensive was a textbook example of military incompetence. Russian soldiers advanced through freezing, forested marshes, against entrenched German infantry, and died by the tens of thousands from capably employed artillery and machine guns.

This debacle at Lake Naroch makes the subsequent triumph of the Brusilov Offensive even more impressive. The shattering success of the Brusilov Offensive grew out of further efforts to coordinate Allied plans. On 28 February/12 March 1916, another conference at Chantilly agreed on synchronized action late that spring, with a major Russian offensive in May to be followed by Allied offensives two weeks later. The Russian plan was worked out at a meeting with the tsar on 1/14 April. Chief of Staff Alekseev was present, as were the three Front commanders and their aides. Kuropatkin, commanding the Northern Front, inspired little confidence with his lackluster performance in the Russo-Japanese War. Aleksei Ermolaevich Evert, commanding the Western Front, had demonstrated his incompetence even more recently with the Naroch Offensive. By contrast, Aleksei Alekseevich Brusilov, commanding the Southwestern Front, had a distinguished record as an army commander and was not infected by the same defeatism and fear of the Germans as his counterparts. Nonetheless, the ultimate plan was to hand the main blow (and corresponding men and equipment) to the Western Front for late May, leaving Brusilov's Southwestern Front to carry out a subsidiary attack assisting the main offensive.

Brusilov was forced to make do with his present resources. Lacking overwhelming material, he substituted systematic training and innovative methods. He sapped Russian trenches as close to Austrian lines as possible. His officers rehearsed with aerial photographs and detailed terrain models. Artillery and infantry carefully coordinated their actions. To prevent the Austrians from shifting reserves to plug a breach, Brusilov ordered all four armies under his command to prepare breakthroughs. Each of those breakthroughs had to be at least 15–20 miles wide, to prevent Austrian artillery on its flanks from covering the entire gap. Finally, he devoted great care to the construction of deep bunkers to conceal his troops up to the moment of the attack.

Brusilov's schedule was rushed by an Austrian offensive against Italy in May. The Italians came under serious pressure and urged Russia to advance its scheduled offensives. Brusilov agreed to begin his attacks earlier, still assuming his offensive was only a prelude to a more ambitious one to follow. On 22 May/4 June 1916, Brusilov's 600,000 men in four armies began their assault on 450,000 Austrians. For once, Russian artillery was highly effective, smashing Austrian dugouts and clearing wire barriers. From trenches pushed close to Austrian lines, Russian infantry rushed Austrian positions, arriving precisely as artillery fire lifted. Thousands of Austrians were captured as they emerged from their bunkers. Within two days, the Austrian forward defenses were broken along the entire front, and the Russians had difficulty even counting their Austrian prisoners. The Austrian 4th Army, for example, suffered 82,000 casualties from a strength of 110,000 within a week. While Brusilov had done a masterful job of preparing his offensive, the Austrians helped with incompetent command and leadership. Their defensive doctrine emphasized forward deployment, putting troops at the mercy of the well-coordinated Russian attack. In addition, heavy artillery and supplies had been cut to the bone to support the Italian offensive.

The Austrian army faced a desperate situation. Its soldiers had melted away into Russian captivity, and the troops remaining in good order had been forced out of trenches to fight in open ground. The only thing saving the Austrians from destruction was that Russian pursuit and encirclement moved only at the speed of a man marching. Russian cavalry was unable to break into open country, even with Austrian defenses in disarray. By the end of the summer, from total manpower on all fronts of 2.8 million, Austria had lost 750,000 men to the Brusilov Offensive, 380,000 as prisoners.

Brusilov's successes carried the seeds of failure. His offensive had its greatest successes in two sectors. On his right, the main blow by the 8th Army took Lutsk easily and pushed on toward Kovel, a vital railroad junction. The 9th Army on his left caught the Austrian troops thinly stretched and made impressive gains. Even the 11th and 7th Armies in the center did well. The Russian high command, however, continued to insist that the main offensive would come from Evert's Western Front, and Brusilov's troops lacked reinforcements and ammunition. Just as they grew exhausted, Austrian resistance stiffened thanks to German officers and men brought in to restore the situation. As German-Austrian counterattacks developed in early June, Brusilov desperately needed the long-awaited offensives by the Western and Northwestern Fronts. They did not come, delayed again and again by Evert's and Kuropatkin's anxious passivity. Only on 19 June/2 July did the Western Front finally begin its offensive, too little and too late. Brusilov's Offensive wound up in late summer, having inflicted terrible losses on the Austrians and advancing 20–40 miles, but without eliminating Austria from the war. The much-anticipated simultaneous Allied offensives also failed to materialize—the British offensive on the Somme began after Brusilov's Offensive had already peaked.

Brusilov's successes convinced Romania to join the war against the Central Powers, but that proved a liability. After two years of weighing options, Romania declared war on Austria-Hungary on 14/27 August 1916. Romania's entry extended the Russian front line an additional 350 miles south to the Black Sea and required creating a new Romanian Front. Romania also needed substantial Russian material assistance. While Romania had an army of 600,000 men, it was poorly equipped and led. Germany and Austria responded to Romania's declaration of war by massing reserves from other fronts on Romania's lengthy frontiers. Bulgaria also prepared to attack Romania's southern border. Russia had no faith in Romanian competence and only grudgingly dispatched troops to defend it. Romania's attacks through the Carpathian Mountains into Transylvania went nowhere. After a Bulgarian attack north along the Black Sea coast, German troops moved south through the Carpathians into Wallachia and then in November raced east toward Bucharest. By December Russia and Romania together held only a fraction of Romania's prewar territory. Germany possessed the Romanian oil fields and Russia's front line had been stretched even farther.

The Collapse

Despite the Romanian fiasco, Russia's position appeared reasonably good in winter 1916–1917. The German failure to defeat France at Verdun, the successes of the Brusilov Offensive, and Romania's entry into the war had led to Falkenhayn's dismissal, and he was replaced by Hindenburg as War Minister and Chief of the General Staff. Germany took a fateful step toward total war and military dictatorship, including eventually the unrestricted submarine warfare which brought the United States into the war. Austria became increasingly a powerless subordinate of an overarching German war. Russia's military could regard its prospects with some optimism. While the war had been very hard on Russia, it had been hard on Germany as well and even harder on Austria-Hungary. The Brusilov Offensive conclusively demonstrated that Russian soldiers could win when competently led. While morale was not good, it was much better at the front than in the rear. All plans for renewed action in 1917 were preempted, however, by the rapid and unexpected collapse of the tsarist regime.

The crisis came not in the front lines, but at the rear. By the end of 1916, prices were four times what they had been before the war, while wages had at best doubled. Worker discontent rose through the winter. On 23 February/8 March 1917, International Women's Day, peaceful marches in Petrograd became bread riots and strikes. Government officials lost control of the city, as policemen were lynched and troops mingled with the crowds. The revolutionary parties were as surprised as the authorities by this spontaneous explosion. Over the next few days, strikes spread and demonstrations grew, while soldiers became increasingly reluctant to confront civilians. On 25 February/10 March, Nicholas ordered the use of force to end the disturbances. When soldiers killed civilians the next day, it meant the end of Nicholas's reign. That night, some units decided on mutiny: to refuse to shoot. This mutiny spread to most of the Petrograd garrison, and the government's authority disintegrated. Nicholas was ignorant of the gravity of the situation. On 27 February/12 March, Nicholas ordered a military expedition to restore order in Petrograd. His generals had other plans. Convinced Nicholas was incapable of winning the war, they disobeyed orders. Instead, his generals confronted him with the need to abdicate to achieve victory. Nicholas resigned in favor of his brother Mikhail on 2/15 March. Mikhail refused the crown, and the Romanov dynasty ended.

Two institutions replaced it, both created on 28 February/13 March. First, the Duma's leadership despised the tsar's regime, but feared social revolution. With anarchy the threatening alternative, they formed a Provisional Government to restore order. Simultaneously, industrial workers and revolutionary parties returned to the model of 1905. Factories elected soviets (worker councils), which in turn sent delegations to a central Petrograd Soviet of Workers' Deputies. Thus, in the first days of the revolution, its essential dynamic was established. The Provisional Government enjoyed legitimacy by virtue of being elected and by taking the formal mantle of government. The Petrograd Soviet lacked formal legitimacy, but enjoyed the loyalty and obedience of workers and soldiers in Petrograd, and even across all Russia. This divide between formal authority and real power crippled the Provisional Government from its foundation.

The new Provisional Government intended to continue fighting until victory. Indeed, Nicholas's generals convinced him to abdicate precisely to win the war, not end it. Russia's allies were less optimistic. Britain, for example, quickly cut the supplies it was providing Russia after the February Revolution. Pavel Nikolaevich Miliukov, leader of the liberal Cadet party and Foreign Minister for the Provisional Government, informed Russia's allies that Russia intended to remain in the war and expected all promises of territorial gains to be respected, particularly Constantinople and the Turkish Straits. Miliukov's stance produced clear tensions with the more radical Petrograd Soviet. It was not yet demanding immediate peace, but endorsed only revolutionary defensism: fighting to defend Russia, not for territorial gain.

The February Revolution undermined officers' authority, but did not yet produce the disintegration of the Russian army. The Petrograd Soviet issued Order #1, requiring military units to elect soldier committees and removing many officer privileges, while asserting the Soviet's right to veto directives of the Provisional Government. Officers and the Provisional Government did not oppose soldier committees, seeing them as a means of keeping the army together. This did create dual power in the army, paralleling that in Russia as a whole, with soldiers' committees and officers competing for authority. Soldiers were on the whole politically sophisticated. They wanted peace, but saw governmental change in Petrograd as the way to achieve that, not simply dropping their weapons and trudging home.

Russian politics were becoming steadily more radical, and by May the growing weakness of the Provisional Government and strength of the Petrograd Soviet produced a shakeup. After riots over Miliukov's refusal to disavow annexations, he and other more conservative figures left the Provisional Government, replaced by socialists of various stripes. Alexander Fyodorovich Kerensky, a radical lawyer who saw himself as the savior of the revolution, became the Provisional Government's War Minister, and Brusilov commander in chief.

Eager to demonstrate his effectiveness and to restore Russian credibility, Kerensky forced an offensive on a reluctant Brusilov, who doubted his troops' willingness to fight. Kerensky turned his oratorical skills to inspiring the troops and appointed commissars to promote patriotic zeal. He provided the Southwestern Front's 7th and 11th Armies with massive reinforcements. Artillery preparation began on 16/29 June, and the infantry attack two days later. Material abundance allowed the Russians to penetrate several Austrian trench lines, but the troops lacked any desire to risk their lives in a war clearly nearing its end. The offensive lost all momentum. A German counteroffensive in July took back the ground Brusilov had gained in 1916.

A notable result of the failed Kerensky Offensive was the experimental use of women soldiers. From the outbreak of war, some women's organizations had called for women's military units, but the February Revolution and desperate manpower shortages made that reality. In May 1917, Kerensky approved the creation of a women's unit under veteran Maria Leont'evna Bochkareva. Bochkareva had enrolled as a volunteer in the Russian army through the personal intercession of Nicholas II, becoming a noncommissioned officer. Bochkareva's 1st Russian Women's Battalion of Death was made up entirely of 2,000 volunteers, mostly middle-class, professional, or noble women. In addition to purely patriotic motives, many fought to prove their suitability for a greater role in Russian society. Once the first unit had been created, others followed. This was a grassroots phenomenon, as middle-class and professional women's groups first organized, then appealed to the Russian government for acceptance. This elite sponsorship, together with a commitment to continuing the war to victory, brought women's units enduring opposition from leftwing parties.

Kerensky's intent was not to substitute women for men, but to shame soldiers into fighting. As a result, the battalion was paraded before the media, but initially held out of combat. The failure of Kerensky's summer offensive, however, convinced him morale needed a boost. Attached to the Western Front's 10th Army, the women went into combat on 9/22 July 1917, northwest of Minsk. The men of their 132nd Division refused to leave their trenches, but Bochareva's troops seized the opportunity to prove themselves and stormed German trenches, accompanied by male volunteers, and, eventually, the rest of the division. After capturing a number of prisoners, the women were eventually forced to withdraw under heavy German fire. All observers agreed the experiment had gone well. The Russian military approved the creation of over a dozen women's military units, four intended for combat. Only Bochkareva's ever saw action, as the military and government abandoned the idea of putting women into combat again and instead directed them to security and garrison duty.

The failure of Kerensky's offensive emboldened conservative forces and radical socialists. The Russian right wing exaggerated accounts of soldier panic and blamed the offensive's failure on revolutionary agitation, openly advocating a military coup by the army's new commander in chief, General Lavr Georgievich Kornilov. In a confusing episode, still not entirely clear, on 27 August/9 September Kornilov openly broke with Kerensky in an effort to seize power. Kerensky was forced to appeal for support to radical parties, particularly Vladimir Il'ich Lenin's Bolsheviks, to defeat Kornilov. Kornilov's mutiny collapsed ignominiously, but Kerensky lost any remaining legitimacy. Only Lenin and the Bolsheviks came out of the crisis with increased support. The Bolsheviks, the more radical wing of Russian Marxism, had since April under Lenin's leadership been advocating the immediate overthrow of the Provisional Government and its replacement by Soviets. Kornilov's mutiny, and the Bolshevik role in stopping it, made that increasingly possible. Russia's increasingly radical workers and soldiers backed the Bolsheviks as the most radical option available.

On 19 August/1 September, the Germans launched a major offensive across the Dvina, upriver from Riga. Using gas shells on a massive basis, and complementing that with innovative tactics, the Germans broke Russian defenses and forced the evacuation of Riga, taking 15,000 prisoners. This inglorious defense was the final battle of imperial Russian history. On the night of 24–25 October/6–7 November 1917, Lenin's Bolsheviks seized power in Petrograd then throughout the rest of Russia. The last defender of the Provisional Government was the 1st Petrograd Women's Battalion, summoned to provide security for the embattled Provisional Government. When its women found their purpose was intervention in internal politics, not the fight against the enemy, many left the city. A small remainder stayed to secure the Winter Palace, headquarters of Kerensky's government. Bolshevik forces stormed the palace against desultory resistance, ending Kerensky's Provisional Government and beginning a new era. Lenin proclaimed a new government, the Council of People's Commissars, and a new order in Russia: the era of Soviet power.

Russia's ordeal was not over. During World War I, Russia waged war simultaneously against three great powers: Germany, Austria, and the

Ottoman Empire. It paid a terrible price. Mobilizing 15 million men, it suffered 1.7 million dead and 2.4 million taken prisoner. Its loss of life was great, but low levels of conscription made this proportionally much less than other powers. Russia's war dead amounted to 1 in 100 of the prewar population, compared to 1 in 30 in France and in Germany. The revolution and the civil war that came from the world war killed far more. Like Germany, Austria, and the Ottoman Empire, the regime that led Russia into war collapsed, though Russia suffered that collapse a year before its rivals. In that sense, tsarist Russia failed the test of war, but it shared that failure with those it fought. Its backwardness crippled its war effort, but the war destroyed states far more advanced than Russia.

CHAPTER **12**

The Soviet Experiment

The twin revolutions of 1917 swept away the Romanov dynasty and with it the imperial army. After October, that army melted away. Many of its soldiers and officers would return, willing or unwilling, to the Bolsheviks' new Red Army, but that was a new organization with a new structure and a new philosophy. Once the Bolsheviks realized they needed an army, they built one on explicitly Marxist principles. Despite inevitable concessions to military and political realities, the Red Army looked very different from the rest of the armies of the world. Some of that distinctiveness faded with time, but it never disappeared. For one, the Red Army was a *revolutionary* army. It served the world's lone communist state, and while intended to defend that state against the capitalist world, it was also an instrument of revolution. It attempted to carry revolution to Poland in 1920, nearly again in 1923, and to Finland in 1939. It successfully brought the Sovietization of Eastern Europe after World War II. For another, its revolutionary nature made the Red Army inherently political in a way Western armies were not. Western societies generally saw their armies as above or apart from politics, serving a general national interest distinct from domestic factions. For the Bolsheviks, committed to class struggle and world revolution, there was no national interest, only class interests. Domestic and foreign affairs could not be meaningfully separated, since the oppressed proletariat abroad was the natural ally of the Soviet state's ruling proletariat. The Red Army served explicitly political goals, it was a political instrument, and its generals needed to be acutely attuned to politics. From the Soviet point of view, an apolitical army was a contradiction in terms. While interests of communism might dictate defense of the revolution's Soviet heartland, the Soviet Union, like a traditional army would do, the revolutionary potential never went away.

The Civil War

When Vladimir Lenin's Bolshevik Party seized power in Russia to create a one-party Communist regime in late 1917, building a military was a low priority. Indeed, the Bolsheviks were more concerned with preventing the old army being used against them than building a new one. For seizing power in Petrograd, defeating armed resistance in Moscow, repulsing Kerensky's desultory attempt to take back Petrograd, and spreading Soviet power across Russia, Red Guards were more than enough. These hastily assembled and loosely organized worker militias were perfectly adequate to establish Soviet power. The Bolsheviks made little effort to preserve the imperial army, which disintegrated rapidly as soldiers headed home. Contrary to Bolshevik expectations, Russia's revolution did not spark Europe-wide revolution. They had to defend themselves not only against imperial Germany, but against domestic foes and Allied intervention. Lenin and his party quickly realized that they were caught in a desperate civil war and needed an army to protect the revolution and to survive. On 28 January 1918, Lenin's new Bolshevik government, the Council of People's Commissars, decreed the formation of a new Workers-Peasants' Red Army.

The Bolsheviks' first task was ending the war with Germany. The German gamble on returning Lenin to Russia from exile in Switzerland had paid rich results, and the Germans fully expected to reap the rewards of victory. They presented Leon Davidovich Trotsky, the Bolsheviks' Commissar for Foreign Affairs, with draconian demands for territorial concessions. Unwilling to accept defeat, and expecting world revolution, Trotsky declared "no war, no peace" and left the negotiations at Brest-Litovsk. The Germans then took by force what the Bolsheviks refused to give them. In February 1918 they pushed east, and the Bolsheviks could not stop them. Faced with imminent destruction, Lenin convinced his party to accept German terms. In the Treaty of Brest-Litovsk, signed 3 March 1918, the Bolsheviks surrendered Finland, the Baltics, Poland, and Ukraine. The Germans had returned Lenin to Russia in April 1917, and from the point of view of the Western Allies, Lenin had taken Russia out of the war and handed Germany territory beyond the wildest dreams of German expansionists. To overthrow what they saw as a German puppet, protect the military material they had shipped to Russia, and resurrect a Russian front against the Germans, Britain, France, the United States, and even Japan landed troops around Russia's periphery. The first British troops landed in Murmansk only days after Brest-Litovsk was signed.

Faced with the German threat, Trotsky had abandoned foreign affairs and on 13 March 1918 became People's Commissar for Military Affairs and thereby creator of the Red Army.

In a way, the German threat simplified his task. Many former officers and soldiers volunteered for the new Red Army to defend their homeland. In the end, they did not fight Germans, but instead fellow Russians in the approaching Civil War. Trotsky began organizing and disciplining the Red Guards and pro-Bolshevik partisans into a real army, using tsarist officers, volunteer or conscripted. Few of these "military specialists" were Bolshevik, and they were not trusted. Trotsky used military commissars, an institution introduced by the Provisional Government, to maintain control. These commissars acted as co-commanders. Without their signatures, orders were illegitimate. They watched for any signs of treason or counterrevolution, enforcing revolutionary control at the muzzle of a revolver.

Over the spring and summer of 1918, the institutions of the Red Army took shape. In April, a central bureau was established to coordinate the work of military commissars. Mass military training for the working population followed. In May, the Soviet government established military districts, emulating imperial models, to handle recruitment and supply for the nascent Red Army. An all-Russian Main Staff managed the organization and training of the army, as well as its operational coordination in the field. Many steps Trotsky took rankled the far left within the Bolshevik Party. European socialism traditionally regarded a people's militia as the only acceptable army. The use of conscription, tsarist officers, and harsh discipline all seemed incompatible with socialist principles. Trotsky's response was simple: winning the Civil War required a disciplined, professional army, not partisan bands. He had the solid backing of Lenin and the party's leadership.

The Bolshevik plight got much worse in May 1918. From the hundreds of thousands of Austrian prisoners taken by the imperial army, a special Czech Legion had been recruited to fight for the liberation of their homeland from Austria. When Soviet Russia left the war, the Czech Legion headed east along the Trans-Siberian Railway to travel around the world to the Western Front and continue its fight. In May, though, clashes with local Bolsheviks led to a full-scale Czech revolt. The Legion's 40,000 soldiers seized control of the railroad, and with it all Siberia. Shielded by the Czechs, anti-Bolshevik Russians, labeled the Whites in contrast to their Red opponents, organized to take power back. The Bolsheviks introduced conscription, and service in the Red Army was made obligatory for imperial officers.

Real fighting began in summer 1918, as Bolshevik Reds clashed with Czech-supported Whites for control of the industrial cities of the Ural Mountains and the Volga River valley. While Trotsky was responsible for building, organizing, and managing the Red Army, actual command in the east went to Ioakim Ioakimovich Vatsetis, a colonel in the tsarist army. He commanded the Red Army's Eastern Front in July–September 1918 and was thereafter commander in chief of all Red forces. These early struggles demonstrated the character of the Civil War's fighting. Both the Reds and the Whites employed improvised armies of unwilling peasants. They were reluctant to fight and eager to desert. This made both armies small and brittle, especially in 1918 and 1919. In Russia's immense spaces, it was almost impossible to hold a defensive line, and once a line was broken, there were neither the men nor defensible terrain to make a new stand. Fronts moved back and forth fluidly for hundreds of miles. Cavalry, useless in World War I against disciplined infantry, was perfect for the open spaces and small armies of the Civil War.

Both sides made allowances for their unwilling rank and file. The Whites developed an officer-heavy army from tsarist veterans. White armies were as a result often highly skilled and highly motivated, but vulnerable to losses. The Reds, on the other hand, relied on political indoctrination as well as discipline to convince soldiers to fight. Special units of communists and industrial workers, the Bolsheviks' natural constituency, were used as shock troops due to their higher levels of motivation. There were other means: the Bolsheviks' fearsome 1st Cavalry Army, the source of much of Joseph Stalin's later military elite, relied less on indoctrination than on a *esprit de corps* of frightfulness and plunder.

Bolshevik support among industrial workers and foreign intervention around Russia's seacoasts meant the Bolsheviks never lost control of Russia's central industrial heartland, and with it the vital railroad network through Moscow and Petrograd. While the Whites relied on material aid from the Western allies, the Reds used Russia's industrial centers to keep their war running. Lenin's government introduced a policy later termed "War Communism" to manage the effort. This involved the total conversion of the economy to state ownership and control and the destruction of the ruble through hyperinflation. The Bolsheviks faced the same challenge the tsarist government did during World War I: how to make peasants exchange valuable grain for worthless money when there was nothing to buy. The Bolshevik answer was requisitions: confiscating grain at gunpoint. At the same time the Reds were battling White opposition around their periphery, they were also fighting the peasantry in territory nominally under their control.

Imperial Germany's war effort collapsed under the cumulative weight of Allied military and economic pressure in November 1918. German troops marched back home from the territory they had occupied after Brest-Litovsk. This threw an immense swath of the Russian Empire, stretching from Ukraine through Belorussia into the Baltics, into anarchy. In some places—the Baltics and Poland—local nationalists seized power and established new national states out of the ruins of collapsed empires. Soviet Russia quickly reestablished control over Belorussia. Ukraine descended into chaos, torn between Reds, Whites, Ukrainian nationalists, and peasant anarchists. With Germany defeated, the Western Allies were free to intervene against the Bolsheviks, but had no stomach for another war so soon after the last. Instead, they continued their previous limited intervention and material support of the Whites.

By the end of 1918, the essential structures of Bolshevik military governance were in place. At the summit was the Bolshevik Party, controlled by its Central Committee, and, later, by the Politburo, a subcommittee of the Central Committee. Final authority over the military always lay with the party leadership. Underneath that, Leon Trotsky ran the Red Army through two linked offices. He was People's Commissar of Military Affairs, the equivalent of a War Minister, heading the bureaucratic machinery of the Red Army. He was also Chairman of the Revolutionary-Military Council, a collective body of the Red Army's top officials that set policy within the military. While this gave him great power, he did not control units in the field. That was left to the Red Army's commander in chief, who was always a military professional. The units of the Red Army had a dual structure. In addition to a commander who ultimately answered to the commander in chief, formations of any size also had a commissar, answering to a separate political chain of command, to ensure loyalty and promote ideological indoctrination among the troops.

The climax of the Civil War took place in 1919. The Reds faced three main centers of White opposition. In the east, a White movement under the tsarist admiral Alexander Vasil'evich Kolchak loosely controlled territory from the Urals east to the Pacific Ocean. To the south, Anton Ivanovich Denikin ruled the north Caucasus. Finally, in the Baltics, Nikolai Nikolaevich Iudenich led a smaller White movement. Had those three coordinated their actions, the Bolsheviks would almost certainly have been crushed. The Whites were, however, by comparison to the Bolsheviks a broad but fractious movement devoid of overarching leadership. The White coalition involved almost every strand of Russian politics to the right of the Bolsheviks, including moderate socialists and monarchists alike. There was no coherent political program aside from restoring Russian unity, and even that rankled non-Russian nationalist movements that might otherwise have gladly fought the Bolsheviks. The generals who dominated the Whites did not easily defer to one another, each having an eye on ruling Russia after the Civil War. The Reds, though split on many issues, recognized Lenin's final authority, and their central location at the hub of Russia's railroad network ensured they could employ their resources effectively.

1919's fighting began in the east, where in March Kolchak's army attacked east against a thin screen of six Red armies stretching 400 miles from north to south. Typical of the Civil War's fighting, Kolchak's offensive easily punched through the Bolshevik line, forcing a headlong retreat that continued 400 miles, nearing the Volga River. Kolchak's problem, though, was that Bolshevik supply lines shortened as his lengthened, and his manpower base, thinly populated Siberia, prevented him from making up his mounting casualties. By late April, as Kolchak's offensive lost momentum, the Reds put professional revolutionary Mikhail Vasil'evich Frunze in command of four of the Eastern Front's six armies. Frunze counterattacked on 28 April 1919, breaking through the southern section of Kolchak's defenses and sending the Whites reeling backward at full speed toward the Urals. Kolchak's defeat created a dilemma: whether to pursue him to the Pacific or pull troops from the east to defend against the growing menace from Denikin in the south. Trotsky and Vatsetis advocated the latter course, setting off a bitter debate within the party that ended in Vatsetis's dismissal. Sergei Sergeevich Kamenev, a tsarist colonel and General Staff officer, took over as commander in chief. Frunze took over Kamenev's position as commander of the Eastern Front and continued the relentless pursuit. Kolchak himself was shot by local Bolsheviks in Irkutsk in February 1920.

Though Trotsky and Vatsetis lost the argument over strategy, they may have been right. Denikin's Volunteer Army in the south pulled together tsarist officers, cossacks, reluctant peasant conscripts, and Allied weapons and supplies into an effective fighting force. Denikin began his drive north in May 1919. Though he enjoyed remarkable success, advancing for five months to within 200 miles of Moscow, the inherent limitations of the White movement held him back. He had only perhaps 100,000 men, not nearly enough mass to overcome Russia's immense space. Weakened like Russian armies before him by geography, Denikin's Volunteer Army thinned as it spread like a fan while pushing north toward Moscow. What made Denikin's attack especially dangerous was that it coincided with Iudenich's attempt to take Petrograd from the west. With only 15,000 men, Iudenich reached the Petrograd suburbs in October before losing momentum and fleeing into Estonia. At almost the same time, a Red counterattack against Denikin smashed through his thinning lines and sent the Volunteer Army into rapid retreat south.

By March 1920, the White movement in the south was confined to the Crimea, and the Civil War seemed over. The Red Army prepared to demobilize. Instead, the Bolsheviks faced an invasion from a resurrected Poland, which had used the collapse of its three partitioning powers to recreate a Polish state. Poland and Soviet Russia had skirmished in 1919 over their borderlands in Belorussia and Lithuania, but in April 1920 Poland invaded Ukraine with aid from Ukrainian nationalists and captured Kiev. In May, the Soviets prepared a counteroffensive west through Belorussia by the Western Front under the dynamic, young Mikhail Nikolaevich Tukhachevskii. At the same time, the Reds' dreaded 1st Cavalry Army counterattacked in Ukraine, forcing Polish withdrawal.

Tukhachevskii, fired by ambition and the tantalizing prospect of carrying revolution to Poland and through it to Germany, drove his Western Front toward Warsaw. This caught him in the same trap that had foiled Denikin. When a state cannot mobilize resources fully (and this was certainly true in the Civil War), armies lack the mass to deal with Russia's space. Tukhachevskii's front grew narrower and thinner as his supply lines lengthened. As he neared Warsaw in July, his forces were too depleted to take it by frontal assault, so he instead angled right to envelop Warsaw from the north, weakening his left, southern flank. Recognizing the danger, the Bolshevik leadership diverted two armies from the Southwestern Front, embroiled in fighting around Lvov, to move northwest to protect the Western Front's exposed southern flank. Instead, Joseph Vissarionovich Stalin, commissar for the Southwestern Front, blocked the transfer. Stalin's motives are cloudy, perhaps involving greater glory for the Southwestern Front at the expense of the Western, but his actions unquestionably had a terrible effect on Tukhachevskii's campaign. On 16 August 1920, the Poles counterattacked from southeast of Warsaw, breaking through Tukhachevskii's paper-thin left flank and sending his entire Front into headlong retreat. Though Tukhachevskii's efforts pushed the limits of what Soviet manpower might achieve, Stalin's obstructionism certainly aided the Polish defense. By spring 1921, the Front had stabilized and the Soviets and Poles agreed to a frontier incorporating substantial Belorussian and Ukrainian populations into Poland.

The remaining Whites in the Crimea, now led by Baron Peter Nikolaevich Wrangel, used the distraction of the Polish invasion to launch their own offensive north in June 1920. This achieved little, and by September Frunze had arrived to push Wrangel's Whites back into the Crimea. On the night of 7–8 November, Frunze's forces stormed the Crimea, breaking through the Perekop. In less than ten days, all resistance was crushed and the Civil War was over. The chaos it produced means that accurate casualty figures are impossible to derive. Perhaps a million Red soldiers died, and fewer Whites from a smaller army. Five million civilians may have died, most from disease and famine. Wrangel's defeat meant the Red Army could finally demobilize, though consolidating Soviet authority over what became the Soviet Union took several years. American, British, and French troops abandoned a losing cause. In Transcaucasia, the Red Army had occupied Azerbaijan, expelling a Muslim national government, in April 1920. In December, nationalist Armenia accepted Soviet rule as an alternative to conquest by the Turks. The Red Army invaded and quickly conquered Georgia, the last holdout in Transcaucasia, in February 1921. In the west, Finland and the Baltics retained their independence with Western support. In Siberia, the Bolsheviks established a buffer state, the Far Eastern Republic, while they worked for Japan's evacuation of territory it had occupied during the Civil War. Fighting continued long after the defeat of the Whites. Soviet Russia was plagued by "banditism," a loose term that covered not only criminal gangs but also peasant resistance to Soviet power. In the spring and summer of 1921, over 100,000 Red Army soldiers were occupied with campaigns against banditism. As the problem was brought under control, the Red Army surrendered domestic duties to special internal troops.

The one place that the Red Army maintained active campaigning was in central Asia against the *basmachi,* Turkic muslim rebels against Soviet control. During the Civil War, Bolsheviks had seized control of Russian-dominated cities in central Asia, but the native population of the countryside remained hostile. Cut off from contact with Moscow by White territory, the Bolshevik cities held on until Kolchak's defeat allowed reinforcements through to impose Soviet rule on the countryside. This generated widespread resistance. Through the early 1920s, 20,000–30,000 Red Army troops were involved in suppressing the *basmachi.* In 1922, *basmachi* rebels, commanded by refugee Ottoman officers, even captured Dushanbe, the current capital of Tajikistan. Generally speaking, though, the *basmachi* had no better luck fighting the Soviets than their fathers resisting Russian imperial expansion. Regular Red Army troops systematically secured cities and communications lines, then eradicated *basmachi* bands. Any serious threat was gone by the late 1920s, though scattered resistance continued as late as 1933.

As soldiers and commanders returned to civilian life after the Civil War, they served as a vital tool of Bolshevik state building. Membership in the Bolshevik Party had more than doubled over the course of the Civil War, from 300,000 to 730,000, and service in the army had been for many the path to party membership. They took the military values of hierarchy, combined with the concrete experience of the life and death struggle against counterrevolution, into civil government.

The NEP Army

Lenin and the Bolsheviks had used War Communism, built around complete nationalization of the economy and forced requisitions from the peasantry, to fight the Civil War. Events in 1921 forced them to rethink that. A stubborn and persistent peasant uprising around Tambov required 40,000 soldiers and the use of poison gas to suppress. On 28 February 1921, the sailors of the Kronstadt naval base mutinied against Bolshevik excesses and had to be suppressed by a bloody infantry assault over the frozen waters of the Gulf of Finland. Lenin became convinced something had to change, and beginning with the Tenth Party Congress of March 1921, he launched the New Economic Policy (NEP). This replaced forcible requisitions of grain with a moderate tax in kind and returned food production, consumer goods, and retail trade to private hands. While this was a necessary step toward economic recovery, Bolshevik veterans of the Civil War resented its concessions to peasants and businessmen—enemies of the revolution.

In the first years after the Civil War, the Soviet Union was an international pariah, its calls for the revolutionary overthrow of foreign governments putting it outside the community of nations. It turned to Germany, another pariah, as a natural ally. From 1922, the two exchanged military advice and technology, with Germany providing weapons designs and expertise, and the Soviet Union providing space to experiment with weapons systems Germany was denied by the Treaty of Versailles. The German laboratories and schools in the Soviet Union were, however, never large, and the Soviet Union bought plans and technology from all Western powers.

Trotsky continued to run the Red Army after the end of the Civil War and used peace to build an army closer to revolutionary ideals. During initial demobilization in spring 1920, before this was interrupted by the Polish War, he transformed armies into labor armies, intended for economic reconstruction. After the end of the Civil War, he slowly shifted toward a militia as more in keeping with socialist ideals than a standing army. While the upheavals of 1921 showed the danger of rapidly moving to a popular militia, Trotsky maintained experimental militia units in industrial centers. In 1923 he began the large-scale transformation of standing units into militia to reduce expenditure and bring the army closer to the Soviet people. By the mid-1920s, over half the Red Army's divisions were part-time militia.

The Red Army's self-image as a revolutionary institution involved the abolition of traditional military hierarchies. The very word "officer" was regarded as bourgeois and was replaced by "commander." Titles of rank were abolished and replaced with functional designations: instead of "general," for example, Red Army commanders were called "brigade commander"—*kombrig*—or "division commander"—*komdiv*. Uniforms were deliberately spare, devoid of the braid and epaulets of other armies. Its new officer corps was remarkably homogenous. It had some Red Commanders—revolutionaries turned commanders, and devoid of formal military training. It also retained a number of military specialists—officers of the prewar tsarist army. Its most important element, though, lay in between. The First World War had created a large number of Russian officers, commissioned and noncommissioned, and those wartime officers were the bulk of the Red Army's officer corps. While possessed of some military experience and formal training, they were not tied to the old regime and old elites the way pre-1914 officers were. After the Civil War, Trotsky began slowly returning autonomy to these safely revolutionary commanders while reducing the authority of commissars. Trotsky also experimented with unusual accommodations to the Soviet Union's multiethnic population. The Red Army created national forma- tion: homogenous units of non-Russians trained and commanded in their native language by native officers. At their height, these accounted for 10 percent to 15 percent of the Red Army's manpower.

Trotsky's management of the Red Army was undermined by a struggle for political power. Lenin suffered the first of a series of strokes in May 1922, unleashing a fight over who would succeed him as head of the Bol- shevik Party. The other members of the ruling Politburo, most notably Sta- lin, saw Trotsky as their most dangerous rival. His reputation as victor in the Civil War, his control over the Red Army, and his arrogance created a broad alliance against him. In autumn 1923, as Germany was gripped by hyperinflation and seemed close to revolution, Trotsky prepared the Red Army for military intervention through Poland to protect any potential German revolutionary government from destruction. Trotsky was forced to demand and use extensive economic powers to prepare the Soviet Union for war, thus confirming the accusation of being a potential dictator that his opponents leveled against him. In early 1924, a concerted attack began on Trotsky's key subordinates, replacing Trotsky's deputy Efraim Markovich Sklianskii with Frunze, allied to Trotsky's opponents. Trotsky was gradually pushed out of the Red Army and resigned at the beginning of 1925. Frunze spent less than a year as formal head of the Red Army before dying during an operation in October 1925. He was replaced by Kliment Efremovich Voroshilov, a thorough mediocrity devoid of civil or military education. His sole qualification was his slavish obedience to Joseph Stalin, who was methodically defeating all rivals to become chief authority in the Soviet Union.

This NEP Red Army, built on Trotsky's model and reliant on First World War technology, was tested under fire in a brief border war with China. In October 1929, the Red Army intervened in Manchuria to protect Soviet interests, particularly in the strategically vital Chinese Eastern Rail- way. The Red Army was remarkably successful, defeating local Chinese forces handily and withdrawing after this demonstration. The Soviets also successfully employed their first domestically built tanks, variants on a Renault model.

While the Red Army of the 1920s saw numerous cases of political repression, it was an institution of astounding intellectual ferment and creativity. The revolution's destruction of old elites and the Bolsheviks' self-conscious identification as the party of the future produced a remark- able flowering of military thought and debate. Frunze had argued that technological developments made it necessary to organize the entire state for war. The mobile fronts of the Civil War and the Bolshevik conviction that war brought revolution combined to produce a general emphasis on offensive, mobile warfare. Tukhachevskii, as a writer, theorist, and briefly the Red Army's Chief of Staff, promoted this new vision. Much of the actual theoretical work was done by Tukhachevskii's protégé Vladimir Kiriakovich Triandafillov. He formulated a concept of shock armies, reinforced with tanks and artillery, attacking in echelons to break through enemy defenses and to carry out deep encirclements. Operations would not stop with the breakthrough, but continue to further operations to pursue and finally destroy the enemy. Triandafillov's ideas served as the seed for mature Soviet doctrine as implemented in World War II and carried through the Cold War. By 1936, a scheme of combining infantry, tanks, artillery, airborne troops, and aviation to attack the full depth of enemy defenses simultaneously—deep battle—was codified into official doctrine in the Red Army's field manual.

Stalin's Revolution and the Red Army

The Red Army's innovative doctrines required modern military technology to implement them. After 1929, the Red Army began a fundamental transformation into something very different. After Joseph Stalin won the fight to succeed Lenin, he launched a campaign of crash industrialization, largely driven by military concerns, putting technology in quantities beyond the dreams of Western armies in the hands of Soviet commanders. Stalin's elimination of his rivals for power had removed those opposed to high military spending and rapid industrialization. This guaranteed that the military remained solidly behind Stalin, even when Stalin's forcible collectivization of agriculture alienated the peasants who made up the bulk of the Red Army's soldiers. In April 1929, the party officially approved the First Five-Year Plan, designed to convert the Soviet Union into a major industrial power. While the First Five-Year Plan had goals beyond simply military ones, its military aspects were central. Military procurement rose steadily, and the Soviet Union created the infrastructure for planning and managing a war economy. Innokentii Andreevich Khalepskii, head of the Red Army's Motorization and Mechanization Directorate, oversaw the purchase of British and American tank designs and their serial production. Iakov Ivanovich Alksnis, his counterpart for military aviation, built a formidable air force, both as a practical means of exerting power and a tangible symbol of the regime's technological prowess. The navy, however, remained small and insignificant, limited largely to submarines and patrol boats for coastal defense in keeping with actual Soviet security needs.

That industrial infrastructure became actual wartime production at the end of 1931. Japan seized control of Manchuria, and the Soviet leadership feared a Japanese attack on the Soviet Far East. While Stalin responded in part with appeasement, he also instituted a crash program of military production, shifting the Soviet economy to wartime levels of production. In 1932, for example, the Soviet Union attempted to produce 10,000 tanks. While it actually managed only 4,000 that year, this still catapulted it into first place among the world's powers. Military production never returned to peacetime levels. The Soviet economy became steadily militarized.

In the mid-1930s, Stalin's Soviet Union abandoned social and cultural revolution, returning to traditional hierarchies and cultural norms, including, for example, higher wage differentials for skilled vs. unskilled labor. The military was no exception, abandoning many revolutionary traditions. Even partly free discussion of military topics became more difficult. Many remaining military specialists were purged. Traditional terms of rank and insignia were brought back. Stalin introduced the rank of Marshal as the highest in the Soviet military. National units were dissolved and replaced by ethnically integrated equivalents, and the territorial militia was abandoned in favor of a regular army with reserves in 1935. The new 1936 constitution eliminated class restrictions on military service, making it the obligation of all Soviet citizens.

While Stalin restored hierarchy, Europe moved closer to another world war. When Adolf Hitler came to power in Germany in 1933, he defied the restrictions of the Treaty of Versailles and openly rearmed Germany. Having underestimated the dangers of fascism's right-wing radicalism, Stalin's foreign policy in the mid-1930s now embraced a "popular front" strategy, uniting all nonfascist forces for collective security against aggression. In 1934, the Soviet Union joined the League of Nations and in 1935 established defensive alliances with France and Czechoslovakia. In July 1936, a partly successful right-wing coup in Spain unleashed the Spanish Civil War, widely regarded as the opening battle in the war between fascism and its enemies, whether democratic or communist. Britain and France, wary of anything that might lead to war, avoided any involvement in defending the legitimately elected Spanish government against its authoritarian and fascist opponents, even when Hitler's Germany and Benito Mussolini's Italy shipped arms, equipment, and advisors to Spain's right-wing Nationalists. Stalin, however, began covert support to the left-wing Spanish Republicans. While Stalin wished to see fascism defeated in Spain, he also relished the opportunity to test his new weapons systems in battle and ensure that the Spanish Republic was dominated by pro-Soviet leftists, not anarchists or Trotskyites.

The first Soviet T-26 light tanks went to Spain in September 1936. Despite a shortage of qualified crews and persistent problems coordinating infantry and armor, the tanks were both psychologically and tactically very effective. Unfortunately for the Soviets, their experience employing tanks in the Spanish Civil War gave them few unambiguous lessons about design or doctrine. Some things were clear: command, control, and communication were vital to tank warfare and required radios. Flags, hand signals, or simply following a command tank were utter failures. The biggest unresolved question was whether tanks should be divided into small groups to support infantry or massed for independent operations. Despite the lack of clear and compelling lessons from Spain, the Soviet military was reasonably confident in its chances in a European war. The Red Army was awash with tanks and aircraft, and its experienced officer corps had developed a sophisticated doctrine for mechanized warfare. Stalin's growing paranoia and megalomania, however, shook the Red Army to its foundations.

The Purges

After the mysterious 1934 assassination of Leningrad party boss Sergei Mironovich Kirov, Stalin radically expanded the powers of his political police. He linked Kirov's death to conspiracies by past political opponents, arrested those old rivals, and put them on public trial. These show trials were travesties of judicial procedure, using confessions extracted through torture to return guilty verdicts and death sentences. The first two major show trials, in August 1936 and in January 1937, began to implicate high-ranking figures in the Red Army. In May 1937, Stalin returned full power to military commissars and arrested several top commanders, putting eight on trial in June. Those eight, including Tukhachevskii, were found guilty of working as foreign agents and plotting the overthrow of the Soviet government. They were immediately shot.

This unleashed a wave of purges and political repression within the Red Army. Those who had at any time been on the wrong side of a past political dispute, or with ties to those already purged, came under suspicion. Any accident or lapse in discipline became evidence of counterrevolution. Crimes and conspiracies were routinely fabricated. This went to ridiculous lengths. One officer was shot for remarking that Trotsky had once been head of the Red Army. Another was found to be in the employ of six separate foreign intelligence agencies. Most cases were resolved by confession, typically extracted through torture or false promises of mercy. Tukhachevskii, for example, confessed to treason when his daughter was threatened with torture.

The scale of the terror is difficult to determine. Some 40,000 officers were repressed in some way, but in some cases that involved only discharge from the military. The number arrested was probably between 11,000 and 15,000, but may have been higher. Some proportion of those arrested were executed, but not all. At least 1,500 returned from prison and torture to serve in the Red Army again. Those included Konstantin Konstantinovich Rokossovskii, who became one of Stalin's top commanders during World War II, and Boris L'vovich Vannikov, a civilian who managed ammunition production during the war. Compared to the 600,000–700,000 killed throughout Soviet society by Stalin's Great Purges, these totals seem quite small. The 40,000 repressed, however, represent 20 percent to 25 percent of the Red Army's 1937 officer corps, and losses were concentrated at higher ranks. What this produced, in effect, was the decapitation of the Red Army.

What Stalin intended is difficult to say. Whatever opposition there may have been to Stalin, it is inconceivable that repressing it required decimating the Soviet state apparatus and killing 700,000 people. Part of the answer is that the process got out of control: when Stalin declared there were spies in the Soviet Union to be rooted out, people found spies, real or not. In the specific case of the Red Army, the purges fell disproportionately on those with independent minds, or with some dispute with Stalin in their past. Tukhachevskii, for example, had tangled with Stalin during the Civil War over the failure of the attack on Warsaw, and then in the late 1920s and early 1930s about the pace of rearmament. Tukhachevskii and all his followers were annihilated by the purges. In addition, xenophobia was important. Of the seven associates shot with Tukhachevskii, the majority were non-Russian. Poles, Balts, Jews, and Germans—generally overrepresented in the Red Army's officer corps compared to the population—were wiped out. We cannot discount Stalin's personal pathology: that he reacted to disagreement with paranoia and deadly force.

This was especially badly timed, since the Soviet Union faced concrete challenges to the west and to the east. In March 1938, Hitler had annexed Austria, a violation of the Versailles Treaty, and that summer demanded that Czechoslovakia cede the Sudetenland, a territory inhabited largely by ethnic Germans. He justified his actions by national self-determination and German unification, disavowing further aggressive intent. To prevent war, Britain and France cajoled the Czechs into a deal with Hitler, which Hitler then rejected on 22 September 1938. War seemed very close, and Britain and France mobilized. The Soviet Union was linked to Czechoslovakia by a defensive alliance, and while the picture is not entirely clear, the weight of evidence suggests that the Soviet Union was preparing to honor its alliance and defend the Czechs if Germany attacked. Geography presented a problem: Polish and Romanian territory blocked any direct link between the Soviet Union and Czechoslovakia. Nonetheless, the Soviet Union mobilized its western districts and prepared to render aid by air. It may have planned to force passage to Czechoslovakia through an unwilling Poland, which had joined Hitler in making demands on the Czechs. War was averted, however, when on 29 September 1938 the desperate British and French governments pulled together a settlement to sacrifice the Czechs in a conference at Munich, a conference to which the Czechs and Soviets were not invited. Though abandoned by its Western allies, the Czech army wished to fight. The Czech government, however, gave in, and Soviet resolve was never tested. Stalin learned a lesson—not to trust Britain and France to stand up to Germany.

At the same time, persistent border tensions between Japan and the Soviet Union broke into serious but indecisive fighting in summer 1938. Japanese troops occupied high ground just west of Lake Khasan, where the Chinese, Soviet, and Korean borders come together on the Pacific Coast. In early August, Soviet troops under Vasilii Konstantinovich Bliukher expelled them in a few days of fighting. Bliukher was subsequently purged, and problems resumed the next year farther west. In May 1939, Japanese troops crossed the Khalkhin-Gol River into Mongolia. Fighting with Soviet and Mongolian forces escalated, and in June 1939 Georgii Konstantinovich Zhukov took over Soviet defenses. He massed a potent strike force of 50,000 men, 500 tanks, and 500 aircraft. On 20 August, he launched a textbook combined-arms offensive, combining infantry, aviation, tanks, and artillery, which encircled and annihilated the bulk of the Japanese force. Zhukov's victory in the Battle of Khalkhin-Gol, also known as Nomonhan, convinced the Japanese to avoid war with the Soviet Union and instead prepare for war in the Pacific.

As war seemed closer in the east and in the west, then, Stalin believed two things. First, his army was powerful and ready, and, second, the British and French could not be trusted to stand up to Hitler in a crisis. The combination of those two beliefs had fateful consequences for the fate of Europe, and for the Soviet people.

CHAPTER 13

The Great Patriotic War

In March 1939, when Hitler occupied what was left of Czechoslovakia, all remaining illusions about his intentions were dispelled. In addition to the clear violation of his previous commitments, there was no way to construe this as uniting ethnically German territory. Britain and France, confronted with the utter bankruptcy of appeasement, were forced to explore other options. Hitler's next target was Poland, and Britain and France offered security guarantees.

If war came over Poland, then the Soviet Union's position was crucial. Britain, France, and Germany all recognized this, but Hitler acted most effectively. Soviet foreign policy in the run-up to World War II is still not entirely clear, but it seems Stalin was perfectly willing to entertain offers from either side. The British and the French were slow to act. Not only did visceral anticommunism hinder efforts to recruit Stalin to the anti-Hitler coalition, but Britain and France had little to offer. Having committed themselves to defend Poland, they were unlikely to use Polish territory as currency to bribe Stalin. Hitler had no such scruples. Geography was another obstacle. Poland did not wish Soviet troops on its soil, and Britain and France had no solution to the problem of how the Soviet Union might actually participate in a war against Germany. In July 1939, a British-French military mission traveled to the Soviet Union by slow boat, without full credentials, to negotiate a military alliance. Stalin rightly took all this as weak commitment.

Hitler, on the other hand, had a strict timetable. In order to attack Poland with good weather, he needed to move quickly. If that meant promising Stalin part of Poland, so be it. Stalin had signaled his willingness to talk in May 1939 by firing his Jewish foreign minister Maksim Maksimovich Litvinov and appointing Stalin's trusted associate Viacheslav Mikhailovich Molotov instead. When in August Stalin suggested a deal, Hitler responded with alacrity. He dispatched his foreign minister Joachim Ribbentrop, who on the night of 23–24 August 1939 hammered out the Molotov-Ribbentrop Pact. The open provisions were devastating:

a nonaggression pact that guaranteed Hitler he could avoid a two-front war against Britain and France in the west and the Soviet Union in the east. Its secret protocols divided eastern Europe between the two dictators, with Stalin's sphere including eastern Poland, Estonia, Latvia, Finland, and Bessarabia.

Hitler accordingly launched his invasion of Poland, starting World War II, on 1 September 1939. Britain and France declared war in response. Poland was the first test of German mechanized warfare, and it proved unable to resist effectively. German armor tore holes in Polish defenses and poured into rear areas to disrupt communications, while German aircraft pounded strongpoints, command posts, and supply dumps. Well-trained German infantry mopped up the remaining uncoordinated resistance. Warsaw fell at the end of September, and all resistance ceased by early October. After the Polish conquest was complete, Hitler turned to refitting his army for campaigning in the west, while Britain and France remained passive, reluctant to engage in serious combat from fear of repeating the slaughter of World War I. Stalin's priority was completing the subjugation of the border territories promised in the Molotov-Ribbentrop Pact.

On 17 September, surprised by the speed of the German advance, the Soviet Union had hurriedly invaded Poland from the east. Shortly thereafter, Hitler and Stalin adjusted their agreement, transferring Lithuania to the Soviet sphere and giving Germany more Polish territory. Stalin wasted no time exploiting his position, forcing the Baltic states to accept mutual defense pacts and Soviet bases on their territory in September and October 1939. In June 1940, Stalin completed the process by occupying, annexing, and Sovietizing the Baltics.

The Winter War

In October 1939, Stalin presented the Finnish government with demands for bases on Finnish territory as well as border adjustments on the Karelian Isthmus opposite Leningrad. Finland refused, and on 30 November 1939, without a declaration of war, the Soviet Union attacked with four armies and 450,000 men. Soviet manpower was concentrated in the 7th Army, which attacked northwest from Leningrad through the 60-mile wide Karelian Isthmus between the Gulf of Finland and Lake Ladoga. Three more armies, the 8th, the 9th, and the 14th, stretched north from Lake Ladoga to the Arctic Ocean. Command of the operation went to Kirill Afanas'evich Meretskov, head of the Leningrad Military District. The Soviet Union now wanted more than bases: Stalin made Finnish communist Otto Kuusinen head of a fictional Finnish Democratic Republic to control occupied Finnish territory.

From the first days of the war, profound difficulties were evident, the result of the coup and the disorganization it caused. Air and naval operations showed real incompetence, and over the course of the war the Finns shot down hundreds of Soviet aircraft with antiquated equipment. Real problems came when the main Soviet ground forces encountered Finnish defenses. The nature of combat was very different north and south of Lake Ladoga. To the south, on the Karelian Isthmus, the 8th Army became entangled in the Mannerheim Line, a fortified belt supplemented by the natural obstacles of forests and lakes. The Soviets took heavy casualties in the bitter cold from skillful Finnish defenders, while failing to coordinate their infantry, armor, and artillery effectively. North of Lake Ladoga, in more open terrain, Soviet performance was even worse. Entire divisions were strung out along narrow roads, where they were cut off, then cut to pieces and defeated in detail. After a month of fighting brought humiliating failure, the Soviets went temporarily on the defensive to reevaluate their plans.

Stalin dismissed Meretskov as commander of the attack and handed the war to Semyon Konstantinovich Timoshenko, a Civil War veteran of the 1st Cavalry Army. Timoshenko's approach was brute force: massive firepower to smash Finnish defenses on the Karelian Isthmus, bolstering the 7th Army with another, the 13th. Soviet troops were hastily retrained in tactics for attacking fortifications in small storm groups. Artillery continued to pound Finnish positions, engineers dug trenches closer, and reconnaissance built a comprehensive picture of the Finnish network of defenses. Timoshenko assembled 600,000 men and 2,000 tanks for the isthmus alone, against perhaps 150,000 Finnish defenders.

Probing attacks began on 1 February 1940, expanding through the next week. The main attack followed on 11 February, and showed the results of intensive training and overwhelming force, together with immediate evaluation and implementation of tactical refinements. By the end of February, Finnish defenses were collapsing under relentless Soviet pressure. As Finnish reserves of manpower and ammunition drained away, the Finns cautiously explored peace terms with the Soviets, who also wanted peace to prevent foreign intervention. On 12 March 1940, the Finns agreed to Soviet terms, and fighting ended the next day.

The settlement granted the Soviets a naval base at Hangö and permanently transferred to the Soviet Union the city of Vyborg and its surrounding territory, pushing the frontier well away from Leningrad. It also included territory around Murmansk, again for purposes of border security. Finland's resistance made the price for peace much higher than the original Soviet terms, but also prevented outright annexation and Sovietization, the fate of the Baltics. The Soviets paid a great deal for their gains. Casualties probably amounted to nearly 90,000 dead and another 40,000 missing. Finland, by comparison, had 50,000 dead from a population of

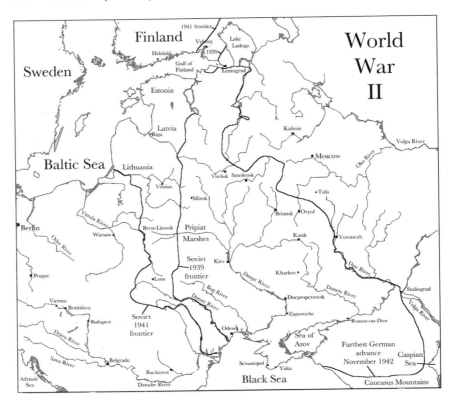

only 4 million. Stalin's humiliation was followed by Hitler's triumph. In May 1940, Germany invaded France, Belgium, and the Netherlands, winning complete victory by mid-June. Britain was left fighting Hitler alone.

The Finnish disaster provoked intense self-scrutiny within the Soviet military, which found deep problems at every level. In May 1940 Kliment Efremovich Voroshilov was removed as Defense Commissar and replaced by Timoshenko, and in August Meretskov took over from Boris Mikhailovich Shaposhnikov as Chief of Staff. An investigative commission reviewed the Red Army's performance and found terrible coordination between infantry, armor, aviation, and artillery and particular difficulties with competent leadership. It was clear, but unstated, that this came directly from the purges. Timoshenko shifted training to emphasize combat skills and nothing else. Discipline and hierarchy were strengthened, including reintroducing the rank of general. By August, Timoshenko had won more autonomy for commanders from their political minders. In an excellent example of fighting the last war, the high command concluded its troops lacked proper training in assaulting fortified positions, and Timoshenko devoted the summer's training to such exercises at the expense of maneuver warfare. Soviet doctrine endorsed the principles of Deep Battle, but stressed assaults on fortified positions over mobile warfare. This proved irrelevant to the Soviet Union's next war. More in keeping with modern warfare, the Red Army reintroduced mechanized corps in July 1940, but had little time to organize and equip them before the outbreak of war.

Growing Tensions

Stalin continued to prepare for war, but in the process contributed to the growing tension with his ostensible partner Hitler. As part of the Molotov-Ribbentrop partnership, Stalin provided huge quantities of raw materials to Hitler's war effort. Germany's most precious commodity, however, was Romanian oil. When in June 1940 Stalin forced Romania to accept the Soviet seizure of Bessarabia, this put Soviet troops close to the Romanian oil fields. Stalin was also increasingly concerned about growing German domination of the Balkans. Soviet-German disputes over southeast Europe led Hitler in July 1940 to plan for a possible invasion of the Soviet Union. In November Molotov visited Berlin in an attempt to resolve outstanding disputes over the Balkans and the Turkish Straits. When Molotov returned to Moscow with nothing settled, Hitler decided Britain was continuing to fight only in the hope of Soviet intervention. Defeating the Soviet Union would therefore not only provide Hitler's Germany with the living space he craved, but also defeat Britain. The Red Army's poor performance against the Finns, and Hitler's contempt for what he saw as hopelessly corrupt Jewish Bolshevism, led him to believe the campaign would be easy: Soviet armies would be destroyed at the border, Soviet authority pushed back to the Volga River, and the western Soviet Union transformed into living space for German colonists and Slavic slaves. Hitler's specific disputes with Stalin over control of the Balkans gave him the reason to do what he wished to do all along: take for Germany the living space—agricultural land and natural resources—that were its due, and in the process destroy the central nest of subhuman Jews and Slavs and the communism that they generated. In December, Hitler set Operation Barbarossa, the invasion of the Soviet Union, for late spring 1941.

Since 1990, one of the most contentious questions of Soviet military history has been Stalin's plans in early 1941. Why did he ignore obvious German preparations for attack? Why was the Soviet military so unprepared? A small number of scholars have argued Hitler achieved such success because he caught Stalin preparing his *own* attack on Nazi Germany, one that Hitler preempted. Hitler himself claimed that his invasion was intended to preempt Soviet aggression. This was clearly a lie; Hitler's aggressive plans had nothing to do with Soviet intent. Reputable scholars, however, have suggested that Stalin was indeed preparing to betray the Molotov-Ribbentrop Pact and was caught off-balance when Hitler betrayed it first.

Much evidence remains locked away in Russian archives, but most scholars have concluded that Stalin's shortsightedness can be explained without plans for an invasion. Stalin certainly expected war with Germany, but not while Hitler was still embroiled in war with Britain. Germany aided this misconception with a program of disinformation. Soviet intelligence was fed accounts of German dependence on Soviet deliveries of raw materials. These had the virtue of truth: many inside the Nazi state doubted Germany had the economic means to fight the Soviet Union and Britain simultaneously. As the massing of German troops on the Soviet border became obvious, German intelligence planted the idea that Stalin should expect an ultimatum demanding territorial and economic concessions, not an attack. Given Stalin's inclination not to expect attack in the summer of 1941, and his intelligence officials' desire to please him, the signs of Hitler's true intentions were ignored.

Soviet doctrine and planning were inadequate for war with Hitler. Soviet doctrine deemphasized defense, anticipating that the Red Army would wage border battles until mobilization, then immediately take the war to enemy territory. After the occupation of eastern Poland, the Soviet Union's old border fortifications were abandoned before new ones were built. This meant Soviet forces were deployed far forward, hugging the border and vulnerable. Serious attention to defense was defeatist and hence personally dangerous. Soviet planning was terribly unstable. The July 1940 war plan had anticipated a German attack north of the Pripiat Marshes, but its October replacement, at Stalin's insistence, instead predicted a German strike south of the marshes into Ukraine. In a January 1941 Kremlin war game, Georgii Konstantinovich Zhukov scored a resounding success with the Blue (German) side, disquieting Stalin and winning Zhukov an appointment as Chief of the General Staff.

The essential Soviet problem was time. The purges removed experienced officers precisely when the Red Army's crash expansion made them vital. Training new junior officers, and giving senior officers experience, took time. Building border fortifications took time. Organizing and equipping the reintroduced mechanized corps took time. Production of weaponry took time. The Soviets had in production, for example, heavy KV-1 and medium T-34 tanks superior to anything in the German arsenal. There were only 1,800 of them, however, by the time of the German invasion. Modern fighters and ground-attack aircraft were likewise only beginning to appear. In short, the Red Army was deep in radical restructuring.

Hitler's smashing success in western Europe did not give Stalin time. Germany's attack on France in May 1940 resulted in complete victory in six weeks, not the long and draining battle Stalin had counted on. The Soviet Union enjoyed a brief respite in spring 1941. Hitler's ally Benito Mussolini became entangled in a failed invasion of Greece. Hitler delayed Barbarossa in order to conquer Greece and Yugoslavia in a lightning campaign in April. Recognizing the approaching danger, on 15 May Zhukov proposed to Stalin a preemptive strike to disrupt German preparations for an invasion. Believing the Red Army unprepared, and hoping to delay war until the next year, Stalin dismissed this out of hand.

Barbarossa

By June, Hitler's armies were ready. On 22 June 1941, Germany invaded. Eventually Hitler's coalition would include Romanian, Hungarian, Finnish, and Italian contingents, even Spanish volunteers. His 3 million men, allied contingents, 3,000 tanks, and 2,800 aircraft formed three army groups—North, Center, and South—broken into seven armies and four panzer groups (the equivalent of tank armies). Each army group had a specific objective. Army Group North drove through the Baltics toward Leningrad; Army Group Center for Minsk, Smolensk, and ultimately Moscow; Army Group South east through Ukraine. Hitler's plan, like Napoleon's, was to annihilate the Soviet armies at the border. He was confident the Soviet regime would shatter at the first blow. His failure to plan realistically is evident in the diverging goals he set. In setting three goals at once—Leningrad, Moscow, and Ukraine—Hitler prepared to fail at all three.

On paper, the Soviets were well prepared. The Red Army had nearly 5 million men under arms by summer 1941, plus additional border guards, and mobilized an additional 5 million in the first weeks of war. The precise number of tanks and aircraft it had available are difficult to determine, depending a great deal on how obsolete machines are counted, but the Soviets possessed at least five times as many tanks and three times as many aircraft as the Germans threw against them. The Soviet western border was defended by four military districts, converted into Fronts on the outbreak of war: the Northwestern, Western, Southwestern, and Southern. On the second day of the war, the Soviets recreated a high command, *Stavka*, along the lines of imperial Russia's model during World War I.

Despite the Soviets' seeming readiness, the first weeks were an uninterrupted string of disasters. The Soviet air force was destroyed on the ground. North of the Pripiat Marshes, German armored formations sliced through Soviet defenses, racing ahead to cut off retreat while disrupting communication and supply. *Stavka* worsened matters by insisting on implementing the prewar offensive plans, sending units forward into German encirclement. Within a week, German armored pincers had pocketed and destroyed the bulk of three Soviet armies, 400,000 men, west of Minsk. Stalin had the Western Front commander, partly responsible for the debacle, shot. Only in the south, where Soviet defenders had more armor and the shelter of rivers, was the German advance slower. Odessa endured two months against Romanian siege before being evacuated by the Black Sea Fleet. The Soviets also maintained a stubborn and active defense of the Crimea. Sevastopol held out under terrible German pressure until July 1942. In the north, though, German progress would have been even faster had leading panzer units not outrun their supporting infantry and been forced to halt and liquidate the huge pockets of Soviet troops they left in their wake.

The disaster was so great that after the fall of Minsk Stalin broke down and fled to his dacha outside Moscow. His Politburo followed him there. Fully expecting to be arrested and shot, Stalin was instead begged to come back. Mastering himself, he returned to power to rebuild Soviet defenses. Stalin established the State Committee of Defense on 30 June 1941 as *Stavka*'s internal counterpart, coordinating the wartime economy. Soon after, he took on the additional posts of People's Commissar of Defense and Supreme Commander. To stem the onrushing tide, he took increasingly draconian steps, including August's infamous Order 270, which labeled all those taken prisoner as traitors and held officers' families responsible for their failures.

In July and August, after desperate fighting and increasingly effective Soviet counterattacks, the Germans again encircled three Soviet armies, this time east of Smolensk. Many of the trapped soldiers were able to break through the encircling ring, escaping to fight again. A similar encirclement in western Ukraine trapped three armies on the upper Bug River.

Hitler was so confident that he ordered a major change in deployments. On 19 July, in a decision reaffirmed on 21 August, he ordered Army Group Center's tank forces (over his generals' objections) to halt their push on Moscow and instead turn north and south. To the south, stubborn Soviet resistance centered on Kiev kept Army Group South's progress far behind its northern counterparts. Kiev, though, was highly vulnerable to an armored thrust from the north, east of the marshes. Two panzer groups converged behind Kiev, meeting on 16 September and trapping four Soviet armies in a pocket east of the city. The Germans claimed 665,000 prisoners. Army Group South then continued east, taking Ukraine's industrial centers and reaching the Donets River. It even briefly crossed the Don River to take Rostov in November before being expelled by a Soviet counterattack.

In the north, the Germans reached the outskirts of Leningrad by early August. By the beginning of September, the first German shells and bombs fell on the city, and Stalin sent Zhukov to organize the city's defenses. Assisted by poorly trained popular militia and extensive belts of trenches and fortifications, Zhukov kept the Germans out of the city (and Hitler did not want to waste his troops in urban warfare). Nevertheless, German troops reached Lake Ladoga. Together with Finnish advances in Karelia, this meant Leningrad was cut off by land from the rest of the Soviet Union, and its citizens would undergo a 900-day siege. Tenuous connections remained across Lake Ladoga, but this was not enough to sustain the city, and at least a million people died from hunger and cold during the siege.

The diversion of Army Group Center's tanks gave the Soviets valuable time to muster reserves, build fortifications, and prepare for the German drive on Moscow. Hitler's detour reaped great gains, but cost him a month's good weather. The renewed drive, Operation Typhoon, used three of Germany's four panzer groups and began 30 September. The thin and brittle Soviet defenses shattered, and another four Soviet armies were encircled and destroyed between Smolensk and Viazma. At this point, the true savior of Moscow intervened: mud. Fall rains turned the unpaved roads into thick mud, bogging down the German advance. This period of *rasputitsa* (literally, "the time when paths disappear") brought the Germans to a halt. Stalin transferred Zhukov from Leningrad to the Moscow defenses on 10 October. The Germans were still so close that Stalin evacuated much of the Soviet government east to Kuibyshev (now Samara), triggering two days of riots and mass panic.

The *rasputitsa* was a temporary respite. Colder weather would harden the ground and enable further German advances. In the meantime, Zhukov scratched together troops to defend Moscow and disrupt German preparations with spoiling attacks. The German offensive began in mid-November with armored thrusts pushing through Soviet defenses both north and south of Moscow. Within three weeks, leading German units reached the outskirts of Moscow—a monument commemorating the Soviet defense lies today on the road between Moscow and its airport. Just as it reached Moscow, though, Army Group Center ran out of men and material to push further. Stalin, informed by his intelligence network in Tokyo that the Japanese would not attack the Soviet Far East, pulled veteran Siberian divisions west to carry out a counterattack.

By 5 December, the German advance had stopped, and some Soviet units began counterattacking north of Moscow. The full counteroffensive began the next day. Zhukov's new Siberian divisions, worker militias, and repaired units caught the frozen and exhausted Germans at their most vulnerable point. Zhukov formed special shock armies and shock groups, reinforced with additional men, artillery, and armor, to break through overstretched German defenses. Front-line German units retreated to avoid destruction. German salients both north and south of Moscow were eliminated, leaving their tanks and heavy guns behind. In the far north, another Soviet offensive gained valuable space around Lake Ladoga, keeping a narrow lifeline of supplies to Leningrad open across the lake. Hitler's generals were unanimous that only further withdrawals to rebuild a coherent defense could prevent encirclement and destruction. Hitler alone disagreed. On 18 December, he ordered all troops to stand fast, fearing that any retreat would never stop, turning into a defeat of Napoleonic dimensions. The Germans were instead to halt in place, fortify towns and villages, and hold until spring. Hitler took over personally as army commander in chief.

Army Group Center's front had cracked and came close to complete collapse, encirclement, and disaster in the cold. Despite the rapidly improving Soviet performance that the Moscow counteroffensive demonstrated, there was still an enormous tactical and operational gap between what the German army was capable of doing and what the Soviets could do. Throughout the fall campaign, encircled Soviet armies quickly disintegrated. Encircled Germans, by contrast, improvised defenses, maintained order, and held out for relief. The Soviets, given inexperienced troops and commanders, were much too reliant on expensive frontal assaults. On a strategic scale, Soviet successes bred overconfidence. In January Stalin attempted to turn this local counteroffensive around Moscow into an attack along the entire front, against the advice of his generals. Soviet troops were wasted in hopeless, piecemeal attacks against well-managed German defenses, and the Soviet Union's scarce airborne forces were destroyed in failed attempts to attack German rear areas. Armies that did penetrate German front lines were pocketed and destroyed. The opportunity to score a more substantial but limited success against Army Group Center was squandered in illusory hopes of total victory.

Evolution of the Soviet War Effort

There was a brief lull in spring 1942 as the thaw and resulting mud halted active operations. That pause provides an opportunity to take stock of the changing Soviet war effort early in the war. The Soviet Army's performance, abysmal in the first days of the war, was steadily improving. The loss of so many experienced officers, in the purges and the early months of the war, meant Soviet operations were clumsy, and depended on mass for success. Attacks were unsubtle frontal assaults; defenses were static and single echelon. Given that the Red Army was a crude instrument, its commanders learned to mass resources at key sectors. In 1941, that meant shock armies: infantry reinforced with all available armor and artillery to achieve narrow breakthroughs at particular points. The wholesale destruction of Soviet armor meant that the small numbers of available tanks were organized into small tank brigades or divisions, used for infantry support. By spring 1942, the improving material situation allowed the creation of tank corps, the size equivalent of a German panzer division. By late 1942, breakthroughs in key sectors were the task of mechanized corps and finally tank armies, the key elements of Soviet mobile warfare for the rest of the war. Air power also reflected the importance of mass, as recovery from the wholesale destruction of the first weeks saw air assets concentrated in key sectors, not scattered along the front.

Because of the limited experience of Soviet officers, *Stavka* made their jobs simpler by reducing the scope of what they were asked to do. Divisions became smaller (a function of casualties as well) and were stripped of support elements to concentrate them at the army level. Corps were eliminated altogether, leaving army commanders with a more manageable job, and they were recreated only when the Red Army had equipment and commanders to justify them. There was a great deal to be learned: how much force was needed to break through German defenses, how narrow or wide a breakthrough ought to be, when to commit mobile forces to a breakthrough—not so early as to get caught in German defenses but not so late as to allow German reserves to close the gap. All this took time and experience, and the Soviets systematically analyzed their own campaigns to educate their commanders.

The Soviets also needed some way to coordinate large-scale operations. Soviet armies were much smaller than German armies and handled a much smaller frontage, but this made them incapable of significant independent action. During World War I, imperial Russia used the "Front" as a level of command coordinating multiple armies, what Western armies called an "Army Group." Russia fought most of World War I with three Fronts in the west (Northern, Western, and Southwestern), creating another for the Caucasus late in the war. *Stavka,* the high command, exercised overall coordination. For World War II, that system was no longer adequate. While World War I's *Stavka* had only three Fronts to manage, World War II's *Stavka* had a dozen. The scale of the war in men and material was far greater, and, second, the fact that Soviet armies were smaller than German armies mean that Soviet Fronts were smaller than German Army Groups. When the Germans invaded the Soviet Union with three Army Groups (North, Center, and South), the Soviets defended with four Fronts (Northwestern, Western, Southwestern, and Southern). By 1942, though, the Soviets had a dozen Fronts stretching from the Arctic Ocean to the Black Sea. Since an individual Front was too small to carry out a strategic operation alone, as early as July 1941, *Stavka* experimented with using "directions" to coordinate actions, handing the Northwest, West, and Southwest Directions to Stalin's Civil War cronies Voroshilov,

Timoshenko, and Semyon Mikhailovich Budennyi. Given their limited abilities, this was predictably ineffective. The solution was the use of ad hoc coordinators, *Stavka* representatives, who managed particular operations by linking multiple fronts for a single strategic purpose. Zhukov played this role in 1941, first organizing the defense of Leningrad, and particularly the defense of Moscow and subsequent counteroffensive. Operation Uranus, the November 1942 Stalingrad counteroffensive, incorporated three fronts (Southwestern, Don, and Stalingrad). Operation Bagration in June 1944, the destruction of Army Group Center, used four.

Stalin himself improved his management of the war with time, a marked contrast from Hitler. Both had a marked tendency to micromanage the war, overruling their professional military advisors. By 1942, Stalin had learned to control this, even reducing the power of military commissars. Though he never ceased an active role in setting military policy, he grew to trust his key military advisors, particularly Zhukov, the top field commander, and the Chief of the General Staff Aleksandr Mikhailovich Vasilevskii, a career professional who coordinated the war effort at *Stavka*.

Those improvements in operational performance would have been meaningless without the manpower and the material to support them. The Soviet Union's ruthlessly centralized economy paid dividends in an astounding effort to mobilize resources. The largely unstudied evacuation of factories and industrial machinery from the eastern Soviet Union to safer zones was a major achievement. Halfhearted efforts in the interwar period to slow investment in threatened zones had had little effect, so much of the Soviet Union's economic infrastructure was taken over by Germany. It would have been much worse without heroic efforts to dismantle and ship entire plants to safety in the Ural Mountains. As early as winter 1941, transplanted factories, reassembled under horrific conditions, were already producing arms and ammunition for the front, and the Soviet Union easily outproduced Germany over the course of the war.

Lend-lease aid from the Western Allies was also vital. Soviet historians downplayed its significance and were correct in discounting, say, the poorly designed tanks they received. Airacobra fighters, however, were an important part of the Soviet air force. The breathtaking power of Soviet mobile warfare later in the war also depended on lend-lease. Radios and other communication equipment to coordinate attacks, the trucks that carried men and supplies across eastern Europe, and the canned meat that sustained the soldiers came from the Western Allies, whether through Murmansk in the far north, across Iran in the south, or over the Pacific to Vladivostok.

The manpower demands of Fatherland War defy belief. The Germans expected to encounter 300 Soviet divisions. By December 1941, the Soviets had mustered 600. Reserve armies behind the length of the 1941 front slowed the German advance just enough to enable survival and continued struggle. The Red Army had 5 million men at the outbreak of war, and over the next four years conscripted almost 30 million more. To meet the Soviet Union's demands for manpower, the Soviets used women in combat, particularly as pilots and snipers. The conscription of so many men meant that the biggest constraint on the Soviet economy during the war was labor. The mobilization of able-bodied young men, followed by less-able older men, required replacing them in the work force. That task was simpler in western Europe and in the United States, where the Depression had produced a substantial surplus of underemployed labor. The Soviet Union, by contrast, had been at full employment for a decade or more. To run its war economy, it pulled in women, students, and retirees, stripping the countryside of men. At the end of 1941, the Soviet government shielded defense industry workers from conscription and a year later centralized control over Soviet labor resources. The Red Army even released 3–4 million soldiers over the course of the war to civilian work. Even so, in 1942 the shortage of labor produced a real crisis, with too many fighting or in arms factories, and too few in the economy supporting them. Fine-tuning restored full productivity, but labor shortages remained acute.

The response of Soviet people to the German invasion was mixed. Those recently incorporated into Stalin's empire—western Ukrainians and Balts—often saw the Germans as liberators, and many assisted the German army in mass executions of local Jews. German brutality, though, quickly erased any wavering among Soviets about which was the lesser of two evils. German practice was to shoot Jews and communists and not to be cautious in assigning people to those categories. The millions of Soviet soldiers captured by the Germans were deliberately starved, and Soviet soldiers realized that surrender was a death sentence. Much time has been wasted debating whether a humane occupation policy would have served Hitler better. What this misses is that Hitler's war was from the beginning a race war directed at the subjugation and ultimate extermination of the Soviet people.

Though Stalin responded to the war by easing restrictions on religion and rehabilitating traditional symbols of Russian patriotism, in most ways life became far harder. Rations fell everywhere, but especially for the millions in Stalin's labor camps. Food supplies shrank and work norms grew, boosting the death rate. Stalin turned his repressive apparatus loose on groups he felt could not be trusted. Early in the war, this meant the Soviet Union's German population, deported *en masse* to Siberia and central Asia. After the brief German incursion into the Caucasus, Stalin was convinced the Chechens had collaborated, and in February 1944 he deported the entire Chechen nation to central Asia.

The 1942 Campaign

In some ways, Hitler was already beaten by January 1942. His army had paid a terrible price for its 1941 successes. As early as the beginning of August 1941, when German progress had been relatively simple, the Germans had suffered nearly 200,000 casualties (compared to 150,000 in the conquest of France), rising to 1 million by the end of the year. In March 1942 the Germans had only 140 tanks still operational among 16 panzer divisions. As of May, Germany's infantry divisions were at 50 percent strength. To make matters worse, there seemed to be no end to Soviet manpower, and the Germans were shocked by the number of new Soviet divisions they encountered. Hitler was reluctant to test his domestic support by moving Germany to a fully mobilized war economy through using women in the industrial workforce and cutting consumer production. As a result, Germany was already feeling the pinch of manpower shortages at the end of 1941. Finding soldiers for the front meant pulling men from industry. Germany had to convert air force manpower into combat units and recruited increasing numbers of Soviet auxiliaries for labor and security duty merely to keep its armies functioning. Removing German labor from industry and replacing it with foreign and slave labor had a pernicious effect on productivity. The German economy was remarkably inefficient, a matter improved only when Hitler's architect Albert Speer took over as Armaments Minister in 1942. The most critical shortage, however, was fuel. Romanian oil was not enough to keep the German war machine running at peak efficiency, and Hitler's strategy in 1942 was driven by his need for oil to win the war.

In April 1942, Hitler declared that his chief target would be Soviet oil fields in the Caucasus. Germany carried out an elaborate deception plan to convince Stalin its spring offensive would be against Moscow. It is worth considering why that was deception, not reality. Moscow was, after all, the Soviet capital, less than 200 miles from German positions. Only Hitler's desperate need for oil and growing German doubts about their ability to beat entrenched Russians in difficult terrain explain his quixotic push for the Caucasus oil fields 1,000 miles beyond Germany's furthest advances. His push, even if it succeeded, would expend scarce fuel to gain fuel and leave a 1,000-mile open flank stretched across the empty steppe. Hitler's only hope was that German operational and tactical skill could save his strategically hopeless war.

Thanks to German deception, Soviet plans for the new year anticipated a renewed German drive on Moscow. Stalin massed his reserves in front of Moscow, leaving little to reinforce his troops farther south. *Stavka* planned a number of limited spoiling attacks in the south to distract supposed German preparation for a Moscow offensive. In particular, the Soviet Southwestern Front planned a two-pronged encirclement of

Kharkov from bridgeheads across the Donets River. Unfortunately, this offensive was launched straight into the teeth of the German summer offensive. The German plan involved splitting Army Group South in two, with the new Army Group B breaking Soviet defenses and pushing east to the Don. Using the Don as a natural shield, it would protect the northern flank and rear of Army Group A, intended to move south through Rostov and continue to the Caucasus oil fields. Army Groups North and Center were stripped of armor and reinforcements for this new offensive. The first priority for the new offensive was clearing the Soviet salients across the Don.

The Southwestern Front opened its attacks on 12 May 1942. Its southern pincer had initial success, with Soviet cavalry exploiting deep into the German rear. As it pushed west, though, it became even more vulnerable to the already planned German drive from the south to eliminate its bridgehead. The Soviet pincer was cut off, trapping 250,000 Soviet soldiers. This Kharkov disaster delayed the German offensive, but even this allowed the Germans time to mop up isolated Soviet strongpoints. In the Crimea, the Germans halted a February offensive out of the Kerch Peninsula, then in May annihilated the Russian foothold there. In June and July, the German 11th Army wiped out the besieged Soviet foothold in Sevastopol.

On 28 June, Army Group South (soon to be Army Group B) began its offensive, Operation Blue, and Army Group A followed two weeks later. Three German armies broke through toward the Don River. Unlike before, though, when these armies reached the Don they found they had trapped few Soviet soldiers. In another demonstration of improving Soviet performance, Stalin was willing to allow retreats to save his armies. Hitler was infuriated at his generals' inability to destroy the Soviet army in place and increasingly took personal control of operational matters. He moved his headquarters to Vinnitsa in Ukraine to be closer to the front lines.

Though the Soviets were forced to abandon the coal and the industry of the Donets Basin, their forces remained intact. Deprived of quick victory, Hitler took the fateful decision in late July to divide his effort further by sending Army Group B east toward Stalingrad and Army Group A past Rostov toward the Caucasus. With the two army groups moving farther apart, burning fuel, lengthening flanks, and stretching supply lines across the steppe every day, Hitler's strategic situation was becoming steadily worse. Stalin did not see it that way. As his armies continued to retreat, he issued Order 227 at the end of July, ordering "Not a step back!" and the creation of blocking detachments to shoot those retreating without orders.

Only continuing German operational superiority delayed disaster. By 25 July, the Germans had generally reached the line of the Don River, which bends east to within 40 miles of Stalingrad and the Volga. Still,

Soviet bridgeheads across the Don threatened the flanks of any further German push past the Don, and Army Group B was short of fuel and ammunition after its rapid push east across the steppe. Army Group A, facing weaker resistance, pushed south all the way to the Caucasus Mountains, but could not capture and hold the Soviet oil fields. After clearing Soviet bridgeheads from the Don, on 23 August the German 6th Army renewed its drive on Stalingrad.

While Stalingrad's name gave it great symbolic significance, Hitler needed it for real strategic reasons. Stalingrad stretched for miles along the western bank of the Volga River where it bent west to approach the Don. If Hitler were to take and hold the Caucasus oil fields, he needed some defensible eastern flank. Allowing the Soviets to keep Stalingrad would allow a perfect bridgehead and staging area for a counteroffensive south from the Volga into the German flank. Hitler could not risk that. Pouring scarce German manpower into a bloody fight for Stalingrad was a terrible gamble, but no more a gamble than Hitler's southern offensive in the first place.

By mid-September, spearheads of the German 6th Army had reached the Volga north and south of Stalingrad, leaving defense of the city itself to the Soviet 62nd Army under Vasilii Ivanovich Chuikov. As the Germans moved from the open steppe into Stalingrad's urban terrain, their advantages in operational maneuver evaporated. The opposing armies became so closely engaged that German airpower could not be brought to bear. The battle became a matter of manpower, and though the 6th Army steadily forced Chuikov's men toward the Volga and split their bridgehead into isolated pockets, the Soviets continued to push reinforcements across the river into Stalingrad. Two months of fighting reduced Stalingrad to rubble and drained irreplaceable German infantry. In order to concentrate German troops in the fight for Stalingrad, the 6th Army's flanks were defended by poorly equipped and demoralized Romanians, Italians, and Hungarians.

While Chuikov commanded defense of the city itself, management of the theater was in Vasilevskii's hands. As the Red Army's Chief of Staff, he coordinated the development of an ambitious counteroffensive, Operation Uranus, to attack those weakly held flanks of Germany's Stalingrad salient and trap the 6th Army. Three Soviet fronts—Southwest, Don, and Stalingrad—were reinforced for the attack.

Operation Uranus began on 19 November 1942, as Chuikov's troops in Stalingrad were at the brink of collapse. The main strike was delivered by the Southwest and Don Fronts north of Stalingrad against the Romanian 3rd Army. It crumbled under the Soviet infantry and artillery attack, and Soviet tank and cavalry corps poured south through the breach. The 6th Army halted offensive actions in Stalingrad and pulled units from the city to repair the damage. The next day, the Stalingrad Front broke through

Romanian lines south of Stalingrad, creating a second pincer to isolate the 6th Army. Hitler ordered the 6th Army to stand fast, and the Soviet pincers met on 23 November. Friedrich Paulus, the 6th Army's commander, begged Hitler for permission to break out to the west before the Russian ring hardened; Hitler refused. Almost 300,000 Germans were trapped in Stalingrad. For the first time, but hardly the last, the Germans were trapped on a grand scale, just as they had done to the Soviets repeatedly in 1941. In the wake of Uranus, subsequent Soviet hammer blows would push the Germans out of southern Russia and the north Caucasus altogether.

Hitler's plan was to supply the 6th Army by air while breaking through it from the west. Both goals were unrealistic. The German air force did not have the planes necessary to keep the 6th Army alive. In addition, the Soviet air force was improving its performance, given a clear mission: keep German aircraft from resupplying Stalingrad. On 12 December, elements of the 4th Panzer Army attempted to cut the Soviet ring around Stalingrad. After a week, German troops had pushed to within 35 miles of the pocket, but Hitler again refused the 6th Army permission to break out toward its relievers.

While the Germans were trapped in Stalingrad, another Soviet offensive west of Moscow went nowhere. The 1941 Soviet winter counteroffensive had left the Germans holding a substantial salient southwest of Rzhev. Zhukov coordinated Operation Mars, an attack by the Kalinin and Western Fronts to cut it off. The attacks began on 25 November but quickly bogged down. The Soviets here ignored the lesson of their early war experience of the need to commit tanks in large masses, not small packets. German reserves sealed off Soviet penetrations, and Mars was called off to use its resources in the south.

Having broken the German front at Stalingrad and pushed the Germans from the Volga back to the Don with Operation Uranus, the Soviets prepared a follow-up Operation Saturn. Though reduced in scope in the face of German counterattacks, Saturn was to seize the Donets River crossings and trap two German Army Groups between the Donets and the Don. On 16 December, the Southwest Front blasted the Italian 8th Army into fragments and raced south behind the German units facing Stalingrad. While threatening to push all the way to Rostov, it captured the airfields used to ship supplies to the beleaguered 6th Army. By the end of December, the entire German position in the south was in danger of collapse, and the Germans hastily withdrew to build a new defense on the Donets. The relief of Stalingrad became an utter impossibility. After stubborn fighting, final German resistance in Stalingrad ceased on 2 February 1943. The 91,000 survivors marched into captivity.

The German retreats continued as Soviet momentum proved unstoppable. On 13 January 1943, the Soviet breakthroughs against weaker German allies continued farther north, as the Voronezh Front shattered the Hungarian 2nd Army, then on 25 January turned north behind Voronezh. The next day, the Briansk Front pushed south, and the two spearheads trapped most of the German 2nd Army west of Voronezh, while both Fronts continued west toward Kursk. Farther south, the German Army Group Don, centered on Rostov, was in imminent danger of encirclement. As Zhukov coordinated relentless pounding, Rostov's sole connection back to German lines was an increasingly precarious corridor along the north shore of the Sea of Azov. Hitler finally approved retreat in early February. Far to the south, Army Group A evacuated the North Caucasus.

Even as the Germans consolidated defensive positions on the Donets, the Soviets again threatened to unhinge them. In early February, a special tank force under the Southwest Front's Markian Mikhailovich Popov crossed the Donets, racing for Zaporozhe and for Dnepropetrovsk, two key Dnepr River crossings supplying German troops in eastern Ukraine. By this point, though, Soviet momentum was waning. The Soviets had been on the offensive for three months, and Soviet soldiers were at the limits of their endurance and their tenuous supply lines. Though the Germans had given up enormous territories, they had generally retreated in good order, keeping units and equipment intact. The result was a substantial German counteroffensive from Kursk south to the Black Sea that stabilized German lines and halted the inexorable Soviet advance. Popov's group was cut off and nearly annihilated. A German drive north from the Dnepr River crossing recaptured Kharkov and restored the German line farther north.

While Soviet forces in the south pushed into eastern Ukraine, another Soviet offensive in the far north opened a narrow lifeline into besieged Leningrad. The German ring around Leningrad was weakest east of the city, where the Germans held a short strip of territory on the shore of Lake Ladoga. In a carefully prepared offensive beginning 12 January 1943, the Leningrad and Volkhov Fronts ground their way into heavily fortified German positions from the east and the west, opening a path along the shores of the lake for land transport into Leningrad, albeit one under constant German shelling.

In spring 1943, as the Soviet offensives stopped, the Germans carefully husbanded their resources for another summer offensive to regain the initiative and turn the war's momentum back in their favor. No one expected victories like 1941 and 1942, only local successes that might produce a stable front or better terms. The Germans consolidated and simplified their lines in the north. Hitler belatedly mobilized the German economy for total war, pulling able-bodied men wherever possible into the armed forces. The shortened front and the newly assembled manpower gave Hitler enough for a new offensive, and he chose the Kursk salient. The previous winter's fighting had left the Soviets holding a giant bulge 120 miles north-south and 60 miles east-west around the city of Kursk. It presented a natural target for the Germans to pinch off from the north and the south. It was such a natural target, in fact, that the Soviets were clear on precisely what the Germans intended. This German Operation Citadel, in fact, shows the desperation of Hitler's war effort by spring 1943. Eliminating the Kursk salient would only shorten the front lines and offer no further strategic advantage. The German army did not have the manpower or equipment to exploit a victory at Kursk. At this point, whether he realized it or not, Hitler was fighting not to lose, not fighting to win.

After lengthy delays, the Battle of Kursk began on 5 July 1943. The German 9th Army struck south from Orel, and the 4th Panzer Army north from Belgorod, both aiming at Kursk. In this clash, 900,000 Germans attacked directly into prepared defensive positions of a staggering scale manned by 1.3 million Soviets. Konstantin Konstantinovich Rokossovskii's Central Front, defending the northern side of the bulge, and Nikolai Fyodorovich Vatutin's Voronezh Front, defending the southern, had spent the spring digging trenches, building dugouts, laying minefields, registering artillery and antitank guns, and training for the attack they knew was coming. The Soviets had massed aircraft, denying the Germans the air superiority they typically enjoyed. The German attacks quickly fell behind schedule, taking more casualties for fewer miles than anticipated.

German progress was slowest in the north. After a week, the Soviets launched their own previously planned counteroffensive by the Briansk and Western Fronts against Orel from the north and the east. The Soviets cleared Orel by early August and approached Briansk six weeks into the counteroffensive. By the middle of August, the Germans had given up the Orel salient entirely. In the south, the German offensive went better, and the Germans broke through most of Vatutin's defensive belts before the final commitment of Soviet reserves, and one of the largest tank battles in history at Prokhorovka, finally stopped the advance. Alarmed by his losses and the slow progress, Hitler canceled Citadel on 13 July. Just four days later, the Soviet counteroffensive south of Kursk began, with the Southwest and Southern Fronts breaking into German lines around Kharkov. On 3 August, the Soviets began a carefully planned push south from the Kursk salient, aimed first at Belgorod and subsequently at Kharkov. Three days of hard fighting broke through German defenses, releasing Soviet mechanized forces and widening the breach. After hastily organized German counterattacks failed, Kharkov fell to the Soviets on 28 August. In all cases, north and south, the Soviet offensives broke through German defenses with staggering concentrations of men and material. The drive on Belgorod, for example, massed over 200 artillery pieces and 70 tanks and self-propelled guns per single kilometer of front. The Soviets failed, however, to encircle and destroy significant

German formations, though their capacity for mobile warfare was clearly improving.

Stalin expanded the local successes of the Kursk counteroffensives to general attacks all along the front line. To the north, these had only limited success, including the recapture of Smolensk and Briansk. The greatest Soviet successes took place where the Germans were already withdrawing, abandoning left-bank Ukraine to rebuild their defenses on the Dnepr River. In central and northern Ukraine, the Central, Voronezh, and Steppe Fronts pushed west, reaching the Dnepr by late September. Matters progressed more slowly in the south. On the Black Sea coast, combined ground and amphibious attacks cleared the port of Novorossiisk in early September. That served as a springboard for crossing the Kerch Straits into the Crimea. The Southwestern and Southern Fronts pushed along the northern coast of the Sea of Azov, clearing the economically vital Donets Basin. A renewed push in October carried the offensive past the Crimean isthmus to the Dnepr River. By the beginning of November, then, the front line in Ukraine lay roughly along the Dnepr River, though each side held isolated bridgeheads. A Soviet feint from one bridgehead south of Kiev on 1 November attracted German reinforcements, followed by the true Soviet breakout north of Kiev on 3 November. Kiev itself was recaptured three days later.

Continuing Soviet offensives gave the Germans no respite from Soviet pressure. German defenses held well in central Russia, but lost substantial ground to the north and to the south. In the north, the siege of Leningrad was finally broken. On 14 January 1944, Soviet troops attacked out of a beachhead west of Leningrad on the Gulf of Finland, followed the next day by troops pushing south from Leningrad and west from Novgorod. Progress was very slow. Soviet troops in the north had less armor and the relatively static front line had provided less experience of mobile warfare than farther south. Nonetheless, Leningrad was finally out of danger after 900 days of siege. In the far north, the Soviets moved to take Finland out of the war in June, smashing through Karelia, the scene of humiliations in 1940, to take Vyborg. By September the Finns realized their attempt to hold on to what they had lost in 1940 was hopeless, and they agreed to terms with the Soviets.

In the south, the steady German retreat since Kursk barely paused at the Dnepr before relentless Soviet pressure resumed. In early March 1944, fighting just south of where Brusilov had led his offensive during the First World War, Zhukov led the 1st Ukrainian Front as it smashed most of Army Group South and continued at full speed southwest toward the Romanian border. At the same time, to Zhukov's left, Ivan Stepanovich Konev's 2nd Ukrainian Front sped through German defenses to the Carpathian Mountains. By May, almost all Ukraine had been liberated. Two German armies (now termed Army Group South Ukraine) were trapped along the Black Sea coast, and Romania was ripe for invasion.

Operation Bagration

The rapid Soviet advance through Ukraine south of the Pripiat Marshes and the slow progress north of them left Army Group Center defending a huge salient extending east almost to Smolensk. The next Soviet objective was the destruction of Army Group Center. The plan involved four Fronts, coordinated by Zhukov and Vasilevskii. In many ways, it was similar to Brusilov's concept in World War I: the penetration of enemy defenses at multiple points to prevent reserves from concentrating to stop the breakthroughs. By 1944, though, the Soviets had mechanized forces capable of exploiting those breaches to break through into German rear areas, something Brusilov lacked. While those four Fronts attacked the Army Group Center's broad salient, Konev would lead the First Ukrainian Front from south of the Pripiat Marshes, swinging around the marshes' western end to produce an even deeper envelopment of the Germans. This plan, Operation Bagration, was breathtaking in scope, involving 15 armies, over 100 infantry divisions, 2.5 million men including reserves, 4,000 tanks, and 5,000 aircraft, deployed over a battlefield stretching 300 miles from north to south. The Soviet industrial machine produced weaponry in immense quantities, and Soviet commanders were increasingly adept at using them in high-speed mobile warfare. German intelligence failed to detect Bagration, expecting instead an attack from Galicia continuing the Soviet advance through Ukraine. Army Group Center thus had only 40 divisions to meet the oncoming attack and had been stripped of its tanks. The Germans were simply not prepared.

The attack opened on 22 June with the 1st Baltic and 3rd Belorussian Fronts flanking the city of Vitebsk on the northeastern section of the salient and pocketing five divisions there. Over the next two days the Soviet attack extended farther south, with the 2nd and 1st Belorussian Fronts penetrating rigid German defenses. Hitler's emphasis on a static defense made the Soviet task of trapping the Germans in huge encirclements only simpler. Soviet aircraft mercilessly pounded German withdrawal routes, and Soviet mechanized formations moved faster than German infantry could retreat. Before a week had passed, two corps of the 9th Army were trapped in Bobriusk. The 4th Army was pocketed east of Minsk, and Minsk itself was liberated on 3 July before the shocked Germans could organize a defense.

Partisan Warfare

Though partisan warfare had been a major part of the war before Bagration, this offensive saw Soviet guerrilla warfare at its height. Partisans had not been part of Soviet planning for war. While there had been some discussion of partisan warfare before the war, it was branded defeatist. The purges ended all exploration of the question. Soviet doctrine envisaged fighting the war on enemy territory, and so Soviet guerrilla resistance to an invader was simply irrelevant. Upon the outbreak of war, furthermore, the Soviet leadership did not expect much popular sympathy and was, in fact, surprised by the patriotism and solidarity its population showed.

As the Germans swept through in 1941, partisan activities were weak and disjointed. Local party and secret police officials went underground to lead resistance. Their lack of training and support, however, meant that they had little effect. The Soviet population under occupation saw little reason to risk their lives to defend a regime that was clearly losing the war. By 1942, though, things had changed. German atrocities pushed more Soviets into active opposition, and the Battle of Moscow suggested the Soviet Union might actually win. The very speed of the German advance had left large numbers of Soviet soldiers and equipment behind, and the effectiveness of the partisans noticeably increased as soldiers brought their military training to bear. In Leningrad, centralized control over partisans showed excellent results, and in May 1942 the regime replicated this on a larger scale, creating the Central Staff of the Partisan Movement to coordinate guerrilla warfare in German rear areas.

While the partisans boosted morale on both sides of the front lines, their military effectiveness was initially limited. Geography constrained their activities. In the south, open terrain and Ukrainian nationalism made it difficult for Soviet partisans to function. In Belorussia, by contrast, extensive forests and marshes and no tradition of anti-Soviet nationalism provided a perfect environment. In 1942, the partisans' key contribution to the war effort was limiting German economic exploitation. Only in 1943, with improvements in support mechanisms and a growing sense of inevitable Soviet victory, did partisans play a major military role. Soviet preparations for Kursk in summer 1943 included directing partisans in support of Soviet operations. This did not aim at disrupting the German attack, but instead at assisting the planned Soviet counterattack. Partisans concentrated on attacking roads and bridges after the German offensive halted, hindering German retreat and the shifting of German reserves. The Soviets repeated this during Operation Bagration, the height of Soviet partisan warfare. The massive Soviet offensive against Army Group Center was carefully coordinated with partisan attacks across Belorussia to prevent an effective German response. Over 19–20 June 1944, the Germans recorded 14,000 separate demolition attempts against their infrastructure. This locked German reserves in place, while keeping front-line soldiers from retreating to allow them to be encircled by advancing regular troops.

The partisans thus had their greatest military impact when the Soviet Union was already winning the war. Their contributions probably sped Soviet victory, but did not make the difference between victory and defeat. Much of the movement's importance was political: the partisans were tangible evidence that Soviet power had not disappeared and would return. This is clear in the Soviet government's efforts to broaden the partisans' popular base in 1943. To prepare for the reestablishment of Soviet power, partisans were directed to extend their recruitment to the religiously observant, former collaborators, and suspect nationalities. As the Soviet armies moved west, partisans were either directed to move west ahead of them, staying behind enemy lines, or absorbed into the Red Army to replace casualties.

Bagration tore the heart out of the German army. On 17 July, Stalin marched 57,000 German prisoners through Moscow as a sample of what his armies had achieved. Bagration had destroyed 30 German divisions outright, while mauling a host of others. The front lines were pushed from just outside Smolensk to the suburbs of Warsaw. There was no longer any question of German defeat. Not coincidentally, a faction of Hitler's generals attempted to assassinate him a month after Bagration opened, convinced Germany had to end the war before complete annihilation.

Though Bagration ran out of momentum by mid-August 1944, its successes opened the door for further pressure on other sectors of the front. In Ukraine, Konev's 1st Ukrainian Front broke through German defenses near Lvov on 13 July, trapping a German corps. The breakthrough swept past Lvov to the north, seizing bridgeheads across the Vistula River and forcing German evacuation of Lvov itself. The pressure continued in the north. In July the 1st Baltic Front fought its way through Shiauliai to the Baltic Sea just west of Riga, cutting off Army Group North in Latvia and Estonia. Though the Germans reestablished contact, in early October the 1st Baltic Front again smashed through to the coast at Memel, trapping the German 16th and 18th armies for good. In late July, elements of the 1st Belorussian Front, north of Konev's push and southwest of Bagration, launched their own attack. Reinforced by a Polish army in Soviet service, Soviet infantry tore a hole in German lines just west of Kovel, and Soviet tanks drove through it, west to Lublin, and northwest to cut off the German retreat from Belorussia. Soviet forces neared Warsaw itself by the end of July.

The approach of Soviet troops triggered one of the most tragic episodes of a savage war. On 1 August 1944, the Polish resistance in Warsaw began open rebellion against German occupation, hoping to liberate Warsaw before the Soviets arrived. The extended Soviet advance stopped, and Stalin made little effort to rescue the anti-Soviet Polish partisans. Poles in Soviet service forced their way across the Vistula in mid-September but had to withdraw after only a few days. After two months of bitter fighting, the Germans finally crushed the Warsaw uprising. The Soviets remained stalled outside Warsaw for the rest of 1944. Stalin's postwar management of Poland was certainly much easier after the Germans wiped out much of the Polish resistance; historians still argue over whether the Soviets could have done more to rescue them.

To the south, German defenses in Romania had been stripped to restore the situation in Belorussia, and Germany's Romanian allies were thoroughly demoralized. To make matters worse, the German position extended east in a wide, vulnerable salient along the Black Sea coast stretching to the Dnestr River. On 20 August, the 2nd Ukrainian Front knifed south behind the Prut River, while the 3rd Ukrainian attacked west from a narrow beachhead across the Dnestr. Romanian troops simply refused to fight, and 18 German divisions were pocketed west of Kishinev and eventually destroyed. Faced with total collapse, a Romanian royalist coup took power in Bucharest on 23 August 1944 and attempted to switch sides to the Allies. The Soviet army swiftly occupied the country, and Bulgaria as well.

German defenses in the Balkans were in complete disarray, and the Soviets quickly took the passes through the Carpathian Mountains in preparation for an invasion of Hungary. After reinforcements and supplies caught up with the Soviet front lines, the Soviet attack reopened in early October. Tenacious German resistance through the Carpathians and in eastern Hungary kept the Soviets out of Budapest itself. Elements of the 2nd and 3rd Ukrainian fronts crossed the Danube and advanced southwest of Budapest. By early December, Soviet spearheads pushed north and south of the city, but still failed to cut it off entirely. On 27 December, finally, a renewed Soviet push finally encircled Budapest with six Axis divisions inside and resisted repeated attempts to break the ring, attempts in which Hitler wasted much of his remaining armor.

The End

Over the winter of 1944–1945, Germany's position was bad but not in danger of immediate collapse. The chances of a fateful dispute between Stalin and his Western Allies grew slim with victory so close. Hitler's Ardennes offensive had taken some pressure off German western defenses, and the sheer exhaustion of the Soviet headlong rush across eastern Europe slowed further advances there. Speer continued to achieve miracles of production despite pounding from British and American bombers. Still, German manpower was on its last reserves, pulling old men and young boys into service. Loss of Romania eliminated Germany's last source of fuel.

The manpower situation was desperate enough that Hitler begrudgingly accepted an option he had previously resisted: arming Russians in the defense of Germany. The Germans had always used Slavic labor, and also organized military units for non-Russian nationalities and even cossacks, but drew the line at Russians fighting as Russians alongside Germans. For propaganda purposes, the Nazis had used Russian anticommunism since early in the war. They even had a figurehead: Andrei Andreevich Vlasov, a Soviet general captured outside Leningrad in summer 1942. Vlasov had willingly lent his name and prestige to the fictitious Russian Liberation Army, but had never been given actual troops with which to fight. By the desperate days of spring 1945, though, Vlasov was allowed two divisions of Russian soldiers.

Hitler needed every man he could get, for the Soviet plan was simple and direct. The Soviet superiority in material was so great, on a much more limited front, that there was little room for tactical subtlety, only the application of overwhelming force. As the scope for maneuver grew smaller, *Stavka* took direct control of the drive on Berlin, dispensing with *Stavka* representatives to coordinate actions. Terrain and German defenses left the Soviets little choice for their main axis of advance. In the north, the Germans had fortified the forests and lakes of East Prussia. In the south, the mountains of Silesia and Austria blocked rapid advance. The sole remaining alternative was an attack directly west across the plains of central Poland.

Stalin set up a competition between Zhukov, now commanding the First Belorussian Front around Warsaw, and Konev, with the First Ukrainian Front in southern Poland. Both Fronts were entrusted with massive resources for a push toward Berlin, while others attacked East Prussia and Austria as distractions. To relieve the pressure on the Allies exerted by the Ardennes offensive, Stalin rushed the schedule, with Konev attacking on 12 January and Zhukov two days later. Both blew their way through German defenses with ease and sped toward the Oder River. By the beginning of February, advance units had crossed the Oder, putting them only 40 miles from Berlin.

At this point, the Soviet advance slowed. Zhukov's generals wished to keep pushing, tantalized by the possibility of taking Berlin "off the march" before German defenses jelled. *Stavka*, however, feared a repetition of Mikhail Nikolaevich Tukhachevskii's defeat at Warsaw in 1920: a narrow and overextended push west defeated by sudden counterattacks from its flanks. The Germans still held stubbornly to Königsberg and Pomerania on the Baltic coast, and to Wroclaw and Silesia in the south. *Stavka* canceled further offensives west and instead concentrated on reducing the German holdouts on the flanks. From February through April, the Soviets methodically destroyed German resistance in the north and in the south in preparation for a final, apocalyptic drive on Berlin. As the Soviets reached German territory, millions of German refugees fled before them. Soviet soldiers exacted crude justice for German crimes on Soviet soil by the systematic rape of German women, making the final defense of Berlin even more fanatic. Final victory became more difficult even as German war potential was ground into dust. The front the Germans had to defend grew smaller every mile the Soviets pushed west, allowing a German defense in depth that had been an unthinkable luxury in the chase across Poland. In addition, the denser population around Berlin produced many built-up areas favoring the German defenders. To add pressure, the Western Allies were themselves only 60 miles from Berlin by the time the Soviet offensive began.

After two days of probing attacks, the Soviet final drive on Berlin opened on 16 April 1945, with 2.5 million Soviets attacking 800,000 German defenders. Just as in Poland, Stalin left Berlin to whichever Front, Zhukov's 1st Belorussian or Konev's 1st Ukrainian, could reach the city first. Rokossovskii's 2nd Belorussian Front was assigned to link with the Western Allies north of Berlin. All three had great difficulty fighting through the extensive German defenses, but eventually Germany's lack of manpower and munitions led defenses to collapse. By 21 April, Soviet spearheads had reached Berlin's outer defenses, and German resistance had lost any coherence. Hitler still gave stirring orders for counterattacks, but they ceased to have meaning. The German 9th Army was pocketed southeast of Berlin, and the city itself was completely surrounded on 24 April. The German high command ordered its generals to release troops from the western defenses to delay the Soviets as long as possible. The next day, troops of the American 1st Army and the Soviet 5th Guards Army met at Torgau, cutting Germany in half. The German disintegration accelerated, as thousands of German soldiers gave up any resistance and headed west to surrender to the Americans and the British if they could.

Having killed additional tens of thousands by his refusal to end a lost war, Hitler killed himself on 30 April. Berlin was surrendered to the Soviets two days later. Early in the morning of 7 May, Alfred Jodl signed the unconditional surrender to end hostilities the night of 8 May. World War II in Europe was over, at a staggering cost to the Soviet Union. Though precise figures are difficult to ascertain, the Soviet Union suffered 27 million dead during World War II, 8 million of those military. An entire generation of men was gone, decimated by the toll of war. Those who survived German prison camps faced an uncertain fate. Collaborators could expect death or a prison camp on their return to Soviet custody. Vlasov, whose Russian Liberation Army had assisted in freeing Prague from the Germans at the very end of the war, fell into Soviet custody and was brutally executed along with his fellow officers. Even those who had not collaborated came under suspicion and faced hard questions from the Soviet secret police about how they were captured and their conduct in German hands, questions that might earn them prison or execution.

The war had one final postscript. In keeping with Stalin's commitment to his Western Allies, he joined the war against Japan three months after the end of the war in Europe. The Soviet Union and Japan had maintained an uneasy neutrality throughout the war, but that ended on 9 August 1945, three days after the first atomic bomb was dropped on Hiroshima. Three Fronts, the Transbaikal, 1st Far Eastern, and 2nd Far Eastern, under Vasilevskii's overall coordination, poured across the borders of Japanese-occupied Manchuria. Against second-line and inexperienced Japanese divisions, these battle-hardened Soviet troops swept through Japanese positions with ease. In the Pacific, Soviet amphibious assaults seized the Kurile Islands, an issue that still haunts Russian-Japanese relations to this day.

CHAPTER 14

The Soviet Superpower

Over the postwar period, the Soviet Union built a military machine of overwhelming size and power. It was, thankfully, never used for its designed purpose: fighting and winning a massive war in central Europe. In fact, the Soviet Union used its military primarily against other communist countries. In East Germany in 1953, Hungary in 1956, Czechoslovakia in 1968, and Afghanistan in 1979, the Soviet Union used military force to protect friendly regimes against their own populations and came close to war with China, another communist state, in the late 1960s. By the early 1980s, even the Soviet army's adequacy for its primary mission, war in central Europe, was increasingly in question. Economic and social stagnation at home threatened to revive perennial Russian backwardness. In 1945, Soviet military power had played the predominant role in annihilating Hitler's Germany. By 1985, it was in serious decline, and something had to change.

The Cold War

As victory over Germany grew closer, tensions among the Allies grew. The ideological conflict between the Soviet Union and the West had been only temporarily eclipsed by the common effort against Hitler. Numerous contentious issues, including the slow development of a second front and the future political status of Poland and Germany signaled possible postwar conflicts. Stalin recognized that the Soviet Union was bearing the brunt of the war against Germany and suspected that the British and the Americans would be happy to let that continue. After all, Harry Truman, then a Senator, had remarked in 1941, "If we see that Germany is winning we ought to help Russia and if Russia is winning we ought to help Germany and that way let them kill as many as possible." After the opening of the second front in June 1944, disputes over the future shape of Europe threatened to wreck relations. President Franklin Roosevelt put a high priority on staying on good terms with Stalin, well aware Soviet troops were doing most of the fighting. At a three-way summit in Tehran in November–December 1943, Winston Churchill and Roosevelt agreed to Stalin's keeping the Polish territory he had seized as a result of the Molotov-Ribbentrop Pact.

The fates of Germany and of Eastern Europe were still unsettled. Unable to reach a consensus on the German question, the three Allies, meeting at Yalta in February 1945, agreed as a stopgap measure to divide the country into occupation zones. At American insistence, France was included as an occupying power. The result was the division of Germany and of Berlin into four zones each, one for each power. This was not intended as a permanent solution, only a temporary expedient until a better solution was reached. Yalta also tried to reach some compromise on Eastern Europe. The war against Germany was clearly won, but Roosevelt's priority had shifted to Soviet cooperation against Japan. Stalin's actions made it clear that he intended to establish friendly governments in Eastern Europe. Needing Stalin's assistance, and with the Red Army occupying Eastern Europe, Roosevelt had little choice but to acquiesce. Churchill and Roosevelt did obtain Stalin's commitment to democratic governments in Eastern Europe. Both sides had, however, very different ideas about what democratic meant. So while there were very real conflicts about the future of Europe, Yalta had achieved at least a temporary solution.

In April 1945, though, Roosevelt died. He was replaced by Harry Truman, who had much less commitment to fostering Soviet-American relations. This coincided with growing evidence that Soviet policy in Eastern Europe was incompatible with Western interests. Given the history of Soviet-Polish relations, no democratic government in Poland could be pro-Soviet, defining democracy in Western terms of free expression and free elections. Stalin's unshakable desire for a friendly and docile Poland thus required active Soviet intervention in Polish politics. Similar processes occurred in the Balkans, where pro-Soviet parties took power in Bulgaria and in Romania. The universal presence of the Red Army made Stalin's task simpler. This Sovietization did not happen uniformly or immediately. Hungary, and especially Czechoslovakia, maintained open, multiparty systems for several years. By 1948, though, Eastern Europe had been thoroughly Sovietized. Poland, Czechoslovakia, Hungary, Romania, and Bulgaria were all run by one-party systems, taking direction from Moscow. Yugoslavia was communist as well, but its large wartime resistance movement under Jozef Broz Tito meant communist rule was imposed without active Soviet involvement, and in 1948 Yugoslavia broke from the Soviet bloc while remaining communist. Overall, though, the Soviet Union replicated its own political system in the territories under its control, and the West was terrified by what it saw.

The West also saw evidence of Stalin's potential hostility outside of the Soviet bloc. Stalin was reluctant to withdraw his troops from northern Iran after World War II. Britain had attempted to maintain its prewar influence in the Mediterranean by supporting Greece and Turkey. The pro-Western Greek government was under threat from a domestic communist insurgency, backed by Yugoslavia. Turkey, by contrast, was facing Soviet pressure for concessions at the Turkish Straits. By 1947, Britain was near bankruptcy and could no longer underwrite Greek and Turkish security. The result was a new commitment by the United States to European politics. Truman agreed to take over Britain's role in the Mediterranean and committed the United States to containing communism more generally. In early 1947 he proclaimed the Truman Doctrine, pledging American support to peoples attempting to maintain their freedom against outside pressures: communism. Massive economic and military aid to Greece and Turkey followed.

Despite the growing tensions, the Cold War was not yet military. It involved a competition for political influence, but the threat of force remained muted. Both the United States and the Soviet Union had demobilized their armies rapidly after the war. Soviet manpower dropped to under 3 million by 1948 and was moreover counterbalanced by the American atomic monopoly.

In mid-1948, though, the Cold War's military side began to become more important. The trigger was Germany. The occupying powers had all imposed their own social and political systems in their respective zones. The difference was that Germans found the Western systems much more pleasant. The Soviet zone saw the steady imposition of one-party dictatorship, while the Western zones enjoyed the slow return of normal social, economic, and political life. As time passed, it became more and more difficult to envisage a way in which the steadily diverging British, French, and American zones, on the one hand, and the Soviet zone, on the other, could be brought back together.

In response to the creation of a unified currency for the three Western zones, Stalin acted to halt the creation of a pro-Western Germany by exerting pressure on the West's most vulnerable spot: the Western-occupied enclaves in Berlin, buried deep inside the Soviet zone. On 24 June 1948, he shut off road and railroad access to West Berlin. Stalin did not see this as a prelude to war, for the Soviet occupying force in Germany made no preparations for war. Indeed, the entire operation seems quite shortsighted; Stalin made no provisions for military complications and cut off Berlin while the United States still enjoyed an atomic monopoly. It was instead an effort either to liquidate the Western presence in Berlin or to force a better deal for Stalin in Germany as a whole. After considering and rejecting the option of testing the Berlin blockade with military force, the United States and Britain organized the Berlin airlift, supplying the city with food and fuel by air. The Soviet military harassed flights into Berlin, but did not halt them. When the blockade had clearly failed, Stalin canceled it on 12 May 1949.

Simultaneously with the Berlin blockade, Stalin remilitarized the Soviet satellite states in Eastern Europe, and the Soviet Union itself. Eastern Europe had generally been demilitarized after the war. Hungary's army, for example, bottomed out at a mere 5,000 soldiers (plus 8,000 border guards). In 1948, however, a major military buildup began throughout Eastern Europe. Soviet military advisors flooded Eastern Europe, and Soviet satellite governments were instructed to build mass armies. Domestic military traditions were obliterated and replaced by the wholesale Russianization and Sovietization of uniforms, doctrine, traditions, and training. Top military officials had Soviet minders. In the case of Poland, Stalin appointed Konstantin Konstantinovich Rokossovskii, a Soviet marshal of Polish ancestry, as Poland's Minister of Defense. Levels of interference varied, depending on the particular country's strategic importance and the level of anti-Soviet attitudes. Bulgaria was relatively free; Poland was tightly controlled. There was at this point no overarching structure; the Soviet Union managed its military ties to Eastern Europe through individual, bilateral arrangements.

Stalin's 1949 cancellation of the Berlin blockade did not repair the damage it had done. Stalin's move had been astoundingly counterproductive. In March 1948, before the Berlin blockade, Britain and France had signed a mutual defense pact with Belgium, the Netherlands, and Luxembourg. The Berlin blockade then led to its expansion into the North Atlantic Treaty Organization (NATO), signed 4 April 1949, uniting the United States, Canada, and Iceland with nine western European countries. NATO pledged its members to treat an attack on any one as an attack on all. In addition, Stalin had succeeded, only three years after the end of World War II, in making Germans into victims. This removed remaining obstacles to the formal unification of the three western zones into the Federal Republic of Germany, or West Germany, in May 1949. Stalin responded by turning his occupation zone into the German Democratic Republic, or East Germany, in October 1949.

The Cold War's front lines in Europe were becoming increasingly rigid, even more so once Stalin possessed his own atomic weapons. Stalin and the Soviets had downplayed the significance of the atomic bomb, briefly in reality and longer in rhetoric, when the Americans first revealed its existence. When the United States possessed the atom bomb and Stalin did not, it was in Stalin's interests to dismiss the bomb as not changing warfare in any essential way. His actions suggest a somewhat different view. Stalin took some convincing as to the importance of atomic research, and serious efforts to build a bomb began only after the two atom bombs were dropped on Japan. Aided by espionage, the Soviet atom bomb project successfully detonated its first weapon on 29 August 1949.

The Soviet military first had to figure out how to fight a nuclear-armed opponent without arms of its own. Even after it possessed the atomic bomb, the Soviets lacked bombers or missiles capable of reaching American territory. Partly as a psychological defense mechanism, partly in recognition of the limited power of early atomic weapons, Soviet doctrine and planning downplayed their importance. The Soviets did step up their attention to strategic bombing and air defense. Soviet aviation during World War II had focused on control of the battlefield, not strategic missions, and the Soviets lacked a strategic bomber. American B-29s that had been interned on Soviet territory during the war were dismantled and reverse engineered to produce the Tu-4, the Soviets' first real strategic bomber in decades. British jet engine designs were purchased to upgrade the Soviet Air Force. In July 1948, Air Defense Forces were reorganized as a separate branch of the Soviet military, on a par with the navy, the air force, and ground forces. At the same time, Soviet military doctrine held that atomic weapons had only limited utility against hard targets like armored vehicles and that speedy operations could overrun air bases and capture foreign territory, greatly reducing the utility of atomic weapons.

Even with the American atomic monopoly broken, the Cold War was still not fully a military confrontation. While NATO represented a joint Western commitment to defense, the creation of NATO did not produce rearmament on any appreciable scale. Some within the U.S. government advocated a major conventional military buildup to counter Soviet strength, but the money and political will for such a step were missing.

A shooting war between the West and the communist bloc changed that. On 25 June 1950, North Korean forces invaded South Korea. Like Germany, Korea had been divided at the end of World War II and had two systems imposed: a communist one-party state in the Soviet-occupied north, a pro-Western and capitalist (though not at all democratic) state in the U.S.–occupied south. After the withdrawal of occupation forces in 1948, both North and South Korea wished to unify the peninsula under their own control. The difference was that Stalin gave the North Korean regime his permission to go ahead, along with the equipment and raw materials to fight a war. Stalin's possession of the atom bomb gave him more freedom to risk military confrontation with the West. After the northern invasion, American troops intervened to defend the South, backed by a United Nations mandate and troop contingents from over a dozen other countries. Though the North almost succeeded in conquering the entire peninsula, in September 1950 a United Nations amphibious landing at Inchon quickly turned the tide, and the North Koreans were driven back in disarray. As the American-led force crossed the 38th parallel and continued north, the recently formed People's Republic of China, with Stalin's backing, intervened on behalf of the North. Early in 1951, the front lines stabilized back at the 38th parallel, where they would remain through a 1953 cease-fire. Stalin saw the Korean War as the beginning of confrontation between the capitalist and communist worlds. Indeed, at the beginning of 1951 he warned the leaders of the communist bloc that war with the West was coming soon, and rearmament had to begin immediately.

In addition to giving Kim Il-Sung, ruler of North Korea, permission for the invasion, Stalin assisted in the construction of the North Korean army and the war effort itself. Even after Soviet troops evacuated North Korea, 4,000 military advisors remained to train the North Korean army. During the war, the Soviet 64th Fighter Corps, based in northern China and from August 1951 in North Korea as well, fought secretly against UN forces. Over 20,000 Soviet servicemen and 300 planes were involved at any one time, though the Soviets were careful not to allow Soviet pilots to fly over enemy territory where they might be shot down and identified. The precise performance of Soviet fighters and antiaircraft guns is disputed; almost 300 Soviet servicemen died fighting in Korea.

In these early years of the Cold War, Soviet armed forces had domestic responsibilities as well. The reimposition of Soviet rule, especially on territories that had not been part of the Soviet Union during the 1920s and 1930s, was a violent process. In the Baltics, especially Lithuania, scattered assassinations and partisan resistance lasted well into the 1950s. In western Ukraine, this looked more like a civil war. There, the Organization of Ukrainian Nationalists (OUN) engaged in a vicious fight that involved ethnic and religious warfare, not simply opposition to Soviet rule. Only massive use of military and police power brought order. Over the decade after World War II, OUN averaged over 1,000 killings per year of Soviet officials and collaborators. The Soviet regime deported at least 300,000 people from the Baltics and western Ukraine in efforts to pacify the region. Most of this fighting was conducted not by the Soviet army, but by special troops of the Ministry of Internal Affairs organized and trained for that purpose. The military itself supported and occasionally participated in these operations.

After the end of the war, Stalin wanted to guarantee a politically reliable military. Unfortunately for Stalin, victory brought great prestige to the Red Army's high command, particularly Georgii Konstantinovich Zhukov. Stalin had tried in the last months of the war to spread credit to other generals—Ivan Stepanovich Konev and Aleksandr Mikhailovich Vasilevskii in particular—but to no avail. Zhukov's own conduct, in which he clearly drew attention to his own accomplishments, exacerbated the situation. In the summer of 1946, Zhukov was brought back from Germany and demoted to running the insignificant Odessa Military District as a lesson to other generals. Stalin also maintained political officers and secret police minders as additional systems of control over his military. Within the armed forces, he used a system inherited from World War II to divide power. Authority over the Soviet military was split between the Minister of Defense, responsible for organizing and supplying the military, and the Chief of the General Staff, responsible for training and operational control. Though the Minister of Defense was nominally superior to the Chief of the General Staff, the real distinction was slightly different. The Minister was typically a more political and administrative figure, while the Chief of the General Staff was a fighting general, intended to manage combat.

The Khrushchev Era

Stalin died in 1953, unleashing a succession struggle. Lavrentii Pavlovich Beria, Stalin's longtime security chief and driving force behind the Soviet nuclear program, moved quickly to solidify his own position, releasing large numbers from the Soviet prison system, making broad concessions to non-Russian nationalities, and moderating the worst excesses of Stalinism in Eastern Europe. This liberalization backfired, however, when a mid-June 1953 uprising in East Germany went beyond the control of East German police and had to be put down by Soviet troops. The disturbances were not entirely Beria's responsibility; they resulted at least as much from Stalin's demands in 1952 for the militarization of the East German economy and the collectivization of agriculture, and the East German regime's clumsy policies. The spark for the uprising, in fact, was the East German government's increase in work norms. Nevertheless, this provided the opening for the other members of the ruling Politburo to purge Beria in June 1953. The military high command played a key role in Beria's arrest and execution, as it was delighted to have revenge on one of Stalin's assassins. Zhukov, who participated in Beria's arrest, was brought back into favor.

With Beria out of the picture, power was split between Nikita Sergeevich Khrushchev, head of the party, and Georgii Maksimilianovich Malenkov, premier and head of government. They began a joint "peace offensive" in the Cold War, aimed at reducing the counterproductive extreme tension Stalin had generated. The Korean War was quickly resolved through an armistice in July 1953, Austria was evacuated and neutralized in May 1955, and in the same month Khrushchev visited Yugoslavia to repair the rupture with Tito. America, Britain, France, and the Soviet Union met in Geneva in July 1955 in an amiable summit, albeit devoid of results. In part, all this was a failed attempt to head off the rearmament of West Germany, a NATO effort to reduce the common burden of defense by passing some of it to the Germans. When this failed and West Germany joined NATO, the Soviets responded by the creation of their own organization, the Warsaw Treaty Organization or Warsaw Pact. This was, at least initially, purely a political gesture. The Soviet Union had managed quite well with bilateral arrangements before 1955.

At the same time, Khrushchev and Malenkov continued a struggle for power inside the Soviet Union. Khrushchev used his party power over key political appointments to win support. He also backed investment in heavy and defense industry to buy off important constituencies. Malenkov, by contrast, pushed for expanding light industry and consumer goods. Though this benefited the general population of the Soviet Union, that population had no influence on the political process. By 1955, Khrushchev had accumulated enough power to demote Malenkov and rule the Soviet Union himself.

Khrushchev's personality and policies contain a mass of contradictions. Carrying himself as a crude peasant, he was quite shrewd. The last of the true believers in communism to rule to the Soviet Union, he was deeply disturbed by the crimes of Stalin's reign. In 1956, he began a campaign of de-Stalinization to expose Stalin's misdeeds and release intellectual life from Stalinist strictures. Many of the victims of the purges, including the military ones, were posthumously rehabilitated. Though he had won power on a platform of promoting heavy industry, he shifted resources toward improving consumer goods, food, and housing.

While the military high command was generally pleased with Khrushchev's rehabilitation of purged commanders, and with his opening discussion of Stalin's mismanagement in the early stages of the war, liberalization had negative effects on the military as well. The release of prisoners from the Soviet labor camp system, combined with the repatriation to Germany of the last prisoners of war, deprived the Soviet state of a large, captive labor force. That gap was filled by the expansion of "construction battalions," military units used to build factories, infrastructure, and military installations. These battalions, not intended for combat, were filled with disciplinary problems from regular units and a disproportionate number of non-Russian minorities. This established excellent conditions for disturbances within units and with local civilian populations—a regular phenomenon in the Khrushchev years. In addition, Khrushchev's liberalization removed the terror of the Stalin years while offering hope of further improvement. The result was a wave of popular disturbances. While controlling these was typically the job of police and special units of the Ministry of Internal Affairs, the military intervened in particularly serious cases. This occurred in Georgia in March 1956 against a nationalist, pro-Stalin reaction to Khrushchev's de-Stalinization campaign, and again in Novocherkassk in June 1962 against food riots gone out of control.

Khrushchev's liberalization also had pernicious effects in Eastern Europe, where attacks on Stalin became attacks on Stalinist policies.

Collectivization of agriculture, an overwhelming emphasis on heavy industry at the expense of food and consumer goods, and vicious political repression were associated with Stalin, and Eastern Europeans wished to see an end to all of them. Khrushchev wanted reforms, but within narrow limits. This proved to be a difficult balancing act. In Poland, for example, Khrushchev was forced to allow Wladyslaw Gomulka, a communist with Polish nationalist leanings, to take over the Polish party as the only way to reconcile de-Stalinization with some measure of Soviet control. The alternative of a Soviet military intervention in Poland, when it was clear the Polish army would fight, was too horrible to contemplate.

In Hungary, by contrast, de-Stalinization went entirely out of control. In October 1956 demonstrations demanded the return to power of Imre Nagy, a liberal communist and a former prime minister. When those demonstrations became violent, focusing on destroying symbols of communist authority, the ruling party's Central Committee brought Nagy back on 23 October. The next day, Soviet and Hungarian troops moved into Budapest to restore order, leading to pitched battles with Hungarian civilians before the Soviets withdrew. Other Soviet units in Romania and the Soviet Union itself moved toward the Hungarian border. Though Soviet troops were pulled out of the capital by the end of October, it was too late. Matters had progressed too far for a compromise solution to work. Hungarian opinion demanded a full break with the Soviet system, and Nagy, caught up in events beyond his control, sided with the Hungarian crowd over his party. On 1 November, Nagy declared that Hungary was leaving the Warsaw Pact and becoming neutral.

Nagy had gone far beyond what the Soviets could tolerate and triggered armed intervention, made simpler by the substantial presence of Soviet troops already in Hungary. On 4 November, three Soviet divisions moved into Budapest in bloody street fighting, and all resistance in the country was overcome within a week. This intervention involved serious combat, though the outcome was never in doubt. According to Soviet sources, 700–800 Soviet soldiers were killed or went missing during the intervention. Hungarian dead are disputed, but the number was certainly in the thousands. Some 200,000 Hungarians fled to the West. Nagy himself briefly took refuge in the Yugoslav embassy. On leaving it with the promise of safe conduct, he was arrested and executed after a secret trial.

These disturbances brought a backlash against Khrushchev. Politburo members from Stalin's old inner circle, including Viacheslav Mikhailovich Molotov, Malenkov, and Lazar Moiseevich Kaganovich, attempted to oust Khrushchev in June 1957. Here military intervention was crucial in saving Khrushchev. Top generals were among those who insisted on moving the debate over Khrushchev from the Politburo, where old Stalinists held a majority, to the larger Central Committee, with a younger and somewhat more liberal membership. Indeed, military planes brought Central

Committee members to Moscow for the climactic debates. Zhukov played a key role in the defeat of this anti-Khrushchev opposition, pejoratively termed the Anti-Party Group, as another way of attacking those responsible for purging the military in the 1930s. Once Khrushchev had defeated and demoted his last Stalinist opponents, he no longer needed Zhukov's services. Zhukov was attacked for neglecting the importance of communism to the armed forces and forced to retire in October 1957. To Khrushchev's credit, none of those defeated in 1957 were killed, marking a transition to a new, bloodless era of Soviet politics.

Khrushchev's odd blend of crude earthiness and true belief in communism extended to his military policy. His commitment to revolutionary ideals involved the Soviet Union in politics around the world, with a scope more ambitious than anything Stalin had entertained. At the same time, in the interests of economy Khrushchev cut the Soviet military's resources for a worldwide struggle. Though terrified of nuclear war, he relied exclusively on nuclear weapons to guarantee Soviet security and risked nuclear war in the interests of the Soviet Union's global standing.

By the 1950s, when Khrushchev took power, the nuclear equation had fundamentally changed. The Soviets exploded a hydrogen bomb on 12 August 1953, only a year and a half after the Americans. The hydrogen bomb, based on nuclear fusion, was a qualitative leap in destructive power. Combined with Soviet intercontinental bombers (available from the mid-1950s), the first Soviet intercontinental missile (August 1957), the public relations coup of *Sputnik* (October 1957), and nuclear-capable submarines, this put the U.S. homeland at risk as much as the Soviet. In December 1959, the Strategic Rocket Forces became a separate branch of the armed forces, equal in status to the army, the navy, the air force, and air defense. War could now conceivably mean the complete destruction of both civilizations, but it took time for that conclusion to bear fruit.

In the meantime, Khrushchev seized on nuclear weapons' potential to solve a number of political problems. First, like U.S. President Dwight Eisenhower, he invested large sums in nuclear missiles. They could bypass America's formidable air and sea defenses, and though individually expensive, they were much cheaper than a conventional military. Both sides of the Cold War used them in the 1950s to keep military spending under control. Khrushchev did this in part through a strategy of bluff, claiming a missile capacity far beyond reality as a means of deterrence.

The other half of this policy was reducing conventional expenditure. Troop strengths and conventional procurement were slashed. While Stalin had toyed with the idea of a blue-water navy, Khrushchev saw it as an unnecessary extravagance. He dismissed the navy's commander Nikolai Gerasimovich Kuznetsov for his intractable commitment to a large navy and replaced him with Sergei Georgievich Gorshkov, who would run the Soviet navy for nearly 30 years. Though strongly committed to a powerful fleet, Gorshkov was politically astute and subtle, biding his time and winning successes gradually. He rejected the construction of aircraft carriers, committing the navy instead to submarines and surface vessels.

Khrushchev's interest in using nuclear weapons to cut military expenditure interacted dangerously with another priority: supporting the worldwide communist movement. Khrushchev went further than Stalin in backing communist and revolutionary parties far beyond Soviet borders. In the mid-1950s, for example, the Soviet Union began a long relationship with Egypt, Syria, and other countries of the Arab world, providing military equipment, advisors, and training in Soviet military academies. Much as they had in the Korean War, Soviet pilots flew in the 1956 Arab-Israeli War and manned Egyptian air defenses.

Despite these efforts, Mao Zedong challenged Khrushchev's revolutionary credentials and Soviet predominance in the world communist movement. After the 1949 establishment of the People's Republic of China, thousands of Soviet military and civilian advisors had worked in China. Soviet-Chinese relations had, however, been in serious decline for some time, and at the end of 1957 Mao had attacked Khrushchev's proclamation of "peaceful coexistence" with the West as a sellout of revolution. Nuclear war was nothing to fear, Mao proclaimed. It might kill 300 million Chinese, but the rest would be more than enough to build socialism. Khrushchev was horrified. In July 1960, he pulled all Soviet advisors from China, marking a clear and final split.

At the same time, Khrushchev was presented with an opportunity in Cuba to humiliate the United States and trump China. After Fidel Castro seized power in Cuba at the very beginning of 1959, he had moved steadily left in the face of American hostility. To maintain Soviet strategic parity and at the same time protect Cuba from American intervention, Khrushchev prepared to deploy Soviet nuclear weapons in Cuba. The decision to deploy the missiles came in May 1962, and the first elements of the Soviet missile force arrived in Cuba on 9 September 1962. American spy planes detected the Soviet missile bases under construction in Cuba in October 1962, before the missiles were fully operational. The Kennedy administration announced a quarantine of Cuba to prevent Soviet missiles from reaching the island. After a few tense days, Khrushchev proposed a compromise, accepted on 28 October: no Soviet missiles in Cuba in return for the secret withdrawal of American missiles from Turkey and Kennedy's public pledge not to invade the island.

Khrushchev's retreat over Cuba was humiliating, but only as a matter of perception, not in reality. He had obtained Kennedy's pledge not to invade Cuba, and his cancellation of a *planned* missile deployment to Cuba was countered by a withdrawal of *operational* American Jupiter missiles from Turkey. Perceptions matter, though, and both the Western world and the Soviet elite believed that Kennedy had won and

Khrushchev had lost. This, together with Khrushchev's capriciousness and unpredictability, led to his ouster in a Kremlin coup in October 1964.

The Brezhnev Era

Khrushchev was succeeded by Leonid Il'ich Brezhnev, whose revolutionary commitments were weak but whose political skills were strong. He was committed to maintaining internal stability by ensuring that key interest groups were happy. In the military's case, that meant immense financial and material resources and a free hand in running its affairs. While Khrushchev had controlled military spending by building nuclear weapons at the expense of conventional weapons, Brezhnev instead offered the military everything it might want. Under two defense ministers, Andrei Antonovich Grechko (1967–1976) and then the industrial manager Dmitrii Fyodorovich Ustinov (1976–1984), the Soviet military did very well. Avoiding hard choices about budgets and priorities avoided conflict, but put an increasingly unsustainable burden on the Soviet economy.

The prime beneficiary of this was the Soviet navy, which finally won the resources it had been denied for essentially the lifetime of the Soviet Union. During the interwar period, the Soviet Union could not afford a navy, and its key geostrategic goals required only the ability to defend its coastlines, not project power by sea. Despite a brief flirtation by Stalin with the idea of a capital ship navy in the mid-1930s, the Soviet Union had never been a naval power. Under Khrushchev, however, the Soviet Union began to act as a world power. This new policy of active engagement in the developing world was not matched, however, by a navy capable of delivering power projection. Only after Khrushchev's 1964 ouster, in the free-spending atmosphere of the Brezhnev era, was Gorshkov able to build a navy of the size and power he desired. Even then, the Soviet Union never matched the American navy. Its ballistic missile submarine fleet was, for example, far less important to its nuclear forces than the American fleet was, and it never possessed a vessel equivalent to an American attack carrier. The Soviets did develop the *Moskva* class helicopter carrier for antisubmarine warfare in the early 1960s. At the beginning of the 1970s, the larger *Kiev* class followed, capable of carrying vertical-takeoff aircraft in addition to helicopters. Only a handful were built, and neither compared in size or striking power to American carriers.

Brezhnev's generosity also extended to the developing world. He expanded Khrushchev's policy of military assistance, based on the three-fold principle of equipment, advisors, and education in Soviet military schools. There were limits. North Vietnam, for example, did not receive the same active support that Korea had—Soviet pilots regularly flying air defense missions. It did, nonetheless, receive large quantities of other forms of aid during its lengthy war with the United States. Soviet advisors were active in Angola, Somalia, and Ethiopia at various times under Brezhnev. Soviet commitments to the Middle East continued. During the 1967 Arab-Israeli War (the Six-Day War), a number of Soviet advisors, particularly with the Egyptian air force, were killed. Soviet pilots and air defense advisors were actively engaged in the subsequent war of attrition between Israel and Egypt. When Gamal Abdel Nasser died in 1970 and was succeeded as Egyptian president by Anwar Sadat, Soviet-Egyptian relations went downhill. After a 1972 Egyptian request for increased aid was refused, Sadat expelled his Soviet military advisors. Soviet aid to Egypt continued nonetheless. In the 1973 Yom Kippur War, when initial Egyptian successes turned into Israeli victories, Soviet threats of military intervention halted the war and saved Sadat's regime. In the wake of the war, when Sadat moved toward rapprochement with Israel and the Camp David Peace Accords, Syria replaced Egypt as the Soviet Union's chief client in the Middle East. Iraq also received substantial Soviet military assistance, temporarily interrupted when Iraq began the Iran-Iraq War in 1980 without consulting the Soviets. In all, tens of thousands of Soviets served abroad as military advisors, chiefly in the Middle East.

The greatest impact of Brezhnev's largesse, however, was nuclear parity and the conventional superiority it gave the Soviet Union over the United States. By continuing Khrushchev's nuclear buildup, Brezhnev achieved a rough equivalence with American firepower, though Soviet nuclear forces were structured differently. The United States relied equally on strategic bombers, submarine-launched missiles, and intercontinental ballistic missiles. The Soviet Union was much more heavily committed to land-based missiles at the expense of other systems. But while Khrushchev had cut conventional forces in the interest of economy, Brezhnev built them up instead. This gave the Soviet Union a clear superiority over the United States in crude numbers of tanks, aircraft, artillery pieces, and troops. The imbalance was smaller when America's NATO allies and the Warsaw Pact countries were included, but was still present.

This changed the nature of Soviet strategy. Under Khrushchev, the reliance on nuclear weapons had produced a commitment to all-out nuclear war. Vasilii Danilovich Sokolovskii, who had been Chief of the General Staff from 1952 to 1960, in 1962 published *Military Strategy*, an official, collective work which saw nuclear weapons as central to Soviet strategy, and condemned notions of limited war or conventional war as bourgeois illusions. Under Brezhnev, however, that emphasis changed. The Soviet Union's growing conventional power now made limited war or conventional war an attractive option, and Soviet strategists envisioned nonnuclear possibilities. This shift should not be overstated. Nuclear weapons were, for the Soviet military, still only weapons, and weapons were for fighting. Certainly, Soviet force structures, including massive reserves, plans to move troops through Eastern Europe in dispersed echelons, and a preference for cheap, plentiful weapons over quality, durable ones suggests an expectation of fighting in a nuclear environment. Much Soviet doctrine and planning for war remains obscure, but evidence from East German and Polish records, now available to Western researchers, suggests that early and frequent use of nuclear weapons was the norm in Warsaw Pact exercises.

By the mid-1960s, a reduction in tension, *détente,* between the two sides of the Cold War was clearly evident. While Khrushchev had been willing to challenge the existing status quo in Germany, a series of crises over Berlin and the Cuban Missile Crisis produced a realization on both sides that the existing division of Europe was far preferable to risking nuclear war. This tacit understanding, together with nuclear parity, reduced confrontation and created the conditions for limited controls on the buildup of nuclear weapons. Some agreements had been reached before: the Cuban Missile Crisis led eventually to test-ban and nonproliferation treaties. In 1972, *détente* produced a pair of U.S.–Soviet treaties. The Antiballistic Missile Treaty put sharp limits on the development and deployment of anti-missile systems, while the Strategic Arms Limitation Talks Agreement (SALT I) froze the number of ballistic missile launchers deployed by each side. In the Soviet case, this led to an increasing number of intermediate-range missiles, specifically to counter the growing military threat from communist China, but also for deployment in Europe. Subsequent negotiations produced the SALT II agreement, signed in 1979. The war in Afghanistan wrecked its chances for ratification, but both sides observed its provisions nonetheless.

While *détente* made it simpler for the United States to focus on a long, draining war in Vietnam, it also removed a serious distraction from the Soviets in dealing with their own crises. In Czechoslovakia, Brezhnev faced a crisis similar to that Khrushchev did in Hungary. After Alexander Dubcek became head of the Czechoslovak party at the beginning of 1968, he began gradual liberalization. This "action program" most notably included an effective end to censorship, bringing a flowering of intellectual and cultural life in the "Prague Spring." Dubcek and the Czechoslovak leadership were careful to avoid the pitfalls that had brought the invasion of Hungary, emphasizing their continued commitment to socialism and the Warsaw Pact. Even within those limits, Czechoslovak reforms were highly destabilizing. Dubcek received a collective threat in July from the rest of the Warsaw Pact to guard against counterrevolution. In mid-August, the Soviet leadership agreed on the need for military intervention, a decision supported by all the other Pact countries besides Romania.

Warsaw Pact forces moved into Czechoslovakia the night of 20 August 1968. Unlike in Hungary in 1956, Soviet troops were accompanied by Bulgarian, Hungarian, and Polish troops, and a symbolic East German contingent. Only Romania refused to participate. Also unlike 1956, there was no organized resistance. The 500,000 Soviet and allied troops took control of the country within hours. Dubcek's reforms were ended, though he was not immediately deposed. Czechoslovakia was forced to accept the permanent presence of Soviet troops. Under 100 Soviet troops and 100 Czech citizens were killed in the intervention.

In the wake of the Czechoslovak crisis, Romania grew increasingly distant from the formal structures of the Warsaw Pact. The Romanian ruling party used nationalism to bolster its legitimacy, and by the early 1970s, Romania had developed a distinct military doctrine of national defense, much like earlier defectors from the Soviet system Albania and Yugoslavia. This was based on the idea of a people's war of resistance against a foreign occupier. Clearly but not explicitly directed against the Soviet Union, this entailed growing self-sufficiency in armaments. While Romania stayed a nominal member of the Warsaw Pact, it rejected any foreign troop presence on its territory. Romania was accordingly rewarded with Western trade and connections, but never transgressed the rules of the Soviet bloc enough to trigger expensive Soviet intervention.

Brezhnev also inherited from Khrushchev an increasingly bitter dispute with China over leadership of the world communist movement, and then over concrete issues of security. Border disputes became increasingly intense in 1964, leading to a steadily escalating rhetoric. In March 1969, the dispute became open combat. Chinese troops occupied tiny Damanskii Island in the middle of the Ussuri River early on the morning of 2 March 1969. They ambushed a KGB (Soviet secret police) border patrol that day, setting off a series of border skirmishes that continued at varying levels of intensity along the Soviet-Chinese border for several months. Most of this story remains unclear. Both sides agree that several hundred soldiers were killed, but each claims the other suffered much heavier losses. Military tensions remained high, especially after U.S. President Richard Nixon brought Chinese-American reconciliation in 1972.

At the end of the 1970s, though, *détente* began to break down, and Brezhnev faced not only continuing tensions with China, but a renewed confrontation with the West, rising discontent within the Soviet bloc, and social stagnation at home. Continuing Soviet activity in Africa alarmed Western governments. Soviet upgrades in missile designs threatened the SALT I agreements, as did the Soviet replacement beginning in 1977 of its intermediate range SS-4 and SS-5 missiles targeting western Europe with much more powerful SS-20 missiles. After heated debate, in 1979 NATO approved basing American missiles in Europe as a counter.

Within the Soviet Empire, the 1978 election of Karol Cardinal Wojtyla, archbishop of Krakow, as Pope John Paul II galvanized nationalist feelings in Poland, the Soviet satellite least reconciled to its status. In the summer of 1980, Poland's economic stagnation forced its government to raise food prices, triggering wildcat strikes. Those strikes quickly became a national movement, Solidarity, demanding the right to free, independent trade unions. Such a request was terribly dangerous in a society ostensibly devoted to the rights of workers. After 18 months of crisis, and tacit threats of Soviet intervention, the Polish army itself intervened to crush Solidarity and introduce martial law in December 1981. While damaging relations with the West further, this made manifest the Soviet bloc's continuing difficulties in winning acceptance from those it ruled.

By far the most damaging crisis for the Soviet Union's international standing, fueling a renewed Cold War, was the disastrous invasion of Afghanistan. In the early years of the Cold War, Afghanistan had been only a backwater. Over the course of the 1970s, though, it had moved more clearly into the Soviet camp. In April 1978, the People's Democratic Party of Afghanistan (PDPA), avowedly Marxist, seized power in a coup. The problem was that the PDPA faced a restive and an uncontrollable population and was deeply split by internal factions. By spring 1979, much of the Afghan countryside was in open revolt against the government in Kabul, and some Soviet advisors were killed. The unpredictable and unreliable president Hafizullah Amin, who had assassinated his predecessor, begged for additional Soviet support to help him to control his country, but by late 1979 the Soviets had concluded that Amin himself was a key obstacle to any stabilization. With the regime on the verge of collapse, the Soviets decided on a quick and decisive intervention to replace Amin, beat the insurgency, and reestablish Soviet dominance. In effect, this would repeat the quick and relatively painless Czechoslovak intervention. The reality proved to be quite different.

Acting against the nearly unanimous opinion of his high command, Brezhnev and his closest advisors agreed on intervention. The presence of Soviet troops in the country as advisors made this quite simple. The invasion began on 24 December 1979, with troops landing in the capital Kabul and five divisions invading across the northern border. Amin was assassinated (made easier by his Soviet bodyguards) and replaced by the more manageable Babrak Karmal. The initial invasion was a striking success, and the Soviets quickly controlled Kabul, the other major cities, and the ring road that circled the country.

The countryside proved far more difficult. The Soviet plan was to make the PDPA a more capable governing party, while using Afghan government troops to control insurgency. Soviet troops, the 40th Army, would garrison major cities and support counterinsurgency efforts. Instead, widespread opposition to Soviet occupation meant that the fragmented and factional antigovernment insurgents (the *mujahideen*) were as a group much more powerful and difficult to eliminate than the Soviets had anticipated, and the Afghan army was much too weak and unreliable to manage the fight alone. The Soviets found themselves fighting a skilled and tenacious insurgency. Keeping the cities and major transport links secure required a buildup of forces to approximately 110,000 by 1982, a strength maintained for most of the rest of the war.

The *mujahideen* quickly learned they could not fight set-piece battles with the Soviets, and the Soviets learned the *mujahideen* simply melted into the mountains and hills if attacked frontally. The war degenerated into a draining and bloody cycle of *mujahideen* ambushes and raids and Soviet counterinsurgency sweeps through the countryside. In material terms, the Soviet army, prepared to fight World War III in Europe, was woefully unprepared for the most mundane challenges of this sort of war. Its troops lacked sunglasses, and they tried whenever possible to exchange their stiff boots for Chinese sneakers, better suited to clambering over the terrain. Soviet armored personnel carriers did not carry spare tires. Medical care was poor, and Soviet troops suffered shocking rates of illness. Intellectually, its officers and men were conditioned to strict hierarchy and obedience to orders, not the flexibility and initiative required in a war waged by battalions, not large formations. The Soviets did learn as the war progressed, however, using helicopter-mobile light forces both as blocking elements in antiguerrilla sweeps and for convoy security against ambushes.

One of the major complications for the Soviets was aid to the *mujahideen* from outside, including the United States and the Arab world. This grew in quantity and sophistication with time. A key moment came in 1986, when British Blowpipe and American Stinger portable antiaircraft missiles appeared in the *mujahideen* arsenal. This immediately and dramatically took away the chief Soviet advantage: command of the air. Without air support in combat or air supply of isolated garrisons, the Soviet war effort became immeasurably more difficult. By this time as well, Mikhail Gorbachev was in power, and he was unwilling to sacrifice his reform agenda to the economic and diplomatic costs of the war. The Soviets finally withdrew in 1989.

While the Afghan population suffered terribly, with millions fleeing to refugee camps in Pakistan, and perhaps a million dying during the war, official statistics claim the Soviets suffered 14,500 dead during the war, or 1,500–2,000 per year. This was easily sustainable from a total population of 300 million, particularly in a country devoid of a free press or democratic process. Other Russian military sources, however, have suggested that as many as 30,000 died in Afghanistan, presenting a picture of a war more costly than previous accounts.

The Soviet military, chief pillar of the system, itself suffered from the general malaise of the Brezhnev years. In an effort to maximize its available reserves to cope with the potential casualties of nuclear war, a new 1967 service law had reduced army service from three years to two, much as military reforms in the late Russian Empire had done. While this brought more of each year's cohort of young men into the military, it had pernicious effects on training and discipline. With few long-serving rank-and-file soldiers or noncommissioned officers, the Soviet military instead became officer heavy. Its soldiers were not in the military long enough to master their tasks. Instead, the Soviets relied on lieutenants and captains to do what in Western armies were the routine duties of sergeants, corporals, or even privates. Officers did not share barracks with enlisted men, and so without noncommissioned officers to provide structure and discipline, second-year enlisted men began a reign of terror over new recruits. This *dedovshchina*, routine and ritualized hazing, not only undermined discipline within the military, but made military service a dreaded ordeal. Intellectual elites had always disdained military service, but *dedovshchina* made draft dodging far more common. An extensive system of educational deferments brought political peace, but left military service disproportionately to those too ignorant or poor to escape it. Naturally, the war in Afghanistan exacerbated the problem. In addition, the ready availability of hashish and opium poppies in Afghanistan spread drug use throughout the Soviet military, further undermining discipline.

By the time Brezhnev died in 1982, the dark side of his policy of providing all things to all groups was clear. The Soviet bloc countries were mired in debt and weighed down by unsustainable military spending. His efforts to confront the West and shore up his own empire produced a renewed Cold War that it did not seem he could win. There was, however, no simple solution to the dilemmas he had created.

CHAPTER 15

The Emergence of a New Russia

After a series of decrepit rulers—Brezhnev died in 1982, his replacement Yurii Vladimirovich Andropov in 1984, and his replacement Konstantin Ustinovich Chernenko in 1985—the Politburo turned to youth. Mikhail Sergeevich Gorbachev was elected General Secretary of the Communist Party, and hence ruler of the Soviet Union, on 11 March 1985. He had just turned 54 when elected, vaulting him ahead of others with substantially more seniority. Gorbachev's election demonstrated that the party's elite understood the depth of the crisis facing the Soviet system, and its need for reform.

The core of the crisis was the slow decay of the Soviet economy. Economic growth had been stagnant for over a decade, and after a period in the 1950s and 1960s when it appeared the Soviet Union was catching up with the West, the gap had been steadily widening. The lag was particularly acute in high technology. At the same time, Soviet society was increasingly plagued by social ills: crime, divorce, alcoholism, and the growing alienation of the population from communist ideology. While many social problems (aside from alcoholism) were minor by Western standards, the trend was troubling. The Soviet Union's international environment was also threatening. China's reconciliation with the West and a growing economy made that country even more of a danger. The Soviets were still involved in a draining war in Afghanistan. Martial law in Poland had temporarily ended the threat of Solidarity, but there was no guarantee that would last.

Specific military threats also demanded action. The American military buildup that had begun under Jimmy Carter and accelerated under Ronald Reagan threatened the Soviets in a number of ways. First, Soviet strategy in the event of a third world war had been predicated on massive waves of troops crashing against Western defenses in Germany. That required mobilizing and transporting millions of men in multiple eche-lons through Eastern Europe. Western advances in technology, including precision munitions and cruise missiles, when combined with increases in the number and quality of weapons systems available to the Ameri-cans, threatened Soviet conventional superiority. When these were incor-porated into a Western doctrine of attacking and disrupting Soviet troop movements across Eastern Europe, preventing the arrival of the follow-on forces essential to Soviet victory, the Soviets could no longer be com-fortable with their odds in the event of a clash in central Europe. In addi-tion, the Reagan administration's commitment to missile defense—the Strategic Defense Initiative (SDI), or Star Wars—terrified the Soviet lead-ership. While opinion in the West generally questioned the system's feasi-bility, Soviet technology was far enough behind that the Soviet Union could not match whatever system the United States devised. Western technological advantages threatened to make the entire Soviet defense establishment obsolete.

As a result, Gorbachev took office backed by a broad popular and elite consensus that the Soviet system required fundamental reform. The prob-lem was that no one, Gorbachev included, understood how exactly to fix the Soviet Union. In addition, few understood the danger that tinkering with the system might in fact destroy it altogether.

Gorbachev's initial reforms were moderate, in keeping with his background. From a poor, rural background, he had risen through the system after training as a lawyer (highly unusual in the Soviet context) in a series of local party jobs in the North Caucasus. His talent was spotted by Andropov, who brought him to Moscow with a number of other bright, young technocrats. Gorbachev soon took the Central Com-mittee portfolio for agriculture, and during Andropov's brief reign served as de facto General Secretary while Andropov was dying of kidney failure. At Andropov's death, conservatives in the Politburo were too strong and the sense of urgency too weak for Gorbachev to win, forcing him to wait a year before taking power while Chernenko died from emphysema.

Andropov had made his career as head of the KGB, and his brief period in power was marked by efforts to reform the Soviet system through greater discipline. When Gorbachev came to power, he followed the same line. He cracked down on alcohol consumption and pushed the accelera-tion (*uskorenie*) of economic development. Even at this early stage, though, there were hints of more radical steps to follow. Gorbachev endorsed *glas-nost'*, or openness, as a tool of reform. *Glasnost'* did not mean free speech, but instead the narrower practice of revealing inefficiencies and abuses in order to correct them. Gorbachev also made tentative steps toward reduc-ing tensions with the West and thawing the Cold War.

An end to East-West tensions, while worthy in itself, was intended to pay dividends in the form of reduced military expenditures. Brezhnev's largesse had produced an overwhelming military burden on the Soviet economy. The opacity of the Soviet economic system, even to its own managers, makes it difficult to specify the precise burden of defense, but it likely was at least 20 percent to 25 percent of gross national product. By contrast, in 1985, at the height of the Reagan defense buildup, defense spending was only 6 percent of American gross national product. Any reform in the Soviet economy required reducing that crushing defense burden, but reducing that defense burden required ending or at least ameliorating the Cold War.

Working in conjunction with Eduard Amvros'evich Shevardnadze, his liberal foreign minister, Gorbachev's efforts to end the Cold War began with a unilateral nuclear test ban. He followed it by a pair of summit meetings with Ronald Reagan: in November 1985 in Geneva and in October 1986 in Reykjavik. In both cases, Reagan and Gorbachev wished to commit to major reductions in nuclear weapons, but this foundered on Reagan's refusal to abandon SDI. Though both summits were in this sense failures, they established a personal relationship of trust between the two, one that paid dividends in other sectors. By December 1987, the United States and the Soviet Union had reached an agreement on the complete elimination of intermediate-range nuclear missiles.

Imposing substantial cuts on the military was a difficult task. Not only was it a powerful institution with substantial allies throughout Soviet society, but military secrecy meant that there were few civilians with a real understanding of the military's workings. Gorbachev had no military experience himself, and the Soviet Union did not have the network of civilian experts and research institutes ubiquitous in Western societies.

Part of Gorbachev's reform involved removing the ossified elite that dominated civil and military life. Sergei Georgievich Gorshkov, for example, was forced into retirement from the navy. This process was accelerated by a fortuitous accident. On 28 May 1987, Matthias Rust, a West German teenager, flew a small aircraft through Soviet airspace and landed on Red Square. Gorbachev took advantage of this humiliating failure of Soviet air defense to dismiss hundreds of high-ranking officials over the next few years, appointing his own Defense Minister, Dmitrii Timofeevich Iazov, to replace Sergei Leonidovich Sokolov.

In keeping with the Soviet emphasis on ideology and doctrine, Gorbachev's efforts to reform the military required an ideological basis. This dovetailed neatly with Gorbachev's desire to end the Cold War and produced a new emphasis on "humankind interests" as opposed to traditional "class interests." This meant that social development, protection of the environment, and, above all, avoidance of nuclear war trumped considerations of proletarian revolution and the spread of the Soviet system.

Gorbachev presented "reasonable sufficiency" as the new standard for Soviet defense. Whatever that meant precisely, it implied a military much smaller than the Soviet Union's 6 million men under arms and tens of thousands of tanks. The ideological and doctrinal rug had been pulled out from under the feet of the Soviet high command.

Though the military as a group was opposed to major cuts, this opposition should not be overstated. The pernicious nature of the Soviet defense burden was clear to all intelligent observers. The military elite did not object to moderate cuts, but instead to hasty or ill-conceived reductions, and especially to the social disintegration that Gorbachev's reforms unleashed inside the USSR. As Gorbachev's early, moderate reforms failed to have an appreciable effect on Soviet economic performance, he began more aggressive measures, including the widespread introduction of joint ventures with Western firms, the legalization of various types of individual and cooperative businesses, and finally flexibility for managers of state enterprises. While this introduced a commercial mind-set alien to Soviet military elites, their chief concern was with social changes, particularly the damage done by *glasnost'*. Gorbachev blamed the failure of his reforms to produce concrete benefits on obstructionist bureaucrats, and so he widened the scope of *glasnost'* and introduced democratizing reforms into Soviet society. This had explosive results. It brought civilian participation in strategic debates, as well as open complaints from junior officers about their substandard living conditions.

The Soviet system's economic problems went far deeper than Gorbachev or anyone else realized, and so as efforts at economic reform seemed only to make matters worse, Gorbachev used foreign affairs and diplomatic successes to compensate for his declining popularity at home. He turned to increasingly theatrical gestures, as in December 1988 at the United Nations when he unilaterally announced major cuts in Soviet armed forces overall and specifically in Eastern Europe. In March 1989, this was followed by the opening of a major new series of talks on substantial reductions to conventional arms in Europe.

This effort was overtaken by events on the ground. Since 1985, Gorbachev urged his more conservative counterparts in Eastern Europe to implement reforms along his lines. It was clear by 1989 that Gorbachev's interests in ending the Cold War made it impossible to imagine Soviet troops intervening to prop up communist regimes. Over the course of the single remarkable year of 1989, every Soviet-bloc government in Eastern Europe collapsed, only to be replaced by pro-Western reformist governments of varying stripes. Gorbachev and the Soviet army did nothing to halt the process. The Warsaw Pact became meaningless, though its formal institutions survived until 1991.

As a group, the Soviet military elite was upset at the loss of the East European Empire, which so many had died to establish. Few felt it could realistically have been preserved, however, and by 1989 their chief concerns were preserving the existing system inside the Soviet Union itself, let alone the Soviet Empire. Gorbachev's increasingly radical political, economic, and social reforms were undermining the existing system without setting up any effective replacements, and the military, along with most other Soviet institutions, was suffering from it. Gorbachev had come to power as General Secretary of the Communist Party, but attempted to shift the basis of his legitimacy to elective institutions.

This new emphasis on popular sovereignty had dangerous implications. For one, the Soviet Union's increasingly free press allowed nationalist voices to be heard for the first time in decades. One of their key targets was the Soviet military, where non-Russian conscripts suffered disproportionately from hazing. Increasing numbers of non-Russians called for serving in their home republics, the creation of national formations along the lines of the 1920s, or even an end to conscription altogether. What began as calls for greater autonomy moved toward full independence, particularly in the Baltics.

As Soviet institutions fell apart in the late 1980s, there were many more questions than practical solutions. The military's dilemmas mounted with each passing day. How in practice was it to achieve the force reductions Gorbachev foisted on it? How was it to cope with a reduced budget? Where was it to house the officers returning from Eastern Europe? What should it do with political officers and communist ideology when the Soviet Union itself was abandoning communism? How should it convert its extensive military-industrial complex to civilian production? None of these questions had good answers. Most disturbing for military elites, Gorbachev did not seem to understand this or care.

The army was also forced to step in to deal with the social unrest unleashed by the disintegration of Soviet society and found itself condemned for that. This began in 1986 in Kazakhstan. As part of cleaning out old elites and bringing in reformist ones, Gorbachev fired the party boss of Kazakhstan. This unleashed Russian-Kazakh riots in the capital Alma-Ata, riots that Internal Affairs troops were unable to contain, forcing the military to step in. Beginning in 1988, Armenians and Azerbaijanis fought a low-level war over the disputed Armenian enclave of Nagorno-Karabakh, lying within Azerbaijan. The military attempted to separate the warring factions, only to find itself a target. In Tbilisi, Georgia, in April 1989, the army and internal affairs troops broke up a massive nationalist demonstration with clubs and shovels, killing dozens. This became a national scandal, and the army again felt itself the scapegoat for political decisions beyond its control. At the beginning of 1991, the military intervened forcibly in the Baltics against growing independence movements and again found itself abandoned by Gorbachev. The lesson commanders learned was to steer clear of politics.

During this period, the actual military readiness of the Soviet armed forces dropped precipitously. Shortages of funds did not allow for training, whether ships' time at sea or pilots' hours in the air. The newly free media revealed the poor living conditions and hazing that awaited conscripts, and draft dodging reached catastrophic levels by 1989. Beginning in 1990, a mass movement of soldiers' mothers pressured the military and government to reform its conditions of service. The military itself was increasingly torn by political dissent within its ranks. It had some liberal reformers, some hard-line Russian nationalists, and a much larger group who simply wished to the defend the military as an institution.

By late 1990, Gorbachev realized just how dangerous his situation had become. He flirted with repression to reimpose order by force, leading Shevardnadze to resign as foreign minister. As anticommunist forces gained strength, though, Gorbachev seems to have decided in the spring of 1991 to compromise with reformist forces. Confronted with Boris Nikolaevich Yeltsin, the newly elected popular and populist president of the Russian Federation, the largest and the most important republic inside the Soviet Union, Gorbachev agreed to a new Union Treaty, intended to redefine the relationship between the central government and the Soviet Union's republics, promoting greater federalism and thereby reducing nationalist demands for a full breakup of the Union. In August 1991, he went on vacation to the Crimea, intending to return on 20 August for the signing of the Treaty.

That signing never happened. Instead, on 18 August, Gorbachev was put under house arrest in the Crimea, and on 19 August, the Soviet Union woke to news that martial law had been declared by an eight-man State Committee for the State of Emergency. This group, made up of the members of Gorbachev's own administration, declared that it was taking power in view of Gorbachev's illness to save the Soviet Union. Their plot was thoroughly amateurish, but might have succeeded if not for Yeltsin's inspired resistance. The plotters failed to arrest Yeltsin at his dacha, so he was able to reach the Russian government's headquarters (the White House) in Moscow and declare the coup an illegal and unconstitutional act. The coup plotters' task was simple: to get through a small crowd of people surrounding the White House and arrest Yeltsin. The plotters included the head of the KGB, the Minister of Internal Affairs, and Iazov, Gorbachev's hand-picked Minister of Defense. None could find soldiers willing to support them if it meant violence. This does not mean that military officers were necessarily opposed to the coup; many were sympathetic. Instead, they had been burned too many times by politicians asking soldiers to do their dirty work. Within three days, the coup had collapsed, and the members of the State Committee were themselves under arrest.

This tawdry episode destroyed all remaining legitimacy of both Gorbachev himself and the Soviet Union. All of the Soviet Union's 15 union republics declared their independence, and Gorbachev found himself a president without a country. This left a great deal unresolved, most notably the status of the Soviet Union's armed forces. Evgenii Ivanovich Shaposhnikov, the new Defense Minister, was confronted with competing demands for the enormous military he nominally controlled, including, he claims, Gorbachev's request for a military coup to preserve the union. The puzzle of what would happen to the Soviet Union was resolved by Yeltsin and his Ukrainian and Belorussian counterparts on 7–8 December 1991. Meeting in secret at a Belorussian hunting lodge, they agreed to treat the Soviet Union as null and void, creating in its place a Commonwealth of Independent States as a loose structure linking them. All other republics of the Soviet Union would be invited to join. Gorbachev attempted to salvage the Soviet Union for another few days, but soon realized the hopelessness of his tasks. On 25 December 1991, he resigned as the Soviet Union's president and the Soviet Union was gone.

Initially, at least, the Commonwealth was intended to provide the structure for joint military forces. Though concrete arrangements were all quite vague, there was some idea that strategic forces (primarily but not exclusively nuclear) of the former Soviet Union would remain under Commonwealth authority, while conventional forces would be under national control. That distinction quickly broke down in the face of the union republics' rush to establish their independence. Shaposhnikov did a great deal to ensure the process was peaceful and reasonably orderly. Russia, seeing itself as dominating the Commonwealth's united military, was the last to surrender this notion. Any military authority the Commonwealth had quickly disappeared. In practice, that left nuclear weapons on the territory of Russia, Belorussia, Ukraine, and Kazakhstan. Under international pressure, Belorussia, Ukraine, and Kazakhstan, which together had possessed a quarter of the Soviet missile force and much of its bomber force, gave up their nuclear weapons, leaving Russia as the lone nuclear power of the 15 republics.

The picture of military developments after the end of the Soviet Union is complex and confusing. In dealing with such a recent period, historical perspective is by definition absent, and reliable sources on military politics are difficult to come by. All this section can do is outline basic features of the period.

In the case of the Baltics, post-Soviet militaries began to evolve toward Western models of organization. The Baltics' motivation was clearly to draw closer to NATO as protection against reimposition of influence by Moscow. In recent years, Georgia has moved in a similar direction. For the rest of the former Soviet republics, the picture is generally one of maintaining Soviet models of training, organization, and internal culture, but without Soviet levels of resources. Despite the creation of new national states, ethnic Russians have continued to hold important positions in these new armies. The domination of the Soviet officer corps by ethnic Russians meant that technical expertise was often a Russian monopoly.

In Russia itself under its first president Boris Yeltsin, the overall picture of the military is one of institutional decay. Yeltsin was a skilled populist, had democratic instincts, and responded well to crises, but was ill suited to building a coherent and a responsible state. Instead, his term in power from the disintegration of the Soviet Union to his resignation on 31 December 1999 was marked by a series of negative developments. Authority over armed force was deliberately divided as a tool of rule. While the Russian military was starved of budgetary resources and equipment, other armed groups did quite well by comparison. The Internal Affairs troops, for example, and the smaller Presidential Guard benefited from official favor as a counterbalance to the army. The one exception to this was the Strategic Rocket Forces. Judging that nuclear weapons allowed Russia a final trump card in defending itself, as well as substantial influence in international affairs, Yeltsin's administration kept that branch in better shape than the air force, navy, or army.

During Yeltsin's years in power, there were innumerable suggestions, projects, proposals, and discussions of military reform. Few had much effect. In 1992, for example, the Russian army began an experiment with professional soldiers, part of a widely supported idea of moving away from a conscript army. The essential difficulty with the concept was expense. As the Russian state was almost bankrupt, the advantage of conscripts was that they did not need to be paid (under the Russian Empire, the Soviet Union, and the new Russia alike, conscripts received only symbolic wages). Professional soldiers needed to be paid enough to entice them to serve. This experiment with *kontraktniki* has had mixed results at best. While accounting for 10 percent to 15 percent of military manpower, many are in fact soldiers' wives: already living on military bases, they may as well earn salaries. In Chechnya, *kontraktniki* are often recruited by the opportunities for plunder and extortion.

In Yeltsin's defense, many of the new Russian army's most serious problems dated back to the Gorbachev period, or even to Brezhnev. Housing shortages, draft dodging, hazing, and corruption were nothing new. The post-Soviet decline in law and order, however, made them more serious, and the free media (one of Yeltsin's achievements) made public what had often been kept secret. The result was a further decline in the prestige of military service, despite growing Russian nationalism.

Conflicts over the direction of the new Russian state, particularly between Yeltsin and his more conservative parliament, the Duma, led to an open clash in September–October 1993. On 21 September 1993, Yeltsin declared emergency rule, dissolved the Duma, and called for new elections. The Duma in turn denounced Yeltsin, leading to a two-week stalemate. Despite pressure from Yeltsin, the Russian army attempted strenuously to remain out of this dispute, following the lessons learned under Gorbachev. Only after the Duma's leadership turned to violence, attacking the Moscow mayor's office and a television studio, did the army reluctantly step in. It dispersed the Duma's supporters, stormed the White House, and arrested its leadership. Yeltsin then took advantage of his victory to rewrite the Russian constitution, giving much more power to the president.

In the wake of this crisis, Yeltsin again lapsed into a policy of drift, while the Russian military continued to decay. This drift extended to the emerging crisis over Chechnya, a small region in the North Caucasus on Russia's border with Georgia. It had been the site of extended warfare during Russia's nineteenth-century conquest of the Caucasus. During World War II, Stalin decided the Chechen people as a whole were guilty of collaboration with the Germans and in February 1944 deported the entire Chechen nation to central Asia amid great suffering and loss of life. This poisoned heritage reemerged with the collapse of the Soviet Union.

When the Soviet Union fell apart in late 1991, it broke into its 15 union republics. Those republics, particularly Russia, contained within them smaller territories populated by minority nationalities (autonomous republics/autonomous regions) which also showed some desire for sovereignty. In most cases, Yeltsin's government negotiated a settlement providing for limited autonomy and shared sovereignty. The one place that did not happen was Chechnya.

Chechnya was ruled by its elected president Dzhokhar Dudaev, a former Soviet air force officer and ethnic Chechen. While appealing to Chechen nationalism, Dudaev also presided over the steady criminalization of Chechen society. Yeltsin's government grew increasingly impatient with Chechnya's rampant lawlessness and attempted a variety of measures to topple Dudaev, including sponsoring Chechen opposition groups. All failed, including armed incursions by other Chechens. Yeltsin and his inner circle were confident that Russian force would resolve the matter. As Yeltsin's Defense Minister Pavel Sergeevich Grachev famously remarked, a couple of hours and a parachute regiment would suffice to end Dudaev's reign. On 11 December 1994, Russian government forces invaded Chechnya.

Instead of an easy success, the war became a debacle. It was unpopular with the Russian public, and Chechen guerrilla resistance was highly effective against poorly trained and unmotivated Russian conscripts. Worst was the Battle of Groznyi, the Chechen capital, in late December 1994. Russian columns moving into the city were cut off and cut to pieces, killing well over 1,000 Russian soldiers. The war degenerated into the massive and indiscriminate use of force by the Russian military, and Russian internal troops, against people who were Russian citizens. As Russian atrocities increased, the Chechens turned to terrorism. In June 1995, Chechen fighters seized a hospital in the town of Budennovsk, well outside of Chechnya, and over 100 people were killed in the ensuing battle. The war dragged on through the summer of 1996. The decentralized nature of Chechen society aided guerrilla resistance and also made it difficult for the Russians to find negotiating partners. Dudaev was killed in April 1996 by a Russian missile homing in on his cellular phone, but the Chechen resistance continued unabated.

At that point, Yeltsin's efforts to win reelection hinged on some resolution of the First Chechen War. After a narrow victory in the first round of elections in June 1996, narrowing the field to Yeltsin and Gennadii Andreevich Ziuganov, leader of Russia's Communists, Yeltsin appealed to the nationalist supporters of the third-place candidate, retired general Aleksandr Ivanovich Lebed. Lebed joined the Yeltsin team with the assignment to secure peace in Chechnya, a seemingly hopeless task, and Yeltsin went on to win the second round and reelection in July.

As Yeltsin was inaugurated in August 1996, the Chechen resistance launched a massive offensive throughout Chechnya, which managed even to take the Russian-garrisoned capital of Groznyi. After this humiliation, Lebed reached an agreement with Chechen leader Aslan Maskhadov giving Chechnya de facto independence. While Yeltsin was unhappy with the concessions Lebed made, he accepted the deal, and the war ended with Russian withdrawal. Having been reelected, though, Yeltsin no longer needed Lebed and so fired him.

This 1996 settlement did not resolve the Chechen crisis. Chechens themselves could not pacify Chechnya any better than the Russians. The region descended again into crime and warlordism, with kidnapping for ransom becoming a major industry. Though Islamic, Chechen society had not had radical Islam. Under the influence of the first war and foreign Muslims, however, radical Islamists became increasingly prevalent in the Chechen cause.

In August and September 1999, a confluence of events brought about the Second Chechen War. In August, Yeltsin appointed the unknown Vladimir Vladimirovich Putin as his new Prime Minister. The same month, a group of Chechens and foreign sympathizers invaded the neighboring Russian republic of Dagestan. Then in September, a series of apartment bombings blamed on Chechen terrorists (though still disputed) killed hundreds of people in central Russia. Putin responded by another invasion of Chechnya, one much more effectively planned than the first. This war was highly popular in Russia and catapulted Putin from an obscure bureaucrat to Yeltsin's successor. Fearing for his legacy and personal safety after the end of his second term, Yeltsin resigned on 31 December 1999, making Putin acting president and triggering snap presidential elections in March 2000. Putin's advantages of office, together with his get-tough policy on the Chechens, brought his easy victory.

The Russian military's conduct of the Second Chechen War learned much from the first. In the initial stages of the war, the Russian army sealed off Chechnya's borders and concentrated on controlling the open terrain north of the Terek River, avoiding hills and built-up areas. Russian forces sought to establish secure zones governed by loyalist Chechens to demonstrate the advantages of Russian rule and win acceptance from the Chechen population. The military also did a much better job of managing the Russian media. Some key Russian journalists had been kidnapped for ransom by Chechens between the wars and no longer had much sympathy for the Chechen cause.

Tactically, the Russian approach was to use overwhelming firepower to reduce losses among Russian troops, though this naturally increased civilian casualties. Standard tactics involved using artillery (quicker to respond than aviation) to pulverize suspected Chechen strongholds before ground troops approached. This extended to the use of fuel-air explosives in built-up areas. Groznyi, which had been badly damaged during the first war, was leveled in the second. For all these improvements, the Chechen conflict is still not over. At a cost of perhaps 25,000–30,000 Russian soldiers dead, and 100,000 or more Chechens, any stability in Chechnya under Moscow-backed Chechens is exceedingly fragile. Horrific terrorist attacks continue, within Chechnya and outside it.

This pattern can be generally applied to Putin's presidency, and the specific case of the Russian military. Putin has brought with him the perception of decisive action, stability, and competence. The question, with regard to Chechnya, economic reform, or the Russian military, is whether that perception is matched by reality or is only a well-crafted image. As Russia's economy is propped up by lucrative oil and gas revenues, and Russia's independent media are gradually brought under Kremlin control, the difference between reality and illusion is increasingly difficult to determine.

Seen in historical perspective, the outlook is gloomy. Fifteen years after his defeat at Narva, Peter the Great had transformed Russia into a major military power and was consolidating his victory in the Great Northern War. Fifteen years after the Crimean War, Miliutin had restructured the Russian army from top to bottom to make it a modern fighting force and would soon lead it to victory in the 1877–1878 Russo-Turkish War. Fifteen years after the 1917 revolutions destroyed the imperial Russian state, the Bolsheviks had won a civil war, demobilized their army to conserve scarce resources, then built an effective fighting force with cutting-edge technology and military theorists on a par with any in the world. Today, fifteen years after the collapse of the Soviet Union, the Russian military looks much like the Soviet military before it, sharing its equipment, structure, uniforms, and culture. The difference is that it suffers from higher corruption, has more trouble recruiting officers, has higher rates of draft dodging, and uses increasingly antiquated equipment. Putin has presented himself as transforming Russia. He has not yet transformed Russia's military.

Suggested Reading

Aside from the chapter on the interwar Soviet Union, where I have done a great deal of archival research, this book is entirely based on the research of a large group of dedicated scholars. What I present in this book would, of course, not be possible without their research, and I am grateful to all of them.

Since this book is intended for a broad reading public, I have not used footnotes, but instead indicated places to go for more detailed discussion of issues and subjects raised in the text. Where possible, I have emphasized recent works using newly available sources.

There is no single book covering both imperial Russian and Soviet military history, one of the reasons that I chose to write this book. There are, however, a number of good syntheses of one period or the other. For long views of imperial foreign policy, see William C. Fuller, Jr., *Strategy and Power in Russia, 1600–1914* (New York: Free Press, 1992), John P. LeDonne, *The Russian Empire and the World, 1700–1917: The Geopolitics of Expansion and Containment* (New York: Oxford University Press, 1997), and John P. LeDonne, *The Grand Strategy of the Russian Empire, 1650–1831* (New York: Oxford University Press, 2004). For a broad selection of topics in imperial military history, see Eric Lohr and Marshall Poe, eds., *The Military and Society in Russia, 1450–1917* (Leiden: Brill, 2002) and David Schimmelpenninck van der Oye and Bruce Menning, eds., *Reforming the Tsar's Army: Military Innovation in Imperial Russia from Peter the Great to the Revolution* (New York: Cambridge University Press, 2004). For a general look at imperial history, see Frederick W. Kagan and Robin Higham, eds., *The Military History of Tsarist Russia* (New York: Palgrave, 2002). For the Soviet Union, see Roger Reese, *The Soviet Military Experience: A History of the Soviet Army, 1917–1991* (London: Routledge, 2000) and Robin Higham and Frederick W. Kagan, eds., *A Military History of the Soviet Union* (New York, Palgrave, 2002).

For medieval and early modern history, there are few works in English on military history. Some of the welcome exceptions are John L.H. Keep, *Soldiers of the Tsar: Army and Society in Russia, 1462–1874* (Oxford: Clarendon, 1985), Michael C. Paul, "The Military Revolution in Russia, 1550–1682," *Journal of Military History* 68, 1 (January 2004), pp. 9–46, and Carol Belkin Stevens, *Soldiers on the Steppe: Army Reform and Social Change in Early Modern Russia* (Dekalb: Northern Illinois University Press, 1995).

Chester Dunning, *Russia's First Civil War: The Time of Troubles and the Founding of the Romanov Dynasty* (University Park: Penn State University Press, 2001) has extensive discussion of military matters.

For the Russian military in the eighteenth century, the reading list in English in some ways starts and ends with Christopher Duffy, *Russia's Military Way to the West: Origins and Nature of Russian Military Power, 1700–1800* (London: Routledge, 1981). See also Philip Longworth, *The Art of Victory: The Life and Achievements of Field-Marshal Suvorov, 1729–1800* (New York: Holt, Rinehart, and Winston, 1966). Military matters are touched on peripherally in broader works on Russian history of the era.

Sadly, there is also relatively little that is new and accessible on the Russian military in the first half of the nineteenth century. Among the exceptions is Frederick W. Kagan, *The Military Reforms of Nicholas I: The Origins of the Modern Russian Army* (London: Macmillan, 1999). The same is true of the Crimean War. In addition to Albert Seaton, *The Crimean War: A Russian Chronicle* (New York: St. Martin's, 1977), see David M. Goldfrank, *The Origins of the Crimean War* (New York: Longman, 1994).

For the late empire generally, the best summary is Bruce Menning, *Bayonets before Bullets: The Imperial Russian Army, 1861–1914* (Bloomington: Indiana University Press, 1992). For imperial warfare, it is Robert Baumann, *Russian-Soviet Unconventional Wars in the Caucasus, Central Asia, and Afghanistan* (Leavenworth: Combat Studies Institute, 1993). On the Great Reforms, in addition to Menning, see John S. Bushnell, "Miliutin and the Balkan War: Military Reform vs. Military Performance," and Jacob W. Kipp, "The Russian Navy and the Problem of Technological Transfer: Technological Backwardness and Military-Industrial Development, 1853–1876," in Ben Eklof, John Bushnell, and Larissa Zakharova, eds., *Russia's Great Reforms, 1855–1881* (Bloomington: Indiana University Press, 1994), as well as W. Bruce Lincoln, *The Great Reforms* (Dekalb: Northern Illinois University Press, 1990).

On the origins of the Russo-Japanese War, see Ian Nish, *The Origins of the Russo-Japanese War* (New York: Longman, 1985) and David Schimmelpenninck van der Oye, *Toward the Rising Sun: Russian Ideologies of Empire and the Path to War with Japan* (Dekalb: Northern Illinois University Press, 2001). On the war itself, see J.N. Westwood, *Russia against Japan, 1904–1905* (Albany: SUNY Press, 1986), Richard Connaughton, *Rising Sun and Tumbling Bear: Russia's War with Japan* (London: Cassell, 2003), Constantine Pleshakov, *The Tsar's Last Armada: The Epic Journey to the Battle of Tsushima* (New York: Basic Books, 2002), and John W. Steinberg et al., eds., *The Russo-Japanese War in Global Perspective: World War Zero* (Leiden: Brill, 2005).

There is a wealth of interesting materials on the late empire, which has been a popular recent field of research. See William Fuller, *Civil-Military Conflict in Imperial Russia, 1881–1914* (Princeton: Princeton University

Press, 1985), Peter Gatrell, *Government, Industry, and Rearmament in Russia, 1900–1914* (Cambridge: Cambridge University Press, 1994), David Alan Rich, *The Tsar's Colonels: Professionalism, Strategy, and Subversion in Imperial Russia* (Cambridge: Harvard University Press, 1998), Joshua Sanborn, *Drafting the Russian Nation*(Dekalb: Northern Illinois University Press, 2003), Jennifer Siegel, *Endgame: Britain, Russia, and the Final Struggle for Central Asia* (London: Tauris, 2002), and Carl Van Dyke, *Russian Imperial Military Doctrine and Education* (New York: Greenwood, 1990),

The First World War is terribly understudied. The starting points are D.C.B. Lieven, *Russia and the Origins of the First World War* (New York: St. Martin's, 1983), W. Bruce Lincoln's popular *Passage Through Armageddon: The Russians in War and Revolution, 1914–1918* (New York: Simon and Schuster, 1986), and Norman Stone, *The Eastern Front 1914–1917* (New York: Scribner's, 1975). See also David R. Jones, "Imperial Russia's Forces at War," in Allan Millett and Williamson Murray, eds., *Military Effectiveness, Vol. I: The First World War* (Boston: Allen and Unwin, 1988). On the domestic side of the war, see Peter Gatrell, *Russia's First World War: A Social and Economic History* (Pearson: Harlow, 2005). There are almost no campaign studies in English using Russian sources. One very good study of the war's opening campaign is Dennis E. Showalter, *Tannenberg: Clash of Empires* (Hamden, CT: Archon, 1991). On the revolution in the military, the standard work is Allan Wildman, *The End of the Russian Imperial Army*, 2 vols. (Princeton: Princeton University Press, 1980, 1987).

On the Civil War, begin with Evan Mawdsley, *The Russian Civil War* (Edinburgh: Birlin, 2000) or W. Bruce Lincoln's *Red Victory: A History of the Russian Civil War* (New York: Simon and Schuster, 1989). See also Geoffrey Swain, *The Origins of the Russian Civil War* (London: Longman, 1996). For the Russo-Polish War, see Norman Davies, *White Eagle, Red Star: The Soviet-Polish War* (New York: Macdonald, 1972).

On the interwar period, see John Erickson, *The Soviet High Command: A Military-Political History, 1918–1941*, 3rd ed. (London: Frank Cass, 2001), Roger Reese, *Stalin's Reluctant Soldiers: A Social History of the Red Army, 1925–1941* (Lawrence, University Press of Kansas, 1996), and David R. Stone, *Hammer and Rifle: The Militarization of the Soviet Union* (Lawrence: University Press of Kansas, 2000).

For the Red Army on the eve of war, see David Glantz, *Stumbling Colossus: The Red Army on the Eve of World War* (Lawrence: University Press of Kansas, 1998), Gabriel Gorodetsky, *Grand Delusion: Stalin and the German Invasion of Russia* (New Haven: Yale University Press, 1999), and Carl van Dyke, *The Soviet Invasion of Finland, 1939–1940* (London: Frank Cass, 1997).

On Munich specifically, see Hugh Ragsdale, *The Soviets, the Munich Crisis, and the Coming of World War II* (Cambridge: Cambridge University Press, 2004).

There is a wealth of literature on World War II, but much less uses Russian source materials. Among the best of what do not are Richard Overy, *Russia's War* (London: Allen Lane, 1998), Earl F. Ziemke and Magna E. Bauer, *Moscow to Stalingrad: Decision in the East* (Washington: Center of Military History, 1987) and Earl F. Ziemke, *Stalingrad to Berlin: The German Defeat in the East* (Washington: USGPO, 1968). The best operational survey in one volume is David M. Glantz and Jonathan M. House, *When Titans Clashed: How the Red Army Stopped Hitler* (Lawrence: University Press of Kansas, 1995), which uses new Soviet archival materials. Glantz has also written a series of voluminous and detailed campaign studies. John Erickson covers the Soviet side of the war (based on published sources and memoirs) in exhaustive detail in *The Road to Stalingrad* (New York: Harper and Row, 1975) and *The Road to Berlin* (Boulder: Westview, 1983). On the domestic side of the war, see John Barber and Mark Harrison, *The Soviet Home Front, 1941–1945* (New York: Longman, 1991). For partisan warfare specifically, see Leonid Grenkevich, *The Soviet Partisan Movement, 1941–1944* (London, Frank Cass, 1999) and Kenneth Slepyan's forthcoming work from the University Press of Kansas.

Sadly, there is still little historical literature in English on the postwar Soviet military, though much is written by contemporary analysts and political scientists. One starting point is Vojtech Mastny and Malcolm Byrne, *A Cardboard Castle: An Inside History of the Warsaw Pact, 1955–1991* (Budapest: Central European University Press, 2005). David Holloway, *Stalin and the Bomb: The Soviet Union and Atomic Energy, 1939–1956* (New Haven: Yale University Press, 1994) has some discussion of the Soviet military's response to atomic weapons. One very interesting work on Afghanistan is the Soviet Union's own staff study: *The Soviet-Afghan War: How a Superpower Fought and Lost* (Lawrence: University Press of Kansas, 2002). See also Dale Herspring, *The Soviet High Command, 1967–1989* (Princeton: Princeton University Press, 1990). The best work on the end of the Soviet military is William Odom, *The Collapse of the Soviet Military* (New Haven: Yale University Press, 1998).

There is likewise a great deal of journalistic literature on Chechnya. Two books with a historical bent are Carlotta Gall and Thomas de Waal, *Chechnya: Calamity in the Caucasus* (New York: New York University Press, 1998) and Anatol Lieven, *Chechnya: Tombstone of Russian Power* (New Haven: Yale University Press, 1999).

Two remarkably good sources on contemporary military developments are the publications of the U.S. military's Foreign Military Studies Office (http://fmso.leavenworth.army.mil/products.htm) and the British military's Conflict Studies Research Centre (http://www.da.mod.uk/CSRC/documents/).

Index

About the Author

DAVID R. STONE is Associate Professor of Russian history at Kansas State University. His first book, *Hammer and Rifle: The Militarization of the Soviet Union, 1926–1933,* was a History Book Club selection, winner of the Historical Society's inaugural Best First Book prize, and co-winner of the Shulman Prize from the American Association for the Advancement of Slavic Studies. The author of numerous articles on Russian and Soviet military and diplomatic history, Stone is currently working on a study of Trotsky's role in the creation and development of the Red Army.